SLOVENIA
Brda

UNITED KINGDOM
England

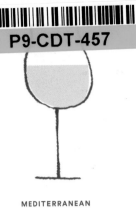

MEDITERRANEAN
Corsica

ISRAEL
Upper Galilee

NORTHERN FRANCE
Champagne

INDIA
Nandi Hills

GERMANY
Rheinhessen

HUNGARY
Villányi

LEBANON
Bekaa Valley

EASTERN FRANCE
Bugey

AUSTRIA
Niederösterreich

MEDITERRANEAN
Sardinia

SOUTHERN SPAIN
Murcia

PORTUGAL
Minho

SOUTH AFRICA
Western Cape

CHILE
Casablanca

AUSTRALIA
Victoria

NORTHERN FRANCE
Riceys

AUSTRIA
Kremstal

NEW YORK
Finger Lakes

WASHINGTON
Walla Walla

CALIFORNIA
Sierra Foothills

OREGON
Willamette Valley

SOUTHERN FRANCE
Provence

SOUTHERN ITALY
Calabria

WASHINGTON
Columbia Valley

SPAIN
Cigales

**REPUBLIC OF
GEORGIA**

Rosé

THE ESSENTIAL GUIDE TO
YOUR NEW FAVORITE WINE

All

KATHERINE COLE

ILLUSTRATIONS BY MERCEDES LEON

Day

ABRAMS IMAGE, NEW YORK

CONTENTS

CONTENTS

Politics, Power, and Pink

Rick Ross has a rap sheet. Tattoos cover nearly every centimeter of his body. His thick neck bears the weight of ten to twenty[i] massive, heavy gold chains. He goes by aliases: "The Boss"—or, as his adoring fans call him, "The Bawse"—and "Rozay."

These nicknames are fitting, because this rapper just so happens to love . . . rosé.

Rozay has allied his personal brand with that of a pink sparkling wine from Provence, Luc Belaire. He composes rhymes about this fizzy drink. He makes music videos celebrating it.

Luc Belaire Rare Rosé is mysteriously cloaked in opaque black glass. Some special-edition bottles have light-up labels so you can spot them across the dance floor. The Boss's homies, the "Black Bottle Boys," periodically trot out in black varsity jackets emblazoned with the Luc Belaire motto.

Gentle readers, please try to imagine Tupac, Snoop Dogg, or Dr. Dre crooning about rosé back in the early nineties. Snoop liked to roll down the street sipping gin and juice. Tupac was a Hennessy man. And wasn't it Dre who warned everyone, "Don't Drink That Wine"? [2]

But fifteen or so years later, tough-guy performers are striking

---

[1] *The self-proclaimed number varies from song to song.*

[2] *It should be noted, however, that Dr. Dre, the Cognac-and-weed man of the 2000s, went on to put his name on Beats headphones in a color dubbed "Champagne." Times have changed.*

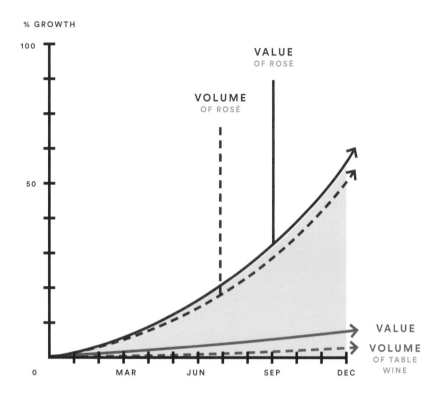

% GROWTH

**ROSÉ VS TOTAL TABLE WINE
MARKET IN THE U.S. IN 2015**

a different chord with their lyrics. "Two in the morning I'm zoned in / Them rosé bottles foaming," raps hip-hop artist Flo Rida. Wiz Khalifa calls for "rosé in my Champagne glass." And then there is Rick Ross with his black bottle. Rozay's rosé entered sixty-six international markets in its first three years of existence, becoming the top-selling sparkling wine on Amazon.com. Between 2013 and 2014 alone, its sales grew by 340 percent, according to a Sovereign Brands spokesperson. Yes, that is correct.

Rosé is a pop-culture phenomenon. Rosé is all the rage. And rosé is, improbably, macho. Rick Ross the Boss, of all people, likes to unwind with pink bubbly.

So does everyone else. Sales of premium imported rosé table wines (that is, decent, food-friendly wines priced higher than $11) shot up 58 percent in volume and 60 percent in value in the United States in 2015 alone, according to data provided by Nielsen and the Wine Market Council. Meanwhile, the total table wine market was plodding along at a nearly flat 1.8 percent growth on volume and a modest 5.2 percent on value.[3]

Rosé is an entire category that offers excellent quality for the price and is nearly foolproof in food-pairing contexts. It can be made from any red grape variety (and many white grape varieties, too) in any winegrowing region. It's a sure winner.

Yet it is marginalized. Despite the fact that rosé sales outstrip those of white wines in France, Business France, the French trade commission, categorizes French wine exports only by red, white, or sparkling. Contemporary media articles all follow roughly the same outline—"It used to be crap, but now it's good, and it's cool!"—failing to dig deeply into pink wine's long, long, long history. Rosé is rarely mentioned at wine symposiums or conferences, and a surprising number of winemakers I interviewed while researching this book told me that rosé vinification was not a part of their education at oenology school.

I find it ironic that wine professionals have largely been ignoring rosé when it's what they need most. After years of tasting professionally, my palate is pooped. I'm overwhelmed by an overabundance of flavor and tannin. At the end of a long day of wine-related work, I crave the crisp acidity and balanced proportions of a fine dry rosé. It might not be the world's most precious wine, but it's the wine that makes me happiest in the moment and recharges my taste buds for tomorrow.

I would argue, too, that the wine-erati is missing out on rosé's intellectual prowess. Adherents to the holy trinity of pigment, concentration, and toasty oak might find rosé to be a lightweight, half-baked sort of wine, but I find it to be relevant precisely because it is irreverent. A *vin gris de gris*—a bona fide French rosé—is closely related to a northeastern Italian ramato, which is an outré orange wine. And there are entire avenues of winemaking techniques that are just now being explored in the rosé sector.

Yet when I asked French winery owners to explain the recent windfall as I researched this book, many of them shrugged and responded, "The women like it." The subtext being, "It's just pretty."

Is this why rosé isn't taken seriously by the wine trade? Because women think pink is pretty? As the fashion and beauty industries have proven, pink packaging resonates with female shoppers. And in the retail manufacturing world, a prevalent strategy for designing

---

[3] *Brager*, U.S. Wine Trends: Battle for the Next Pour, *20.*

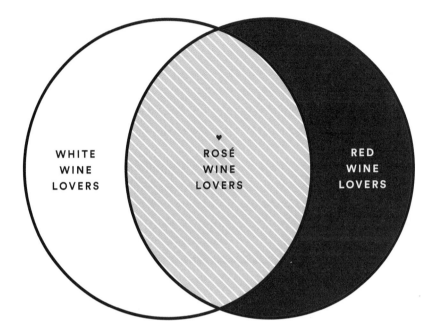

WHITE
WINE
LOVERS

ROSÉ
WINE
LOVERS

RED
WINE
LOVERS

women's mass-market products is known as "shrink it and pink it."

It is true that women tend to make their wine-buying decisions based on appearances, while men are more likely to be swayed by an impressive price or a "shelf-talker" (display tag) reporting a high score. Why? The answer cannot be reduced to a simple "girls like pretty things." Rather, as advertisers and marketers have known for decades, women connect to wine socially and emotionally, while men like to collect, analyze, and brag about wine. "Women seemed to focus more on the relationship element, whereas men's comments were more pragmatic," observes the author of a 2012 study of wine consumers published in the *Journal of Wine Research*. Men, the article states, are attracted to wine's "snob appeal," and are willing to pay more per bottle than women are, no matter what the occasion.[4]

So men buy wine to show off their purchasing power, while women are scouring bottle-shop shelves thinking, "Hmm, what should I give my friend for her birthday? Which wine should I bring to book club? What would make a great hostess gift?" They are not choosing pink because it's implicitly feminine, but because a rosé wine is simply undeniably beautiful, an aesthetic confection swathed by savvy marketers in a crystal-clear bottle. Its value as a "pretty thing" is cashed in not as some sort of fashion accessory, but as an offering of friendship.

As a wine professional, I suppose I should advise you not to purchase a wine based on its looks. But I'm also a woman who goes to book clubs and birthday dinners. And I'm drawn to rosé not because pink is feminine, but because it cheers me up, as do those apple blossoms that announce the arrival of spring, the promising glow of sunrise, the ripe peaches of summer. When I buy wine, I want a visual feast as well as a gustatory one, and I want that vision to be uplifting.

But as you'll learn in Chapter 1, men increasingly want in on that good feeling. Thanks to *Details* magazine, we even have a term for this phenomenon: "brosé." Guys made up nearly half of rosé consumers last time I checked.

Rosé is white and red, masculine and feminine. It is yin and yang, high and low, chic and shabby. It is as agreeable to the classical-music crowd as it is to rappers. A Venn diagram separating red and white wine lovers is fat in the middle. Throw a party and you'll notice that the pink wine disappears first.

Just ask the Rozay.

Luc Belaire Rare Rosé ($$$)

Rick Ross's favorite sparkling pink comes from the same marketing minds who brought us Armand de Brignac, aka Ace of Spades.[5] Its provenance is cryptic (the website offers nothing but vague promotional speak), but Burgundy bubbly powerhouse Veuve Ambal, which produces a Provençal sparkling wine labeled Rivarose, appears to be behind the winemaking. As for the name, I'm willing to bet that the Hotel Bel-Air in Los Angeles served as inspiration. Luc Belaire Rare Rosé is made from a blend of grapes that's mostly Syrah, but that's not the point. The point is: This wine is *sex-ay*. The bottle is black. The color is perfect Provence peachy pink. The nose is red berries and warm pastry with a touch of boudoir. The mousse is luxuriant. And there's just a hint of lemon-chiffon sweetness on the finish that brings to mind Moscato. Bottom line: It may not be original, but it's anthemic.

---

[4] *Thach*, Journal of Wine Research 23, *134–154.*

[5] *That is, the overpriced Champagne brand that's now owned by Jay Z. It's packaged in an opaque gold bottle—his delicious revenge after being dissed by Cristal Champagne, which comes in a gold cellophane-wrapped bottle.*

About This Book

I had been covering wine as a journalist for fifteen years when I began this book, fueled by a sense of frustration that rosé hadn't received its due. As I write this, in 2016, there are no English-language wine guides in print on the subject of rosé. I have attempted to fill that void in the following pages.

This book tracks rosé's recent rise from obscurity to pop-culture phenomenon. It presents a brief history of pink wine, outlines the various ways rosé is made, and explores the many styles of rosé produced in nations all over the globe. It highlights distinct regions to know and introduces you to producers and particular wines that have caught my interest.

Because my goal is to challenge the prevailing assumption that one rosé is indistinguishable from the next, I have zeroed in on wines that stand apart from their peers in terms of quality, methodology, or backstory.

Wine is a finite specialty good, and no bottle shop has the capacity to stock every producer on the planet, so—as with any wine guide—I cannot guarantee that every name mentioned in this book will be readily available at a moment's notice. That said, with just a few rare exceptions, I aimed to include wines with distribution in multiple cities throughout the United States.

At the ends of chapters, I have included images of a selection of the wines discussed, featuring some of the most attractive bottles and labels in rosé-dom. I hope these pages will help you recognize some safe bets on the shelves of your local wine shop.

A good merchant can procure a hard-to-find wine for you—if not from current stock, then by special order. Don't be shy about requesting one that has piqued your interest. If that fails, ask your wine merchant to recommend something comparable. The descriptions in this book of regions and styles will still inform your tasting experience. If you've never sampled a Rosé des Riceys before, one is likely to taste quite similar to another. And for every wine described in these pages, there were five more I wished I'd had the space to include.

Speaking of space, I tried not to bog down the book with explanations of geographical classifications. If you are wondering what an AOP or IGP is, turn to pages 282–283 for a quick tutorial. If you choose not to wonder, I don't blame you.

Rosé is largely seasonal. It is produced in limited amounts with the expectation that it will sell out immediately. I tasted vintages that in most cases will not be available to you. So I have left specific years out of the discussion, choosing instead to offer a general sense of what to expect from each wine.

Last but not least, let's talk price. Rosé is a category that tends toward the affordable, and there are many treasures in the sub-$15 range. In this book, I recommend plenty of those wines, and I don't hold them to the same stringent standards I apply to $30-to-$50 bottles. A $10 rosé should be merely refreshing and pleasant. A $40 rosé should get your gray matter going with its complexity.

I have also included some of the most precious pinks on the planet, which can sell in the $75 to $100 range (or more, if we're talking Champagne). This is still reasonable by the standards of the cult wine world. Even with the recent arrival of the luxury class of still rosés, pink continues to represent value.

While I wasn't able to include every worthy rosé region and winery in the world, this book is a start. After all, most wine encyclopedias don't give rosé more than a quick nod. I believe it deserves more. So let's dive in.

PRICE GUIDE

Wine prices are subject to change. So instead of listing specific prices that might vary depending on where and when you're shopping, this book provides ranges according to the formula shown here.

$	≤	$15
$$	=	$15–$25
$$$	=	$25–$40
$$$$	=	$40–$75
$$$$$	≥	$75

Rosé Through the Ages

On two days in June 2014, hundreds of well-heeled New Yorkers piled onto the decks of a mega-yacht to cruise up and down the Hudson River. There were fresh oysters on ice. There was a photo booth and a DJ. Someone was handing out pink Wayfarer-style sunglasses.

And there were buckets and buckets and yet more buckets of chilled rosé. Some of the wines were sparkling, with gold chips floating around in them. Some were flat. Most were from France, but some were from Lebanon, Morocco, and Turkey.

The first ninety-minute cruise filled to capacity. As did the second. And the third. And the fourth.

"La Nuit en Rosé," as the whole affair was dubbed, sold out again in 2015 and 2016, attracting 4,500 attendees to five cruises aboard an even more mega-size mega-yacht. The party was duplicated and triplicated in Los Angeles and Miami both years. In July 2016, impresario Pierrick Bouquet[6] rolled out "Pinknic," a waterfront rosé and music festival on Governors Island, New York, at which more than 8,000 partygoers picnicked on pink blankets.

"Rosé is trending now because it makes people feel good, dream about summer vacations," Bouquet explained. "It's approachable, price-wise, and versatile. And rosé is not pretentious like other categories of wine that require more knowledge to be understood." The association with partying on the Riviera, he added, didn't hurt either.

Rosé is the new face of wine: accessible, attractive, affordable, and aspirational. In addition to the

---

[6]   *Yes, that's right. One of rosé's most prominent promoters is actually named "Bouquet."*

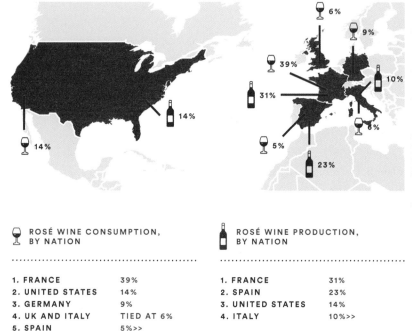

Source: OIV/CIVP/FranceAgriMer - Abso Conseil, 2015

ROSÉ WINE CONSUMPTION, BY NATION

....

1. FRANCE   39%
2. UNITED STATES   14%
3. GERMANY   9%
4. UK AND ITALY   TIED AT 6%
5. SPAIN   5%>>

ROSÉ WINE PRODUCTION, BY NATION

....

1. FRANCE   31%
2. SPAIN   23%
3. UNITED STATES   14%
4. ITALY   10%>>

yachts, there are the movie stars and the money. In 2013, when Angelina Jolie and Brad Pitt released their Château Miraval rosé, the first 6,000 bottles sold out within five hours. In 2014, a single bottle of Sine Qua Non California rosé sold at auction for a record-breaking $42,000. That summer, multiple news outlets reported on—god forbid—a severe pink-wine shortage in the Hamptons, where rosé is also known as "Hamptons Gatorade."

And in a July 2015 interview on the popular podcast *WTF*, the multi-talented boyish movie star Jason Segel confided to comedian Marc Maron that he finally sought help for his alcoholism after consuming an entire case of . . . you guessed it. That's right: from rosé to rehab.

This pink-wine craze had all the ingredients of a passing fad. But rosé is no flash in the pan. For the past two decades, rosé's come-back has been declared annually. It's a rite of spring. If I had a dollar for every time I have read about the "rosé revival," I'd buy myself a year's supply of pink Cristal.

Along with each new vintage's release comes the publication and posting of articles proclaiming the return of dry rosé, as if it had gone missing. All follow the same script: The trouble started in the late 1940s, when the Portuguese megabrands Lancers and Mateus débuted. These wines were fizzy, pink, and celebratory—just what everyone needed after the depredation and deprivation of World War II. At first, they were embraced. Later, wine connoisseurs would deride this genre for its short shelf life and lack of character.

Then, in 1975, California producer Sutter Home stumbled upon the formula for off-dry "White Zin." By 1987, Sutter Home White Zinfandel was America's bestselling wine, with annual production at two million cases. But, like Lancers and Mateus before it, the success of this beverage perplexed connoisseurs. In the words of the influential critic Robert Parker, Sutter Home is the "distressingly commercial . . . McDonald's of wine," producing "the cloyingly sweet" beverage.[7] (For tasting notes on today's Sutter Home "The Original" California White Zinfandel, turn to page 239.)

Psychologists tell us that categorization is a basic human need. We can't help but put things in boxes. We are hardwired to develop prejudices. So, having suffered through one too many semisweet "blush" wines, whether Portuguese or Californian, the foodie elite of the 1990s wrote off *rosé* as a four-letter word. Regardless of their provenance, pink wines belonged in the same grouping as Hummel figurines, leisure suits, the Cadillac Seville, and Barry Manilow albums.

Then, just as it hit rock bottom, pink wine bounced back. Stealthily, French rosé production overtook white by volume in 1994. In 2008, it claimed its position after red as the second-most-popular wine color being consumed within the borders of France, leaving white in the dust.

That same year, fortified wine marketeers jumped on board, as Croft introduced the first-ever pink Port. In 2011, Lillet, the venerable apéritif producer, added pink to its longstanding portfolio of red and white.

In 2013, the stately British paterfamilias of wine punditry, Hugh Johnson, used a rosé as the cover model for his perennial *Pocket Wine Book* for the first time ever. He would repeat the performance two years later.

By 2014, more than 30 percent of the wine being guzzled in France was pink. Not only had it surpassed white, but rosé now threatened the dominant position of red. That same year, an Instagram account started by a couple of blond New York–dwelling besties as a joke, @yeswayrosé, went viral and made the pages of *Vogue*. Rosé became a meme, a cocktail-party punch line.

And out came a new rash of articles declaring astonishment at the return of rosé. Again.

---

[7] *Parker,* Parker's Wine Buyer's Guide No. 7, *1,266.*

When was the last time you saw an article discussing "red wine" or "white wine" as though it were a recent discovery? What halfway decent historical account begins only seven decades ago? And what if I were to tell you that rosé has been riding up and down the waves of public adulation for thousands of years?

Beginning at the Beginning

The stories behind some of our best comestibles start not with an enterprising human, but a fearless animal. Consider a legend that takes place more than twelve hundred years ago in the Ethiopian Highlands. Kaldi, a young goatherd, found his flock hungrily feasting on plump red berries, their chins dripping with juice. The goats were bleating, hopping up and down, butting their heads against each other's flanks, and frolicking, their tails wagging. They looked like frenzied dancers at an evening celebration.

Kaldi grabbed a twig laden with the strange red berries and popped one in his mouth. The flesh was crisp and juicy. He crunched down on two large seeds, then spat them out and waited. The goats were still dancing around and, Kaldi noticed, crunching hungrily on the seeds.

Shrugging, Kaldi tried again, this time biting down on the seeds with his molars. A deeply bitter taste was followed by a jolt of excitement. Kaldi had stumbled upon the stimulating effect of coffee beans.

Kaldi's name and story are well known, and have been passed down through folklore. But the same plot, with anonymous players, has been enacted countless times all over the planet. Herbs, fruits, and spices have revealed their medicinal and mind-altering properties through similar random occurrences: an accidental ingestion observed by a sharp-thinking human. A line drawn between cause and effect.

A large mountain ash, *Sorbus scopulina*, grew behind my childhood home. In late spring, it bloomed with sprays of delicate white flowers. Then, in August, these developed into bright orange berries, as plump as tiny pumpkins. By late October, the berries began to rot and emit a sweet vinegar-like odor in the afternoon sun.

And then they came: the inevitable loud thuds, shuddering

through the house, as though someone were throwing softballs against our tall dining-room windows. Suicidal birds were flying straight at us like kamikaze pilots.

In other seasons, the birds were smarter. They saw the reflection of the glass and avoided it. But in the late autumn, swallows and robins hit our windows like squash balls projected by a merciless unseen racquet. Post-impact, they lay comically splayed on our dining-room balcony, knocked out stone cold, until they eventually roused themselves and dazedly hobbled around for a few minutes before flying off.

After a few of these incidents turned out to be lethal, my parents hung up tiny aluminum-foil flags. They didn't help. Because these birds were drunk. Sloppy drunk. They were flying while intoxicated, high on fermented ash berries. The FAA would not have approved. My mother renamed our tree the "Rocky Mountain Crashberry" in honor of them.

In Europe, the ash goes by another name: rowan. It has been associated with gods and mystical powers since prehistoric times. Like rose hips, rowanberries are better suited to tea or jelly than raw consumption, but early humans did eat these sour fruits, benefiting from their rich supply of vitamin C.

Perhaps these early ancestors did not bother to eat the berries that hung too high to be picked by hand. Until one day late in the season, a sharp-eyed person, someone like Kaldi, saw a group of birds snacking on shriveled late-season berries and then looping giddily around. Perhaps this person put two and two together, climbed the tree, gathered some of these fermented berries, and had a bit of fun with them.

Flip through books about foraging and you'll inevitably find a timeless recipe for rowanberry wine. It's an orangish pink color, incidentally. Could it have been the world's first berry wine? And, at the same time, the world's first rosé?

The First Grape Wines

Patrick McGovern, the scientific director of the Biomolecular Archaeology Project at the University of Pennsylvania Museum of Archaeology and Anthropology, believes that grape wine's creation story followed a similar arc. Tens of thousands of years ago, Paleolithic humans may have observed birds feasting on shriveled grapes, then flying in wobbly loops. Perhaps they gathered these grapes, McGovern posits, and placed them in the hollow of a rock, as a makeshift bowl.[8]

Returning the next day, these proto-oenologists found that the sweet fruit had collapsed into itself, forming a pale, sticky paste at the bottom. Plunging a finger into this, then tasting it, resulted in a mild, pleasing sense of intoxication.

What color would the earliest wines have been? Today's vine-tenders carefully train and prune their vines to maximize sunlight exposure, then discard excess clusters just before harvest so that the few remaining bunches will be sure to ripen fully, thus achieving their darkest colors and richest flavors. Wild vines climbing tree trunks in dappled light don't get the same treatment. And grape pulp is generally pale, regardless of the color of the skins.

We can only imagine how the first accidental fermentations evolved into something more purposeful. In the cellar, today's winemakers carefully control their maceration and fermentation temperatures, lengthening soaking times to maximize color intensity. Then they punch down or pump over the cap of skins that floats to the top of a fermenting tank to further enhance color. In past centuries, this same action was achieved through hours and hours of foot treading. Before Neolithic vintners[9] worked out a few basic techniques, could the very earliest wines have been pink?

In cool climates, it's no easy feat to make a bloodred wine; it probably took generations for the earliest northern winemakers to work out how much effort and time are required to extract color, flavor, and tannin from grape skins. They weren't able to practice every year, either. Because unlike rowan-berries, which ripen on the tree annually and reliably, wild grape-vines, like people, are gendered; male vines don't produce fruit. When both male and female vines are flowering, a gust of wind must carry the pollen of the male to the flower of the female. It's a tedious long-distance love affair that might result in fruit only every few years.

---

[8] *McGovern*, Ancient Wine: The Search for the Origins of Viniculture, 8.

[9] *In American English, "vintner" is synonymous with "winemaker."*

Primeval Viticulture and Multicolored Oenology

There are, however, wild grape subspecies notable for their high percentages of hermaphroditic plants.[10] The earliest humans to have found these fecund vines knew they were onto something good. As Neolithic societies transitioned from hunting and gathering to a more settled existence centered on domesticated agriculture, these hermaphroditic grapevines surely attracted the attention of enterprising farmers.

Archaeologists believe that the first of those groundbreaking vignerons[11] lived in what is now known as the Republic of Georgia. Here, evidence of grape cultivation and fermentation has been traced back 8,000 years, providing the first dot on the wine-history timeline. Vine tending is so intrinsic to the culture here that the delicate looping shapes of the Georgian alphabet are said to be modeled after the curled shoots of a grapevine.

Viticulturally speaking, Georgia is a complicated place. Indigenous domesticated wine-grape varieties number in the hundreds. In the 1890s, botanists realized that phylloxera—a devastatingly destructive root louse that feasts

on noble grapevines—endangered this treasure trove of plant material and began collecting samples of traditional varieties. By 1960, a publication entitled *The Ampelography of Georgia* listed more than 525 wine-grape varieties bred in the region since the beginning of the agricultural era. A few of those endemic cultivars appeared to be closely related to hermaphroditic wild vines. Any one of these could have produced the first wines made not thanks to a lucky accident, but with intent.

Perched at an elevation of 2,743 feet (836 m), overlooking the lush Alazani Valley and the snow-capped Caucasus Mountains, the fortified hilltop town of Sighnaghi is a popular travel destination in the Republic of Georgia. It has been settled since the Paleolithic period, but it is notable today for its eighteenth-century architecture. Tourists flock here to snap photos at the turreted church and convent, wander the narrow, sloping cobbled streets, and shop

---

[10] De Lorenzis, Chipashvili, Failla, and Maghradze, BMC Plant Biology, 154.

[11] Vinetenders.

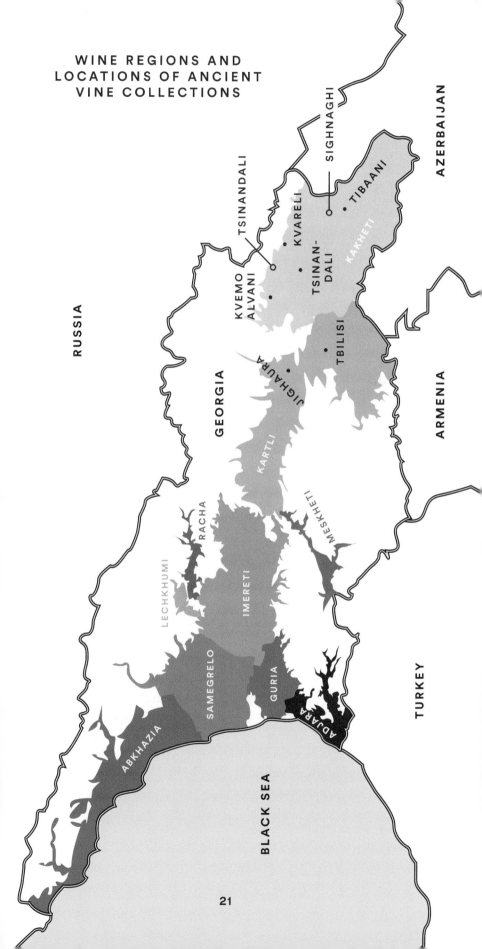

WINE REGIONS AND LOCATIONS OF ANCIENT VINE COLLECTIONS

RUSSIA

AZERBAIJAN

SIGHNAGHI

TSINANDALI

KVARELI

TIBAANI

KAKHETI

KVEMO ALVANI

TSINAN-DALI

TSINANDALI

GEORGIA

TBILISI

JIGHAURA

ARMENIA

KARTLI

MESKHETI

RACHA

LECHKHUMI

IMERETI

SAMEGRELO

GURIA

ABKHAZIA

ADJARA

TURKEY

BLACK SEA

21

for handwoven carpets, artisanal ceramics, and wine.

Riotously colorful, Sighnaghi couldn't be further from a Westerner's notion of what a former Soviet outpost might look like. Elegant balconies, brightly painted and garnished with lacelike woodwork, festoon plaster-fronted, pastel-painted townhouses. Red-tiled roofs stand in stark relief against white mountaintops, blue sky, and the ubiquitous green of cypresses.

It's no surprise that a well-known artist should have been drawn to this dazzling backdrop. What is odd is that when this artist decided he wanted to stay in Sighnaghi, he learned that he couldn't, unless he opened his own winery.

With his reddish-blond beard and ponytail and the proportions of a well-fed yeti, John Wurdeman could play the part of a Viking on film. The American artist, whose works are represented by galleries in the United States, first traveled here to satisfy a longing to hear live performances of Georgia's haunting polyphonic music. He met a singer and dancing troupe leader in Sighnaghi and fell in love. He wanted to get married. But he couldn't, because he didn't have enough of the right sort of wine.

Everyone in the Republic of Georgia drinks. A lot. It's an agrarian society, where most farmhouse cellars store terra-cotta pots full of homemade wine. You can even find fermentations percolating in the basements of the drab Soviet Bloc public housing of Tbilisi.

Plus, the music that drew Wurdeman here is closely connected to the tradition of the *supra*, a feast centered on a proscribed system of toasting, singing, and heavy drinking. So, in order to marry his lovely bride, Wurdeman had to supply scores of high-tolerance guests with rustic country wine; to do otherwise would have been an insult to the people of Sighnaghi. But Wurdeman, the expat Yank, didn't have a basement full of clay pots.

In 2005, while painting in a vineyard, Wurdeman struck up a friendship with an eighth-generation vinetender and wine-maker, Gela Patalishvili. One thing led to another, and two years later, the men were business partners and vineyard owners. Wurdeman got his wedding day.

The winery the men run together, Pheasant's Tears, is located outside Sighnaghi's city gate and past its formidable rock walls, in the hamlet of Tibaani. The north-facing vineyard, looking out over the Alazani Canal at the Caucasus, is primarily planted with the prominent Georgian red grape, Saperavi. The northernmost acre or so (half hectare), however, is devoted to a living library—one of just a handful in the nation

(see map on page 21)—of ancient indigenous grape varieties.

Pheasant's Tears has made a name for itself in the West by resurrecting these endangered varieties and following vinification practices that have been in use since preantiquity. To witness winemaking here is to get a sense of the protocols the earliest oenologists followed thousands of years ago.

The winery is a simple stone barn that appears, at first glance, to be confusingly empty. Where are the tanks and barrels? Instead, circular holes in the floor mark the gaping mouths of massive egg-shaped terra-cotta vessels, called *qvevri*. Nestled deep in underground cavities, cradled in sand for stability, and topped with clay lids, the *qvevri* stay cool year-round.

This form of winemaking disappeared under Soviet rule, when traditional *qvevri*-fermented dry wines were deemed "dirty" and their sale outlawed. Georgia's vineyards were converted to factory production, eventually fulfilling 75 percent of the demand for sweet wines in the Soviet Union. Georgians didn't drink the stuff, continuing to quietly ferment wines in clay pots in their home cellars.

The tradition of fermenting in buried pots, however, was not fully revived until 2006, when Russian president Vladimir Putin banned imports of Georgian wine, effectively killing the commercial industry. The artisan winemaking movement that arose from the ruins revived Georgia's proud history of oenological innovation.

For anyone familiar with the fundamentals of contemporary winery design, the elegance and efficiency of this empty room come as a stunning revelation. Why do Western winemakers pay thousands of dollars for French oak trees to be cut down, toasted, bent into shape, and shipped overseas, only to discard their barrels after three years of use? Why expend the energy to refrigerate massive stainless-steel tanks? Buried *qvevri* are naturally temperature-controlled, and the same clay vessel can last for centuries. Why did anyone ever think to make wine any other way?

Of course, today's consumers like the smoky spice and silky texture of a barrel-aged red. And they crave the crisp, fresh whites that can only be made by pressing the juice off the grape skins and fermenting it in airtight stainless-steel vats, then dosing it with sulfur. But at Pheasant's Tears, most of the white grapes are treated the same way the reds are. The juice macerates on the skins, soaking up color, texture, and tannic structure. This ensures that the wine will be long-lived, despite the lack of modern winemaking equipment. It also makes for a flavorful—if rather confusing—beverage that doesn't jibe with our idea of what a white wine should be.

The poets of antiquity had no word for *blue*. Likewise, the modern American tourist has no lexicon to describe the appearance of the traditional wines of Georgia. These wines, then, could have no better ambassador than John Wurdeman, a professional painter. The guy knows his colors.

A grape that would, in the rest of the world, be categorized as "white" makes a wine that can be as cloudy as apple cider and dark as "amber," or it can blaze like a "fire opal," as Wurdeman describes it. And how to describe that unusual red that seems to glow from within? It's "like a garnet with the sun backlit through it."

In the traditional cellars of Georgia, white grapes are vinified as though they were reds, and in some cases, red grapes are treated like whites. Because thousands of years ago, early Georgian winemakers didn't feel beholden to critics who dole out points based on the concentration of color. They still don't.

Rkatsiteli, for example, is a grape variety that's a yellowish-gold color with splashes of rosy pigment, like a Comice pear. Because the juice is not pressed off the skins but is allowed to wallow in that gorgeous autumnal color, the finished wine ranges in appearance from apricot to amber. A cultivar of the same grape, called Rkatsiteli Vardisperi, bears blushing pink fruit and makes a raspberry-candy–colored wine. Pheasant's Tears is the first estate in a looooong time to have a significantly sized planting of this grape. "Even if you do a long skin-contact maceration, it never becomes red," John Wurdeman says.

Then there's the highly unusual Tavkveri: It's a modern *Vitis vinifera*[12] variety that's female rather than the now-typical hermaphroditic. Could it have been the world's first domesticated wine grape? (Rkatsiteli is also in the running for this title, as are other Georgian varieties.)

At full ripeness, Tavkveri is midnight blue. But there's a long tradition in Georgia of fermenting only its free-run juice—that is, juice that hasn't had time to soak pigment from the skins. The resulting wine is a rosé.

The murky, mysterious liquids at Pheasant's Tears are just a few of the many endemic Georgian varietal wines that look unlike anything most of us have ever poured in a glass. They're impossible to categorize.

But then, what would ancient oenophiles think of today's wines? Imagine pouring New Zealand Sauvignon Blanc for a Roman nobleman lounging in his toga. In a world where white wine looked

---

[12] *Nearly all fine wines today are made from the domesticated* Vitis vinifera *species.*

like apple cider, he'd probably think he'd been handed a cup of piss.

The idea that wine must be either as pale as water or as red as blood, and classified as such, by color, is a recent one. These stark hues didn't exist in wine until contemporary vinification techniques and equipment made them possible. Until relatively recently, most wines fell somewhere between cloudy gold and ruddy amber, with a large spectrum in the pink-to-cranberry range. "These distinct wine genres we have today are a bit crude," says Wurdeman. "They leave out the thousand other shades in between."

Two Rosés Made in the Style of Antiquity

A. D. Beckham "Amphora" Willamette Valley Pinot Gris ($$$)
Vinetender and winemaker Andrew Beckham also happens to be a master ceramicist who handcrafts his own massive terra-cotta amphorae. Beckham doesn't crush his fruit, instead transferring whole Pinot Gris grapes to an amphora to macerate and ferment on the skins, a process that takes approximately one month. Half the vintage continues to rest in amphorae while the remainder ages in neutral acacia barrels. Pinot Gris is typically pressed off the skins and vinified as a white wine, but this grape has dusty-pink-to-lavender skins, so this wine is a blushing apricot color. The texture is initially matte, but softens with air. The watermelon-and-citrus palate finishes floral; the haunting fragrance includes notes of rose hips, cardamom, and ripe stone fruit.

Radikon "S" Venezia-Giulia Pinot Grigio ($$$)
The Radikon family practices biodynamics in Oslavia, the spot in northeastern Italy where Friuli borders Slovenia. Again we have a Pinot Gris (Pinot Grigio is the Italian term for this grape variety), but this skin-fermented wine ages in large oak casks for approximately eighteen months, making for coppery color in a wine that's dry on the palate, despite notes of spiced cherries, ripe strawberries, and marmalade. Bottled unfiltered without any preservatives, the "S" can be funky—a pleasurable challenge to your preconceptions about what wine should be. To taste it is to travel back in time.

Classical Colors

While our Platonic ideal of wine might be red, the wine Plato actually drank probably wasn't. The wines of antiquity weren't strictly made from crushed grapes. Water, spices, and fruit juices were added; as we have read in Homer, this *krasi* was "honeyed" for sweetness.

Mas des Tourelles, a domaine in France's southern Côtes du Rhône, runs two winemaking operations. One produces standard table wines. The other, inspired by an important archaeological site located on the estate, is a precise reproduction of a Gallo-Roman winery, following descriptions outlined by Cato.

Winemaking is carried out—in costume—according to classical treatises on the subject, following the recipes of first-century agronomist Columella. Get out of the way when the grapes in the wine press are being squashed by the lowering, by pulley, of a massive tree trunk that could easily crush your bones.

The winery is also a museum where visitors can peruse materials on ancient winemaking techniques and materials. Among them are a list of color additives, which includes saffron to add color and vine-stock ash to remove it.

Owner Diane Durand guided me around her remarkable cellar, where that year's clay-orange–colored wines were quietly fermenting in squat open-topped amphorae that were half buried in a bed of small pebbles. Then she poured tastes of her classical wines: "Produit en Gaule," as the labels so aptly put it.

One, called "Turriculae," was as bold yellow as a yield sign. Mixed with seawater—yes, actual seawater—and fenugreek, it smelled like hay and tasted nutty and salty, like a Sherry.[13] Another, called "Carenum," looked like a watered-down cola. The addition of quince concentrate had halted fermentation, resulting in a sweet drink that finished dry, not dissimilar to a tawny Port.

An ancient Roman might not recognize today's red and white wines, just as we find the wines at Mas des Tourelles to be bizarre. But Columella and Pliny both described one style that would be familiar to us: the young pinkish-orange *protropos* (*protropum* in Latin), made from "the must that runs spontaneously from the

---

[13] *A quick shout-out to all you wine geeks: It was also a bit reminiscent of a really heady Vin Jaune from the Jura.*

grapes before they are trodden out."[14] Other famous writers of antiquity such as Galen and, again, Pliny mention the range of colors in wine, and Aulus Gellius specifically cites a "vinum medium" thought to be a rosé that was popular back in fourth-century BC Greece.

The Bible is full of wine mentions but frustratingly lacking in detail. What descriptions we have, however, lead us to believe they weren't all bloodred. Wines are watered down, "full of mixture," and flavored with spices and pomegranate juice. And there are multiple references to "new" wine, a descriptor that denoted quality, since older wine had an annoying tendency to turn brown or become vinegar.

"For thousands of years, people drank wine within the first year," winemaker Jean-Baptiste Terlay of Gérard Bertrand in France's Languedoc region tells me. "The test of a good wine was for it to be fresh and fruity." The best-known "new wine" today is the French Beaujolais Nouveau, which is released every November, just a couple of months after harvest. While it's red, it tends to be translucent rather than opaque, and as it lacks pigment-stabilizing tannins, it can fade quickly.

Unfortunately, tasting notes with the appropriate color descriptors weren't a thing back then. To this point in history, all we have to go with are a few written descriptions, a few artworks, some ancient amphorae coated with reddish residue, and a lot of conjecture.

Historian Rod Phillips points out that Byzantine writers classified wines as either white, yellow, red, or black,[15] leaving one to wonder what the word "red" really meant. One thing we can be certain of: "Mega Purple,"[16] the most notorious of contemporary wine color additives, was not present in the wine at the Marriage at Cana.

Time travel to France in the Middle Ages and we're on firmer ground. It is at this point that the northern European wine industry takes shape, thanks to the proliferation of Christianity and the establishment of monastic orders. Wherever a monastery was established, its inhabitants planted vines and devoted themselves to the study and improvement of the arts of viticulture and oenology. Their wines began to look more like what we drink today—less spice and seawater, more pure

grape juice. Except there was a notable difference: The majority of the wines of Europe were not red, nor white, but pink. And France—the center of wine production from the Middle Ages on—made rosé what it is today.

According to historians, nearly 90 percent of medieval Bordelaise wine was a pink co-fermentation of red and white grapes. This was most likely a field blend—that is, a mishmash of different grape varieties grown together.[17] It was nothing like the dark Bordeaux "claret" of today; indeed, a red Bordeaux wine would have been quite unpleasant. The grape varieties of the era were exceedingly tannic,[18] and since the jumbled assortment of varieties would have all been harvested at the same time, as Phillips points out, only a portion would have been ripe at harvest. They were not destemmed, and those stems tended to be green and bitter.[19]

So the finest wine was made from grapes that had macerated for no more than one night.[20] This clairet—also called vinum clarum, or vin clar—was that which flowed freely from the press. The darker pressed juice was astringent from its extended exposure to the skins and stems and could be used in small amounts to color clairet, but wouldn't be drunk on its own. Even worse was the final press of smashed dregs. Impoverished but resourceful drinkers mixed this with water to ferment a dreadful beverage called piquette.[21]

And rosé wasn't prevalent in Bordeaux alone. Phillips states that clairet was the predominant style throughout France, citing cellar inventories and wine-geeky accounts of the era. An agronomist writing in 1600, according to Phillips, is torn over which shade of clairet is "more exquisite"—partridge eye, hyacinth, orange, or rising sun—putting this wine writer to shame with his evocative metaphors.[22]

Cellar temperature was another factor in rosé's rule over northern

---

[14] Pliny (the Elder), The Natural History of Pliny, 250.

[15] Phillips, French Wine: A History, 75.

[16] Its full name is "MegaNatural Purple." Mega Purple is essentially a food coloring concentrate derived from grapes. It's a favorite punching bag for wine writers decrying the commercialization of viniculture and the rise of unnaturally dark, syrupy wine.

[17] By contrast, most vineyards today are divided into individual sections, also known as "blocks," by grape variety and even by clone (cultivar).

[18] Lukacs, Inventing Wine: A New History of One of the World's Most Ancient Pleasures, 61–62.

[19] The modern-day destemmer had not been invented.

[20] Phillips, French Wine: A History, 42. Phillips suggests that fermentation may have begun during this maceration and continued after the pink wine had been "racked off" and stored in barrels.

[21] Johnson, The Story of Wine, 79.

[22] Phillips, French Wine: A History, 42–43.

Europe. Visit Epernay, the *Capitale du Champagne*," in October, just after harvest, and you'll find that the average temperature is around 51°F (11°C), dropping to 43°F (6°C) by November. And the subterranean chalk cellars are even chillier. This explains why historians of Champagne so often mention that all Champagne was pink until it was white (and rosé): To get pink wine from dark-skinned grapes, contemporary rosé makers "cold-soak" their crushed fruit in tanks refrigerated to 50°F (10°C) or so. Vintners working in cold cellars were inadvertently following the recipe for rosé-making, until the monk Dom Pierre Pérignon came along in the seventeenth century and determined that Pinot Noir grapes could be gently pressed to make white wines. Today's winemakers can control the temperature of their fermentation tanks. For vintners working through the "Little Ice Age," which set in around 1300, this was not an option.

Cold wasn't the only force of nature dictating rosé. Down on France's balmy Mediterranean coast, the thirteenth-century Benedictine monks of L'Abbaye de Psalmody began cultivating grapevines in the wetlands of the Camargue and making *vins de sable*—sand wines—first mentioned in print in a 1406 royal decree. The vines, improbably, live and produce fruit in the white sand, where they aren't able to muster up much pigment or tannin. "For centuries, they only made rosé here," says Martial Pelatan, director of Domaines Listel, the giant of the Camargue. "We have always thought of rosé as a noble wine."

And noble it was. Tavel, the sole rosé-only appellation[23] of the Rhône Valley, was a favorite of fourteenth-century Pope Innocent I and a series of Russian czars. Not to mention French kings, beginning with Philippe IV, who ruled from 1285 through 1314. The long-reigning (1643 to 1715) Louis XIV was famously a fan, as was, apparently, XV: A royal edict issued in 1737 instructed estates only within a 13-mile (20-km) radius of Tavel to stamp "C.d.R." on their barrels in an effort to protect the purity of the wine. The reds and whites of the rest of the larger Côtes du Rhône region would not be officially recognized for their distinction for another century.

The quality of wine improved over the centuries, with clear-cut red, white, and sweet styles emerging. That said, the whites tended to be pink-tinged. As Hugh Johnson points out, the top white grape of northeastern France was the pink-skinned Pinot Gris, and Dom Pérignon didn't truly master the art of separating skins from juice until the seventeenth century. And despite the arrival of quality red wine, the economic stratification dividing light- and dark-wine imbibers lingered. Rod Phillips cites one French agronomist, writing in 1605, who describes "full-bodied red and black wines" as "appropriate for working people," while "white and claret wines" are sought out by "people of leisure." (One can't help but imagine a group of corseted high-collared Bourbons and Jacobeans relaxing on the beach at Antibes with chalices of pink.) And a sixteenth-century French physician recommends hearty, earthy, blood-thickening red wine for robust peasants, while fragile, light-colored wines are better-suited to the delicate constitutions of aristocrats.[24]

By the eighteenth century, France's predominance as a wine-production powerhouse was threatened by the arrival of dark, strong, fortified Port, which traveled better and became the darling of the wine-thirsty Brits. Hugh Johnson cites a 1760s-era inventory of a London gentleman's cellar stocked with 400 bottles of Port and a mere forty-eight bottles of *clairet*.[25] Then civil unrest descended upon France, and the fashion for drinking rosé died out along with the aristocrats.

---

[23]   *The word "appellation" is a universally accepted way to refer to a governmentally recognized wine region; most European wine styles are named after the region from which they originate. There are, to my knowledge, only three rosé-specific appellations in France that do not produce true red or white wines: Tavel, Rosé de Riceys, and Bourdeaux Clairet.*

[24]   *Phillips,* French Wine: A History, *96.*

[25]   *Johnson,* The Story of Wine, *164.*

The Vagaries of Public Opinion and Rosé's Bumpy Ride

France emerged from revolutionary chaos as a red-wine-drinking nation. By 1855, the dry reds of Bordeaux were so prized that Napoléon III ordered that its châteaux be classified by price and quality, setting up the insanity that is today's Bordeaux futures market. But pockets of rosé appreciation remained.[26] Writing in 1851, English journalist and wine pundit Cyrus Redding is dismissive

---

[26]   *Various references to* "vin de la première goutte," *or unpressed wine, pop up in French and English texts of the eighteenth and nineteenth centuries.*

ROSÉ'S RISE AND FALL
AND RISE AND FALL

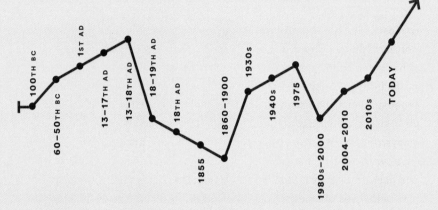

100TH BC RISE
Neolithic accident. Pink wine good. Cavemen like.

60–50TH BC RISE
Prehistoric vintners in the Caucasus have their priorities in order. While someone else is figuring out how to smelt copper, they make copper-colored wines.

1ST AD RISE
Columella, Pliny, et al. enjoy *vinum in polymitam*: pink, brown, bright yellow, etc., in addition to red. Wines in the Bible are young and watered down.

13–17TH AD RISE
Bordeaux is all about *clairet*, a blend of white and red grapes. In Champagne, it's impossible to make anything other than flat pink wine.

13–18TH AD RISE
Bold pink Tavel is prized by kings and other important people.

18–19TH AD FALL
French Revolutionaries prefer the earthy, robust reds of the peasants. Pale wines go the way of priggish aristocrats.

18TH AD FALL
The Brits drink Port.

1855 FALL
Dry reds from Bordeaux are coveted by Napoléon III. Red wine reigns.

1860–1900 FALL
Phylloxera does a number on wine in general. On the bright side, it's the golden age of cocktails.

1930s RISE
Distinctly shaped Ott bottles arrive in New York; A. J. Liebling notes that rosés are "popping up like measles" in France.

1940s RISE
Lancers and Mateus make pink chic. Post-war festivities make Lancers and Mateus rich.

1975 RISE
Sutter Home White Zinfandel is born.

1980s–2000 FALL
Machismo. Power suits and Robert Parker's full-throttle reds are in fashion. Blush wines are so last season.

2004–2010 RISE
Pink Lacoste shirts are ubiquitous. "Parker-ization" becomes a bad word. Big rosé brands are born.

2010s RISE
Unusually colored wines like Sherry and ramati come back into fashion. Light, low-alcohol styles like Riesling and Moscato are big.

TODAY RISE
Winemakers all over the world are making like it's 1999—BC, that is—and fermenting pinkish-orange wines in terra-cotta amphorae.

of most of the red wines of the northern Rhône: "The fact is, the wines in the country round Vienne, in all directions, may be reckoned together in one class as to quality." He is far more bullish about the vineyards of the rosé-only region of Tavel, which are "first in quality," and goes on to praise the *vins gris*[27] and rosés of other regions.[28]

Phylloxera arrived in France from the United States in the late nineteenth century. The pernicious pests multiplied rapidly and ate their way through the nation's vineyards until it was discovered that French vines were effectively immunized if they were grafted onto hardier native American rootstock. In the meantime, Spain and Italy stepped up production to meet the demand created by the gap in French winemaking. Their rustic, regionalized wine production quickly became commercialized and exportable; many of the prominent rosado and rosato houses mentioned in this book trace their beginnings back to the late nineteenth century.

Slowly, shakily, French rosé production resumed. American literary pundit A. J. Liebling knew of only two French rosé-producing appellations in the late 1920s. But "[i]n the late thirties, the rosés began to proliferate in wine regions where they had never been known before, as growers discovered how

marketable they were, and to this day, they continue to pop up like measles on the wine map."[29]

World War II ushered in the proliferation of both nuclear weapons and the frothy, semi-sweet, pink Portuguese wines Mateus and Lancers. The Port trade was floundering, and as wine writer Oz Clarke puts it, "In the depths of wartime, despite Portugal being neutral, you can come up with some desperate schemes to make a buck."[30]

The two brands flourished in the Cold War period, satisfying an American thirst for frivolity. In 1954, *LIFE* magazine[31] convened a panel of experts to judge wines and come up with a list of serious selections with which to start a cellar, a precursor to what wine publications do as a matter of course today. Four of their choices were German (or German-style) Rieslings and six were sweet dessert-style and/or fortified wines. Finally, two were pale styles: an Almaden California Grenache

---

[27] A vin gris, *or gray wine, is a pale-pink rosé.*

[28] *Redding,* A History and Description of Modern Wines, *80, 141, 190–91.*

[29] *Liebling,* Just Enough Liebling: Classic Work by the Legendary New Yorker Writer, *46–48.*

[30] *Clarke,* The History of Wine in 100 Bottles: From Bacchus to Bordeaux and Beyond, *113.*

[31] LIFE, *112–121.*

rosé and a 1951 "Tavel," with no specific producer named. In short, half of the twenty-four wines recommended were either sweet or pink.

In 1963, *Ebony* magazine's "Date with a Dish" profile featured hunky musician, composer, "world traveler and bon vivant" Phil Moore in his home, where he was mixing not martinis but Sparkling Rosé Wine Punch. "Rosé drink," the caption reads, "is made of grenadine syrup, ginger ale, lemon juice, tasty California Rosé wine."[32] It was the punch bowl version of Mateus or Lancers.

Meanwhile, French viticulture suffered. Vignerons returning to war-torn family estates, struggling to revive ailing vines after years of neglect, overcorrected by relying too heavily on chemical fertilizers and pesticides. "Don't drink the pink; it's full of chemical shit and the hangover is worse than the comedown off a speed binge," vows a 1960s-era Edward St. Aubyn character, who summers lavishly in Provence without ever managing to find a decent bottle of dry rosé.[33] For Anglophones of the 1950s through the seventies, decent dry Provençal pink, so ubiquitous today, achieved unicorn status. (Only Julia Child and M. F. K. Fisher, it seems, had access to the good stuff. During a stint living in Aix-en-Provence,

Fisher observed, "A glass of the cool pink wine I plan to drink with the meal is also very good indeed beforehand."[34])

As we will learn in Chapter 2 (see page 44), a vinification process called *saignée* concentrates red wines and produces rosé as a byproduct. This tool proved useful to post-war winemakers who couldn't afford to prune back their crop[35] and struggled to coax ripe fruit from their weakened vines. In the early 1970s, in St. Helena, California, Bob Trinchero used *saignée* to vinify a rich red Zinfandel and a very pale, dry rosé at his Sutter Home winery. In 1975, when he thoughtlessly added some juice to an almost-full tank of fermenting rosé zin, the fermentation stopped and Trinchero was stuck with semisweet wine. Oh well—he sold it anyway. And thus the White Zinfandel we know today was born. Hot on the heels of Lancers and Mateus, White Zin had a heyday in the late seventies through the mid-1980s. Thereafter, it began to be seen as supermarket slosh.

"Unable to move their zinfandel in its natural form, which is decent red wine, the industry has hit upon what it calls white zinfandel to bail it out," wrote *New York Times* columnist Frank J. Prial in 1985. "What we have here is an identity crisis. The wine is not white. It's somewhere between white and rose, a category the industry has christened 'blush wines.' And, while it's made from the zinfandel grape, white zinfandel sure isn't the zinfandel of yore."[36]

The fall of White Zin coincided with the rise of powerful critic Robert M. Parker Jr., whose 100-point scale favored wines he described as "inky," "extremely dense," "massively concentrated," "muscular," or "full-throttle." To achieve this ideal, wineries were outfitted to look like nuclear launch facilities, with digital screens and gleaming, humming hardware: micro-oxygenation devices to soften tannins, reverse-osmosis machines to maximize "jamminess." It was a tough time for a pale, understated wine that's essentially a stripped-down red. "Rosé was not really considered a wine," recalls Patrick Léon, the longtime managing director for Baron Philippe de Rothschild. "People would not identify it by producer, year, or AOC.[37] They would just say 'rosé.'"

In the meantime, gender politics had come into play. There is nothing inherently feminine about the color pink. Until the 1950s, in fact, infants were clad in both powder pink and baby blue without regard to gender. But the 1980s brought us the catchphrase "real men don't eat quiche," Chuck Norris, and the *Die Hard* franchise.

Tom Wolfe's *Bonfire of the Vanities*, which repurposed the He-Man[38] catchphrase "Masters of the Universe," was published in 1987, just months before the predatory financier Gordon Gekko made his big-screen début. The shoulder-padded power suit worn by *Wall Street's* Masters of the Universe was the antithesis of the puffy pink dress donned by Disney's hapless Princess Ariel in 1989.

By the nineties, pink drinks (daiquiris, Cosmos, rosé) were for "girlie men,"[39] while cutthroat Gordon Gekko types preferred burly, smoky, leathery 100-point Robert Parker–approved reds. The ever-rising prices for these bigger-is-better wines were badges of pride in the decade of greed and decadence.

But then convicted rapist Mike Tyson bit part of Evander

---

[32] *Robinson*, Ebony, *188–190.*

[33] *St. Aubyn*, The Patrick Melrose Novels, *58.*

[34] *Fisher*, Musings on Wine and Other Libations, *105.*

[35] *High-quality wine production usually necessitates meticulous pruning.*

[36] *Prial*, New York Times, *1985.*

[37] *Appellation d'Origine Contrôlée, or distinct winegrowing region (see pages 282–283).*

[38] *The animated television series* He-Man and the Masters of the Universe *débuted in 1983.*

[39] *A phrase favored by bodybuilder-turned-governor Arnold Schwarzenegger, as well as by his* Saturday Night Live *alter egos, Hans and Franz.*

Holyfield's ear off and we decided that we preferred metrosexuality to machismo. According to Jo B. Paoletti, a professor of American studies who researches the history of textiles and clothing, "Pink dress shirts and ties have enjoyed a revival, beginning around 2004,"[40] the same year, incidentally, in which states began legalizing marriage between same-sex couples. Today, Dwayne "The Rock" Johnson—the kinder, gentler, metrosexual alternative to He-Mannish Mike Tyson—likes to sport crisp pink button-downs.

Twenty-first-century sexuality is seen as a continuum rather than a dichotomy. Gender lines are blurring. Men and women don't feel compelled to wear their assigned team colors. And rosé is the liquid counterpart to the men's Lacoste pink piqué polo.[41] It's a personal expression of open-minded joie de vivre—or, perhaps, a display of confidence in one's masculinity.

In the ultimate about-face, rosé has become the darling of Rolex-wearing Gordon Gekko types, thanks to a new tier of luxury bottlings that have emerged in the $50 to $100 range. "I would not presume to estimate the breakdown of purchase by gender," says Simon Field, MW,[42] a buyer at Berry Bros. & Rudd, London's toniest wine atelier. "But anecdotally it seems that the male of the population is less bashful than he may once have been when faced with the prospect of purchasing a blushing rosé, especially in a large format." Translation: Banker bros in Savile Row suits flaunt their Benjamins these days by purchasing pink by the magnum.[43] Ah, progress.

Magnums may be big bottles, but rosé isn't, in the Parker sense, a "big" wine. Its popularity is an outgrowth of the "less is more" cultural ethos of the aughts. Where the rich reds of Bordeaux, the Napa Valley, and the Rhône complemented the excesses of the two prior decades, delicate German Riesling and flowery Pinot Noir were emblems of the decade of restraint. The magazine *Real Simple* first hit newsstands in 2000. In 2004, McDonald's phased out the term "super size." That same year, the documentary film *Mondovino* captured the mood of the winemakers, sommeliers, and critics who dissented from the "Parkerization" of the industry. The new catchwords in wine were "subtlety" and "balance."

Although it doesn't always feel that way, the decade we're in now has been notable for society's embrace of diversity. In 2012, the US Census Bureau announced that whites will no longer be the majority population in 2043. In our ever-more-multicultural society, rigid color divisions are unappealing. In wine,

too, monochromatic reds and whites have been pushed aside for in-between shades like pink, tawny, and amber.

Today's critics coo over rosé, Sherry, and roasted-carrot-colored ramato-style Pinot Grigio.[44] These stripped-down, minimalist wines are the anthitheses to yesterday's "extremely dense," "full-throttle," "inky," "massively concentrated" blockbusters. Rosé is a ghostly whisper of a red. Dry Manzanilla Sherry is as ethereal as a cobweb. Orange wines taste downright primordial, as though they are in an embryonic state.

The past decade has also been marked by a golden age of wine archaeology and the revival of long-forgotten winemaking techniques. With groundbreaking discoveries being announced each year, we know more today than ever about wines that fermented in amphorae.

Get a group of today's young winemakers together and you'll hear them talking about the raw authenticity of wines vinified using archaic practices, from biodynamically farmed grapes. For these enthusiasts, the holy land of winemaking is the Republic of Georgia, where the *qvevri* still rest quietly in their tombs. And for them, today's most exciting pink wines reflect rosé's genesis as—quite possibly—the most ancient wine on the planet.

[40] *Paoletti,* Pink and Blue: Telling the Boys from the Girls in America, *98.*

[41] *It is available in four different shades of pink.*

[42] *Master of Wine (MW) is a professional title similar to PhD.*

[43] *The equivalent of two bottles.*

[44] *See page 48.*

A Primer on Pink Wine

For most of us, it's enough to enjoy rosé as it is, at face value. Don't ask questions . . . just drink and enjoy. Above all else, rosé should be fun.

That said, it would be irresponsible of me to start this book off without some solid technical information. If you are not down with learning the ins and outs of fermentation temperatures, please, be my guest. Flip ahead a few pages and catch up with me toward the end of this chapter. My feelings won't be hurt.

For the rest of you, let's get down and dirty.

PROFILE

ROSÉ

COLOR
translucent gold, rose-petal pink, fiery copper, electric fruit punch, light ruby

AROMATIC PROFILE
berries, stone fruits, melon, sea spray, salty olives, spiced rhubarb, savory almonds

VINIFICATION
limited exposure to red-to-black grape skins, a lot of exposure to pink grape skins, and/or a blending of red and white grapes, either prior to or (less commonly) following fermentation

---

The Many Colors of Rosé

The world's sole rosé research facility is located in the town of Vidauban, halfway between Nice and Marseille, in Provence, the world capital of pink-wine production. Created in 1999 by the Conseil Interprofessionnel des Vins de Provence (CIVP), the Centre de Recherche et d'Expérimentation sur le Vin Rosé does a great deal with a very small budget.

Every year, the center's scientists analyze a thousand samples of rosé wines from more than twenty different nations for composition, color, aroma, and flavor. The staff also vinifies two hundred experimental rosé micro-cuvées annually, measuring all the possible outcomes that can arise from changing just one variable at a time. Professional winemakers, experts, and consumers all taste and rate the center's experiments.

But no matter how often aroma, flavor, and biological composition are discussed, the bottom line at the Centre du Rosé, as it's nicknamed, is color. Rosé stands apart from all other wine styles in its breathtaking diversity of hues,

MANDARINE

MANGUE
(MANGO)

MELON
(CANTALOUPE)

PÊCHE
(PEACH)

POMELO
(PINK
GRAPEFRUIT)

GROSEILLE
(RED
CURRANT)

THE PROVENÇAL ROSÉ SPECTRUM

tints, shades, and tones.[45] A wine that is any color from nearly clear to sunflower yellow to purple can qualify as a rosé. So during analysis, each sample is plotted on a color chart.

In an effort to categorize and illustrate their findings, the researchers at the center have developed a number of color guides. There are gel samples, displayed in wineglasses and vials, that display the spectrum of the majority of Provençal rosés: *mandarine*, *mangue*, *melon*, *pêche*, *pomelo*, and *groseille*. There are also more expansive printed color charts and fans that resemble the visual swatches developed by Pantone and used by paint companies.

The spectrum found in samples culled from all over the world is surprising and represents the startling diversity of this wine style. Broadly speaking, northern nations such as Germany, Switzerland, and Austria produce the palest rosés, while southern

Europe—Italy, Greece, and Spain—make the darkest pink wines. However, Provence and, increasingly, the rest of southern France, has adopted a style of wine that teeters precariously close to translucent, shaded with mango and gray.

"Today, if you want to make a successful rosé, you have to get the color pale and you have to have some salmon hints," the winemaker Jean-Baptiste Terlay of the Languedoc's Gérard Bertrand confides. "If it is too pink, it looks like there is something wrong."

But it's dangerous to generalize. Just when you think you've identified a trademark regional tint, you come across a wine that looks nothing like its neighbors. The capacity for diversity and surprise is one of rosé's strengths.

---

[45]   *Strictly speaking, a hue is one of the twelve primary, secondary, and tertiary colors. Tints are whitened colors, while shades are darkened colors. Tones are muted colors.*

How Should Rosé Smell and Taste?

It's quite unusual to begin a chapter about the technicalities of wine with a discussion of color. But I've just done so. Why?

"With rosé, it's easier for us to talk about color than aromas and flavors," says Nathalie Pouzalgues, staff oenologist at the Centre du Rosé. "Which is unusual—with red wine, aroma comes first."

Alas, aroma—which should be floral, fruity, or minerally in rosé—is often sadly lacking. Some winemakers, it seems, are so focused on hitting that stylishly near-clear look called "petale de rose" if translucent pink, or "pelure d'oignon" if pale gold, that they have forgotten the value of grape skins to impart character.

Grape pulp alone brings liquid, sugar, fruitiness, and acidity to wine, but, in my opinion, not a whole lot in the way of character to rosé wines. Grape skins impart flavor and color as well as grippy tannins and aromatic complexity. Juice destined for red wine wallows luxuriantly with the pigment-rich grape skins prior to fermentation. But the predominant methods used in rosé-making—short maceration, saignée, and direct press, which

we'll learn more about later in this chapter—aim to circumvent exposure to red grape skins.

As a result, I have found that many ultra-pale rosés taste more of winemaking techniques than they do of place. It's not uncommon to come across a wine that's a mere 12 percent alcohol by volume[46] but has the aftertaste of a vodka shot. Why? Because when the skins left the picture, so did some of the counterbalances that might have offset the alcohol. A wine that leaves a lingering sensation of heat on the palate is out of balance. It lacks symmetry.

But just when you've bad-mouthed ultra-pale rosés, you taste one that makes you swoon. The best examples, in my own experience, are evocative of freshly sliced fruit, flowers, and the seaside. The worst smell of chemicals, cloying candy, or overwhelmingly of sulfur.[47] Or all of the above.

---

[46] Today's table wines tend to range, roughly, from 12 to 14.5 percent alcohol by volume. A 12 percent wine should taste light and fruity, not highly alcoholic.

[47] Unpleasant sulfur-like wine aromas can result from the winemaking process, the bottling process, and/or the addition of sulfur as a preservative.

On the palate, a good basic rosé should convey fruitiness and the impression of slight sweetness, even though the wine is vinified to be completely dry. (The French call this sleight *sucrosité*.) It might hint at citrus as well as minerality or salinity. Mouthwatering acidity is important, and a slight bitterness to the finish can be, like quinine, immensely refreshing.

Last but not least, let's talk texture. Inexpensive rosés please with a bit of prickly "spritz," or carbon dioxide that has been captured in the bottle to ensure freshness and underscore light fruity flavors.

As you move up in price, you find wines with less obvious fruit but a luxuriant mouthfeel, from silky to mouth-coating to velvety. If a rosé has nothing going for it, texturally speaking, it had better be well made, because any imbalance between acidity and alcohol is more noticeable without spritz or smoothness.

A good test of a rosé is to allow it to warm up to room temperature. Is the aroma still fresh? Is the alcohol still balanced by the acidity? If so, you've got a winner. If that wine falls apart at 68°F (20°C), however, it's not worth revisiting.

100 FRAGRANT AND FLAVORFUL REASONS TO LOVE ROSÉ*

1	alcohol	20	chives	41	jasmine	64	plum	83	star anise
2	allspice	21	cinnamon	42	juniper	65	pomegranate	84	starfruit
3	almond	22	citrus blossom	43	kombucha	66	quinine	85	strawberry
4	aloe vera	23	coconut	44	lavender	67	raspberry	86	sumac
5	basil	24	cola	45	leather	68	red currant	87	sun-dried tomato
6	black currant	25	coriander	46	lemon	69	rhubarb	88	tangerine
7	black pepper	26	crabapple	47	lemon curd	70	river rocks	89	tarragon
8	blackberry	27	cranberry	48	lily	71	roasted red pepper	90	terra-cotta
9	blood orange	28	cream	49	lime	72	rose-hip tea	91	thyme
10	brambles	29	fennel	50	maple	73	rosewater	92	toasted oak
11	brine	30	fig	51	milkweed	74	saffron	93	turmeric
12	cantaloupe	31	ginger	52	mint	75	sage	94	smoke
13	caper	32	grapefruit	53	nectarine	76	sagebrush	95	violets
14	cardamom	33	grass	54	nougat	77	sandalwood	96	volcanic rock
15	cayenne pepper	34	gravel	55	nutmeg	78	seashells	97	watermelon
16	chalk	35	green apple	56	orchid	79	sea spray	98	white pepper
17	chamomile	36	green olive	57	oregano	80	sherry	99	white tea
18	cherry	37	hay	58	paprika	81	slate	100	yeast
19	cherry tomato	38	hibiscus	59	peach	82	soil		
		39	honeycomb	60	pear				
		40	huckleberry	61	pimiento pepper				
				62	pine				
				63	pineapple				

These aromas and flavors are common in rosé and, in fact, were pulled from the descriptions of wines found throughout the book.

How to Make Rosé

It is just as demanding to produce rosé as it is to make white and red wine. And many winemakers argue that rosé requires even more technical precision. The best pink wines can only be made with forethought in the vineyard and attention to detail in the winery.

IN THE VINEYARD

Rosé might taste best in balmy parts of the world where people have a tendency to sun themselves until they look like prunes, but it's a wine style that doesn't benefit from over-baked grapes. So site selection is important. In the South of France, the best vineyards are located by the sea, atop breezy high plains, or on hillsides.

Soil type is important, too. The schist, limestone, and chalk in the soils of Provence, for example, impart minerality to the wines. Along with location and climate, the soil also helps determine the wine's final acidity, alcohol content, and color.

Vinetenders can control certain factors. Those in sun-soaked locations can train their vines to maximize the leaf canopy and protect the fruit from excessive exposure. Fertilization, whether through organic compost or commercial fertilizer, increases the nutrients available for the yeasts to consume when it comes time for fermentation. Pruning down the crop load (that is, reducing the number of grape clusters per vine) can also be important in regions where grapes struggle to ripen; some producers cut their vines back aggressively to ensure that each grape is packed with as much natural sugar (Brix) as possible.

Every winemaker has a different opinion about when to harvest, but earlier rather than later is a good rule of thumb. The flavor should be full, but the acidity should still be bright and fresh. Think of a container of strawberries from the market: If you were to make a rosé wine from half of them and a red wine from the rest, you'd probably set aside the dark, soft ones for the red and keep the firm, tart ones for the rosé.

Climate change has had a profound impact. Many growers are harvesting not only earlier in the season, but earlier and earlier in the day. Some send their pickers out at six A.M. to bring the grapes in during the cool morning, to ensure firm skins and brisk acidity. Others harvest as early as two A.M. and chill the fruit before it ever makes it to the winery.

IN THE CELLAR

Some of the world's most revered wines are made using rosé vinification techniques. Champagne is typically made from clear juice pressed off blue-skinned Pinot Noir[48] grapes. And certain reds from France's Rhône Valley are in fact blends of Syrah (red) and Viognier (white).

If you were vinifying red wine, you would crush the grapes and allow the stew of pulp, juice, and skins to ferment. Since the skins hold the pigment (most grapes have translucent greenish pulp), you'd leave them in the mix for as long as possible to extract all the color you could. If you were making white wine, you would press the clear juice off the skins, then allow that juice to ferment on its own. The following rosé-making techniques combine red and white vinification methods:

SAIGNÉE: You're making red wine, but you want to embolden its color and concentrate its flavor. Maybe it has been a cool growing season and your grapes are not as ripe as you'd like them to be. So you crush your red grapes and allow the skins to macerate in the juice, then siphon some juice out. The grape skins in the first vat continue to macerate, imparting more color, tannin, and flavor to the reduced quantity of liquid. This will be your red wine. The juice in the second vat only spent a short period of time in contact with the skins before it was siphoned—"bled off," as winemakers say. This pale pink juice will be your rosé.

Note that in rosé-centric regions, the *saignée* method is often pooh-poohed. The *saignée* camp, it is argued, are a bunch of opportunists who overcrop. That is, they don't prune their fruit for quality, instead allowing more, and less flavorful, fruit to ripen, so that they can get both red and pink wine out of it. In addition, vineyard-management techniques have evolved to the point where the term "bad vintage" is largely irrelevant. By keeping their crop loads low, increasing sun exposure, and harvesting later, vinetenders should be able to deliver more tannic grapes with higher sugar levels and concentration. And contemporary cellar technologies ensure that every vintage can result in a bold, powerful wine if the winemaker so chooses—no *saignée* required.

In regions where red grapes struggle to ripen and/or thin-skinned grape varieties grow, winemakers strongly disagree. They can prune aggressively but still have difficulty achieving flavorful, fully

---

[48] *Pinot Noir is not the only grape used in Champagne, but it's the most prevalent.*

RED, WHITE, AND ROSÉ WINE MAKING AT A GLANCE

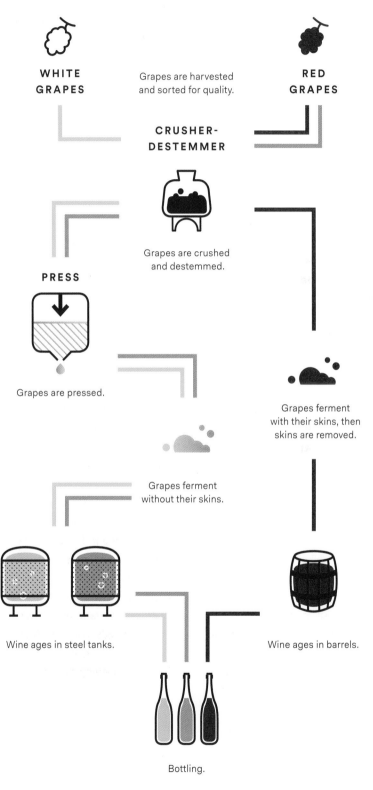

WHITE GRAPES

Grapes are harvested and sorted for quality.

RED GRAPES

CRUSHER-DESTEMMER

Grapes are crushed and destemmed.

PRESS

Grapes are pressed.

Grapes ferment with their skins, then skins are removed.

Grapes ferment without their skins.

Wine ages in steel tanks.

Wine ages in barrels.

Bottling.

45

ROSÉ MATH

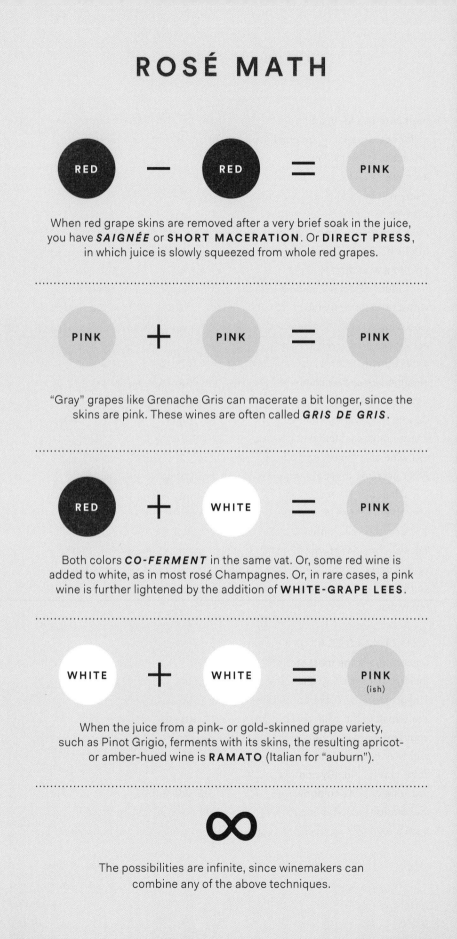

RED — **RED** = **PINK**

When red grape skins are removed after a very brief soak in the juice, you have *SAIGNÉE* or **SHORT MACERATION**. Or **DIRECT PRESS**, in which juice is slowly squeezed from whole red grapes.

PINK + **PINK** = **PINK**

"Gray" grapes like Grenache Gris can macerate a bit longer, since the skins are pink. These wines are often called *GRIS DE GRIS*.

RED + **WHITE** = **PINK**

Both colors *CO-FERMENT* in the same vat. Or, some red wine is added to white, as in most rosé Champagnes. Or, in rare cases, a pink wine is further lightened by the addition of **WHITE-GRAPE LEES**.

WHITE + **WHITE** = **PINK** (ish)

When the juice from a pink- or gold-skinned grape variety, such as Pinot Grigio, ferments with its skins, the resulting apricot- or amber-hued wine is **RAMATO** (Italian for "auburn").

∞

The possibilities are infinite, since winemakers can combine any of the above techniques.

pigmented wine. In addition, cellar equipment can be costly and unnecessary. For them, *saignée* is an essential tool. In addition, many winemakers prefer *saignée* rosé for its color and aromatics. Please note: For the purposes of this book, "saignée" refers only to a wine that is made as a byproduct of red winemaking, with the exception of Champagne (see page 182). Some winemakers, however, use this term in a different way. For instance, French winemakers and websites sometimes use the term "saignée" to denote the inverse. That is, some warm-climate winemakers make red wine as a byproduct of rosé. After pressing most of the juice off the skins to make rosé, they leave a small amount of juice to macerate on the skins until it is red. Because grapes for rosé were harvested early, this red juice is quite acidic and is used to add acidity to red wines.

SHORT MACERATION: Maceration is the most straightforward rosé-making technique: The grapes are crushed and the skins soak in the chilled juice long enough—generally between two and twenty hours—to pick up color and tannin. (By contrast, red wine gets its color over a maceration period that can range from a few days to weeks or even months.) The juice is then drained off and the skins are gently pressed prior to fermentation.

DIRECT PRESS: Too gentle of a press would give you a white wine (à la white Champagne from Pinot Noir grapes). But a very, very slow press of whole red grapes gives the broken skins time to impart some of their color to the juice prior to fermentation.

BLENDING: I know what you're thinking. The easiest way to make rosé is to blend red and white wine, right? But white wines are vinified to be white. Red wines are vinified to be red. They are two different end products and thus don't mix well, according to the experts. However, there are a few exceptions to this rule:

1) The most common method for making pink Champagne is to simply add a bit of red wine to white, just for color.

2) In certain wine regions, such as in Provence and the Rhône, winemakers vinify red and white grapes together. That is, they throw the raw grapes together in the same tank prior to fermentation. This is called co-fermenting.

3) Finally, there's an interesting little trick for extracting color from a dark rosé, no matter what method was used to make it: The winemaker adds the lees (yeast

sediment) from a white wine to the fermenting pink juice. The lees soak up some pigment, but there is the danger that they will also leech flavor from the juice. You don't come across this method very often, but I find it to be an interesting example of winemaker ingenuity.

GRIS DE GRIS: We think of grapes as being either white or red. But go to your local produce market and take a look. You'll see that there are no white grapes. There are no red grapes. There are, instead, grapes with yellow, green, mottled, pink, lavender, purple, blue, midnight, and everything-in-between skins. Those in the dusty-pink range include Grenache Gris. (The French use the term *gris*, meaning "gray," just to confuse us.) Vinify a pink-skinned grape like Grenache Gris almost as though you were going to make very light red wine and you get a *gris de gris*, or a "gray wine made from gray grapes."

RAMATO: Ramato is Italian for "auburn," and this wine is also referred to as "orange" or "amber." It's made from white- to pink-skinned grapes such as Pinot Grigio that are crushed and allowed to macerate and ferment on the skins for weeks, or even months, in an open-topped container, resulting in a wine that's orange, or mango, or sunflower colored. Is this wine white? Not in the contemporary sense. Is it red? Texturally, maybe, but visually, no. Difficult to categorize, it is often lumped in with rosé on wine-bar menus and the like.

THE FINE PRINT

In addition to the major vinification procedures outlined above, the winemaker can make a number of smaller adjustments in the cellar. Here are some of them.

TEMPERATURE: To extract color and flavor gently, winemakers chill their maceration and fermentation vessels. It's like making black tea: Pour boiling-hot water over a tea bag and you'll quickly have a dark, robust beverage. Use cold water and you'll extract (or "fix") less color, flavor, aroma, and harsh tannin.

The maceration stage is also called the "cold soak." As discussed, white grapes generally macerate briefly, if at all. In red winemaking, the cold soak is optional but not necessary, since the skins are present throughout fermentation, imparting pigment, flavor, and tannins to the juice throughout the process. In rosé vinification, however, the cold soak might be the only opportunity to extract any color and character from the skins. The fermentation vat is chilled to around 50°F (10°C) if the goal is to make a very pale wine. At this temperature the "must settles" more readily—that is, the solids separate from the liquid and fall neatly to the bottom of the tank. The juice soaks up flavor and a bit of color from the skins, but not too much. Once the juice is pressed off the skins, it's time for fermentation. This process produces heat, so rosé makers must be diligent about monitoring tank temperatures. In general, 55 to 65°F (13 to 18°C) is favored. White wines are vinified at roughly the same temperature range, to preserve delicacy and freshness. For bolder-hued rosés, slightly warmer maceration and fermentation temperatures ensure that more pigment makes it into the bottle. And red wines do best fermenting at 70 to 90°F (21 to 32°C) to maximize color and tannins.[49]

Another chilling technique used by most rosé producers is cold stabilization. It's also a key step in making white wine, or any wine that is routinely refrigerated by consumers. Because wines tend to drop tartrates—harmless crystals—when chilled, wineries get the process over with before bottling the wine so that customers won't be alarmed by the sight of them later.

STEMS: High-volume wineries use automated harvesters. The best of these machines pluck each individual orb from the stems so that the grapes look like piles of marbles. Small-scale producers, however, employ pickers who trim entire bunches from the vines by hand.

In most cases, these are tossed into a crusher-destemmer. But in some cases, the winemaker prefers to place whole bunches into the press. The natural latticework created by the stems eases the pressing and draining process, making for more juice with lighter color. It also allows a bit of oxygen into the winemaking process, which, in higher-end wines, can be a desirable thing (more on this later, page 51). Some winemakers also like the structure, spice, and slight astringency the stems add to the juice. This is a delicate process that must be watched carefully. Squeeze too tight, or include stems that aren't lignified,[50] and the wine could pick up "stemmy" flavors.

PRESSING: High-end wine producers brag about how gently they press their grapes and how little juice they get from their fruit. This does not seem to make sense from a business perspective. But from

---

[49]   If allowed to rise above 100°F (38°C), fermentation can get "stuck"—that is, stop.

[50]   Fully ripe grapes have tan, woody "lignified" stems. Less-than-ripe grapes have green stems.

MOST ROSÉ IS MADE FROM RED GRAPES

PRESS

RED GRAPES

Red grapes are crushed and destemmed.

Red grapes are pressed—NOT crushed.

VERY SHORT

VAT

Red skins macerate in juice.

ALL juice is siphoned off the skins. The skins are discarded.

Stems, skins, and seeds are discarded.

BARRELS

SOON

Pink juice ferments to make a rosé wine.

The juice is pink because it did not macerate for very long. It ferments to make a rosé wine.

Some juice is siphoned off and fermented separately to make rosé.

The juice and skins remaining in the original tank ferment to make a dark red wine, then the skins are discarded. The red wine ages in barrels, before bottling.

TANKS

TANKS

TANKS

The rosé rests in tanks. Bottling.

The rosé rests in tanks. Bottling.

The rosé rests in tanks. Bottling.

DIRECT PRESS

MACERATION

SAIGNÉE

a quality perspective, the thinking is that if you squeeze too much, you'll end up squashing skins and seeds, which will render juice that's astringent and unpleasant. Terms to know: "Free run" juice just spills out of the press as soon as you've loaded the grapes into it. "First press" juice comes from the first application of the press (duh).

MALOLACTIC FERMENTA-TION: Most rosé producers look at you in horror if you mention "malolactic fermentation." This secondary fermentation, which converts tart malic acid (think apple juice) into soft lactic acid (think milk), is de rigueur in red winemaking, but is usually blocked in white winemaking—unless the wine in question is Chardonnay, or a similarly full-bodied variety that lends itself to a soft, pillowy texture. But "malo," or "ML," as the wine trade calls it, may be the next big thing in rosé production. More on that in a minute.

YEAST: At present, most rosé production relies on the introduction of commercial yeast strains just after maceration, to kick-start fermentation and control its outcome. These can be chosen for their tendencies to impart specific aromas, such as rose petals, cherries, or candied strawberry. As with the best-known Champagne

houses, many rosé estates aim for a signature style that can be reproduced reliably from year to year, and commercial yeasts aid them in achieving this consistency. However, winemakers can also simply wait for wild yeast spores—which float around in wine cellars, vineyards, and your house, looking for something sugary and moist to land on and ferment—to settle on the vat of juice and start the party spontaneously. Although waiting for indigenous yeast to work can be somewhat risky, since there's no knowing how it might affect the finished wine, its proponents believe that a spontaneously fermented wine is more layered, nuanced, and "real." To kick wild yeast into action, the winemaker simply allows the temperature of the juice to warm up a bit.

Once the yeast has done its job and died, it falls to the bottom of the tank or barrel in the form of lees. If the end goal is a crisp wine, the vintner "racks off" or removes the lees. If a silkier, creamier texture is desired, the wine ages *sur lie*, or on the lees, for a few months prior to bottling.

OXYGEN AND OAK: Your typical fresh, drink-now rosé has a bit of spritz that feels like pleasant pinpricks on your tongue. It was likely fermented and aged in sealed stainless-steel tanks and

STEEL
TANK

CONCRETE
TANK

EGG

AMPHORA

FOUDRE

BARRIQUE

DEMI MUID

allowed as little oxygen exposure as possible prior to bottling. This is called "reductive" winemaking. Higher-end rosés, however, are given more of an opportunity to breathe: They ferment in oak tanks and/or age in barrels, where oxygen is not verboten. Typically these barrels are large and neutral—that is, they have been used previously and thus don't impart woody flavors or aromas to the wine. The barrel-aging camp is also big on battonage, or the stirring of the lees, for an even smoother, silkier effect. A rosé that has had time in barrel typically stands up to robust foods.

CLARIFICATION: A very pale hue is seen as desirable in rosé, but at what cost? A number of processes—such as micro-filtering, or adding a fining (coagulating) agent or enzymes—clarify wine, preserve it, and can also remove pigment. Sulfites, added during winemaking, can act as a preservative and also de-intensify color. The result of these processes might be a nearly crystal-clear wine. However, especially when used in conjunction with "reductive" winemaking, the overuse of these methods can result in a nearly flavorless beverage that would be odorless if it weren't for the profound so-called "reductive" stink of sulfur. Everything in moderation.

Élevage Eloquence

Élevage: The period of time a wine spends in the cellar after fermentation and prior to bottling. (In English we call this "aging," but most rosés only spend four or five months waiting to be bottled.) It's typical for a wine to ferment in one type of vat and then be moved to another for its élevage.

Steel Tank: Sealed tight and used to ferment and quickly age fresh, simple rosés anaerobically (without oxygen exposure).

Concrete Tank: Mostly used in Europe to ferment and age fresh, simple rosés. Like a stainless-steel tank, a concrete tank is "neutral" and imparts nothing to the wine.

Concrete Egg-shaped Fermenter: The egg shape, reminiscent of an amphora, is thought to promote more natural movement of the wine during fermentation and/or élevage, imparting minerality and mouthfeel to rosé. The egg shape is the most popular, but winemakers are experimenting with various other shapes, such as pyramids, as well.

Terra-cotta Amphora: Used for fermentation and aging. Plenty of oxygen exposure and skin contact make for orange-to-amber ramato-style rosés. Don't be surprised by the texture of an amphora wine, as it can often be matte—something like licking the side of a terra-cotta pot. As one does.

Foudre or Botte: The French and Italian terms for a wooden vat. These are so large (up to 4,000 gallons or 15,000 L, or, in some cases, even bigger) that they don't impart any oakiness to the wine. However, a bit of oxygen exchange happens through the pores of the wood, making for a wine with a softer texture and/or more longevity than a steel-tank-fermented wine. It's typical to see upright wooden foudres or botti used for fermentation and horizontal ones for élevage.

Demi Muid vs. Barrique: Barriques are small oak barrels that, when new and heavily toasted, can make some Chardonnays and Cabernet Sauvignons smell and taste like campfire. Rosé makers almost never use these. More typically, they'll use an air-dried, neutral demi muid, which is twice the size of a barrique. Like a foudre or botte, a demi muid imparts softness and longevity to a rosé rather than oakiness. It can be used for fermentation but is more often used for élevage.

Natural Wine and the Pursuit of Imperfection

Wines that are allowed to spontaneously ferment without the addition of commercial yeasts, then bottled without additives, fining, filtering, and so on are praised by certain pundits as the real deal. These "natural" wines are more authentic and artisanal, it is argued. Most wines—including rosés—were made this way until a new, technical form of winemaking took hold in the sixties and seventies. Today, consumers expect rosé to be the crisp, translucent result of temperature- and oxygen-controlled winemaking.

But change is in the air. Top rosé producers are looking to build complexity into their wines by means of whole-cluster fermentation. They're moving back to oak barrels and trying out egg-shaped concrete vessels and terra-cotta amphorae. They're skipping the commercial yeasts and the addition of sulfur. Rosé is poised to enter the "Natural Wine" fold in a big way.

Kermit Lynch, the legendary American wine importer, believes that the best rosés are messier, more rustic, and more tangible than the brittle glasslike confections we have become accus-

tomed to. In short, they resemble those of the past. Fining and filtering, claim Lynch, suck the essence out of wine and block it from doing what it wants to do: Go through its secondary malolactic fermentation. "I'm really looking for a pleasurable, delicious wine that kind of flows," he said. "Rosé ought to be velvety as it goes down, fleshy, not hard and austere. With malolactic finished, you can bottle a rosé unfiltered if you want. Filtration takes out everything: some of the nose, some of the body, some of the fleshiness."

To this end, Lynch has been experimenting with a natural rosé-making style at his own winery, Les Pallières, in Gigondas, in the southern Rhône Valley. And shortly after visiting Lynch at his hillside home in Provence, I stopped in to taste with Jean-Marc and Kristin Espinasse, former Rhône winemakers who were now beginning to make wine in Bandol.

Jean-Marc had farmed his vines biodynamically and made his wines naturally previously, so, with the naïveté of someone new to the area, he made his first experimental vintages of rosé, in 2014 and 2015, the way he would make a "natural" Rhône red: zero sulfur; no commercial yeasts; whole bunches, with stems. He harvested the fruit early to be sure to capture enough acidity, then allowed his tanks to go through full malolactic fermentation.

The wines were remarkably un-rosé-like. Where most rosés eventually wilt and die over time when exposed to oxygen, Espinasse's grew more beautiful as they sat in the glass in the afternoon heat. They were creamy, smoky, and silky, with initial notes of grapefruit pith opening up into ripe white peach. They were wines to sit with, luxuriate in, and talk about.

A couple of weeks later, I received an e-mail from Lynch. "I was in the Loire this week and had a 1947 rosé!! Not only that, it was delicious," he wrote. In the cellar of Lamé Delisle Boucard, a winery a couple of miles north of the Loire River in the village of Ingrandes-de-Touraine, Lynch had tasted "a big, fleshy, low-acid Bourgueil rosé that had lovely aromas, still. In those days they didn't block the malo because they didn't know how, and it was vinified in *foudre*. It wasn't just of historical interest, you know—still alive at age sixty-eight, it was a great drink."

On Biodynamics

Biodynamics is part homeopathic medicine for plants, part environmental mysticism. With its herbal remedies and reliance on the moon and stars for guidance, it's more holistic and labor-intensive than organic agriculture. It's an approximation of the style of farming practiced by traditional societies for 10,000 years, before World War I brought us fertilizers made from chemically synthesized nitrogen. Many natural wine aficionados praise biodynamic viticulture because it is thought to reap grapes of pure flavor and unparalleled delicacy. I'm open to this idea when it comes to rosé, since it's inherently a delicate style of wine.

Can I Age This Rosé?

A rosé that has been allowed to breathe during vinification, through whole-cluster fermentation, oak vessels, and the like, can stand some bottle age, and might even benefit from it. Talk to your local wine merchant while purchasing rosé: Was the wine fermented in *foudres*? Aged in large barrels? Did it go through malolactic fermentation? Does the producer recommend that this wine be cellar-aged? For how long?

En garde, as you might remember from films that involve swordplay, means "caution." A fencer who is *en garde* is prepared for anything. In France, oenophiles use the term *vin de garde* to describe a wine that's resilient. It has the experience and tools to allow it to age—it won't be felled by the stray swipe of a sword. Here are some of the ways a *vin de garde* differs from a garden-variety rosé:

TYPICAL ROSÉ WINE

- Vinified anaerobically (without oxygen exposure).
- Brisk aromas and flavors of fresh-cut fruits, flowers, and seafoam.
- Color tends to be bright or blue-toned.
- Should be consumed immediately, chilled.
- Unfinished bottles should be corked, refrigerated, and consumed within twenty-four hours.

VIN ROSÉ "DE GARDE"

- Savory aromas and flavors of nuts, sherry, cream, sandalwood, and river rocks.
- Color tends to be muted or gold-toned.
- Can cellar-age for a year or more—ask your wine merchant how long.
- Tastes just as good at room temperature as it does chilled.
- Changes and develops as it sits in the glass, aerating, for thirty to sixty minutes.
- Open bottles should be corked and chilled but will continue to be enjoyable for three days to a week.

SUMMER

FALL

SPRING

SPRING

WINTER

SUMMER

SOLD out!

FALL

Seasonality

Age-worthy styles aside, most rosé is a seasonal wine that's released each spring, in limited quantities. This works well for wineries, as it frees up cellar space and sells out quickly, bringing in cash while the reds rest in their barrels for a few more months.

Increasingly, rosé is showing up on wine lists year-round. Consumers don't want to constrict their rosé consumption to summer, but supply has not caught up completely with demand. Wholesalers and retailers, fending off queries from thirsty customers, still wait breath-lessly for container ships to arrive from Europe in March, April, and May bearing the newest vintage.

This is the nature of rosé: Wineries would rather produce too little of it—with the assurance that it will all be consumed within a year of harvest—than risk that it could sit on a shelf somewhere and go stale before it's sold.

Insider tip: Rosé devotees can get through the winter by seeking out fresh wines from the Southern Hemisphere, where harvest happens in the spring and the new rosés are released in the autumn.

Burgundy Bordeaux Mosel Champagne PUNT Ott

Glass

BOTTLE MATERIAL

Why is rosé sold in a clear glass bottle? Because there's nothing prettier, of course. But clear is dangerous. Like most white wines, most rosés are made in a fresh, delicate style, meant to be drunk young. Ipso facto, like a teen-heartthrob vampire, they lose their luster with too much exposure to light.

For many decades, the Portuguese sensation Lancers traded the light-exposure problem for what some wags have deemed an oxygen-exposure problem. Instead of translucent glass, they chose (it has been said) porous crockery. Today, Lancers is sold in frosted glass, which might be an elegant solution to the problem if the wine inside the bottle weren't Lancers.

Glass is unnecessarily heavy and fragile. As we become increasingly conscious of sustainability, it's glaringly obvious that to ship just 750 milliliters of liquid in such a cumbersome container is wasteful. And wines in cardboard boxes, no matter how splashy the pink images thereon, may be utilitarian, but they lack cachet.

The new darlings in the rosé-container category are the aluminum can and the recycled and recyclable plastic PET (aka PETE) bottle. Unfortunately, even though it's thicker and better-looking than the juice and soda containers you might be envisioning, the PET is still a plastic vessel, best suited to five-dollar wines on supermarket shelves. That said, I'm not ready to close my mind to this option. Put this problem to the best design minds in the world, and I'm sure there's a solution out there. Maybe it's a variation of the lightweight white-glass bottle used by some producers in the Saint-Tropez area.

On the other end of the spectrum, the rosé revolution that is taking place in Provence has ushered in a new form factor. Don't get your hopes up: It's still clear. And it's still glass. Except now, it's even heavier and less efficient to ship. Because nothing says "luxury" like greenhouse gas emission.

BOTTLE SHAPE

Most rosés are sold in standard cylindrical Bordeaux-shaped bottles. But then there are the outliers. Back in 1972, Kingsley Amis

noticed that French rosé producers had a propensity to make up for their wine's lack of gustatory interest—they weren't as good then as they are now—by using voluptuous, visually interesting, hourglass-shaped bottles.

Seasoned travelers and wine drinkers might find this shape familiar. It's evocative of the Verdicchio bottle widely produced in Italy's Marche region and fondly known as "La Lollobrigida." As the story goes, this design was commissioned in the 1950s to commemorate Ancona's importance as an ancient Greek port. Its resemblance to an amphora paled next to its likeness to the top-heavy form of film siren Gina Lollobrigida.

But it turns out that curvaceous glass proliferated in Provence long before La Lollobrigida took hold in Italy. Going way back, Provence has as much of a claim to the amphora shape as Italy's Marche region does, given that wine production there dates back to the ancient Greek invaders of antiquity.

Fast forward to the late nineteenth century, when, as Jean-François Ott of Domaines Ott tells it, "My great-grandfather was selling his wine in very small barrels—so small that they could fit on top of a bar. Every week, he traveled to each restaurant in the region and refilled all the barrels. It was crazy! Each bar, three barrels: One white, one rosé, and the third was red. Finally, he thought, 'Nobody knows this is our wine.'"

Having identified the marketing problem, Marcel Ott began bottling his wines in the 1920s. Determined to bring Provence up to speed with France's more illustrious wine regions, he initially used the Burgundy-style bottle: wider-bottomed than Bordeaux, with sloping shoulders. But it wasn't quite right.

Perhaps, subconsciously, Monsieur Ott realized that, in a part of the world where swimwear is a perfectly acceptable outfit for the day, sloping shoulders and a wide bottom isn't a good look. Even in a Victorian woolen bathing costume.

By this time, Marcel's son René had joined his father in the business. The younger Ott decided that Provence needed its own signature wine-bottle shape, to keep up with Burgundy, Bordeaux, and the Mosel. His design was suggestive of an amphora: wide in the middle and narrower at the base and top. He was ahead of the curve.[51] When, in 1932, he introduced his eye-catching bottle, colleagues at other wineries weren't willing to spend the extra money to adopt the new silhouette region-wide. Ott was left to go it alone.

Today, the base of every Ott bottle is stamped with a trademark differentiating it from the many em-ulators that have cropped up over the decades. (Mid-twentieth-century wag A. J. Liebling decried "cheap" also-ran rosés "presented in fancy bottles of untraditional form—a trick learned from the perfume industry."[52]) Echoing waves, sand dunes, or La Lollobrigida–type bathing beauties, the parabolic shape is apt for the South of France. One need only sit at a Riviera beach club, order a bottle of rosé, and watch the bodies marching by to confirm the resemblance.

The latest trend in Provençal packaging is a bottle that's heavy as all heck, made from thick-walled glass with a deep punt (depression) in the base, for not much purpose other than to weigh the bottle down so that the winery can charge more. Carry a couple of these trophies around and your biceps will be bulging. It's a silhouette that calls to mind Champagne. Rosé is no longer just an accessory to half-naked bodies on beaches; it's now something to be splurged on and opened with celebratory flair. It's a special-occasion wine. It might be weightless on the palate, but it's a wine of weight in the hand. The new rosé bottle calls for a strong arm and a firm grip.

STEMWARE

Now let's take glass to a more personal level. The crystal stemware producer Riedel makes two

A PRIMER ON PINK WINE

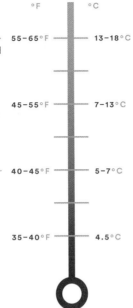

°F | °C

BARREL-AGED
.... 55–65°F ─── 13–18°C

TO SERVE: Leave a refrigerated
bottle out for 30 minutes to
an hour or serve from your
cellar (if you have one).

45–55°F ─── 7–13°C

TO SAVE: Recork, refrigerate,
and consume within 5 days.

DEEPLY PIGMENTED
....

TO SERVE: Leave a refrigerated bottle out on the counter.
Taste-test it as it warms up.

TO SAVE: Recork, refrigerate,
and consume within 3 days.

SPARKLING
.... 40–45°F ─── 5–7°C

TO SERVE: Refrigerate, then
savor slowly to fully experience its aromatics as its
temperature creeps up.

FRESH, LIGHT, SPRITZY
....

35–40°F ─── 4.5°C

TO SERVE: Chill in an ice bath.

TO SAVE: Cork with an
airtight, silicone-sealed
stopper, refrigerate, and
consume within 2 days.

TO SAVE: Don't save!
Consume immediately.

ROSÉ SERVING TEMPERATURE AND LIFESPAN, ONCE OPENED

specific shapes for rosé tasting.
One, in the Sommeliers series
($77 each), has an impossibly long
stem, with a flared-top bowl that's
shaped like a tulip. The other, in
the Vinum Extreme series ($69
each), has a diamond-shaped
bowl; this model is also sold as
an ice wine/dessert wine glass.

Both, like those uniquely
shaped bottles, make a statement
about rosé. They uphold the beauty of this wine by setting it on a
pedestal. If looks are what matter
when it comes to appreciating
rosé, these are the glasses for you.

However, if you're truly inter-
ested in the aroma, flavor, and
mouthfeel of rosé, I recommend

you try sipping it from a standard
all-purpose wineglass, preferably
a crystal one, with an ample bowl,
thin walls, and a precise lip. No
fancy shapes, please. In my tasting
experience, the elegant, minimalist U shape underscores the silki-
ness of texture, delicate ripe fruit
on the midpalate, and spiciness on
the finish of a fine rosé.

---

51   *This is not to say that Ott was the
first to utilize a curvaceous glass vessel.
Coca-Cola introduced one back in 1915.
And apologies for the pun.*

52   *"Memoirs of a Feeder in France: Just
Enough Money,"* New Yorker, 49.

Food Matches

Every rosé-producing region has its own culinary specialties, so when you travel to places like Corsica or Navarra, you'll find local seafood or vegetable dishes that are, without question, rosé's soul mates. But which stateside foods should rosé accompany?

American cuisine has changed radically over the past five decades or so. Sure, there are still old-school joints serving food the way people used to eat it, neatly delineated and bluntly seasoned. Have a glass of white with the salad course. Then order a red. Take a bite of prime rib. Take a sip of a robust red wine. Take a bite of baked potato. Take a sip of red wine. Take a bite of creamed spinach. Take a sip of red wine.

Today the calculus is more complex. We're worldly food sophisticates, eating more comprehensive dishes that are flavored with layers of artful spice. You can't, for example, separate a Korean taco into divisible units. Will a big red wine get you through that experience with your taste buds intact? You might want a red with the bulgogi. But you crave a white to complement the kimchi and the lime. And what about the taco part? Now you're thirsting for a beer.

Fragrant stews, soups, and pilafs present a similar problem. You've got your saffron-and-rice dishes, like paella, cioppino, and biryani, and your herbaceous citrusy soups, like tom yum and pho. They're savory, sour, salty, citrusy, and sweet, all at once. Part of you wants to drink red with those mushrooms and pork or sausage bites. The rest of you craves a white, for the broth, the vegetables, and the seafood.

These sorts of meals are metaphors for what our world has become: globalized. The recipes read like accounts of explorers on the spice routes. Their reinterpretations here, in the United States, reflect our multicultural makeup. Americans are Mexican and Korean. They are Spanish and North African. They are French and Vietnamese. We are what we eat, and what we eat can no longer be compartmentalized.

Rosé is both red and white, so it's exceptionally versatile. A fruity dry rosé is so accommodating that it will work alongside any food, really, apart from a very sweet dessert. Actually, I take that back: I just tasted a rose petal, berry, and hibiscus truffle bar from Xocolatl de David, a boutique chocolatier

in Portland, Oregon, alongside a rosé. The pairing was sublime.

And let's talk about the most notoriously difficult-to-match mainstream foods on this planet. Artichokes, asparagus, and cabbage are all known to mess with people's taste buds and release pungent odors. Rosé has the social grace to dampen the bitterness of these ornery vegetables.

Bracing and fresh alongside a salad? Sure! Silky and opulent alongside a roasted chicken? Of course. Its charm is its Zelig-like ability to adapt to any circumstance.

Rosé still carries a stigma in some quarters: It's considered fatuous, flavorless, a winemaker's afterthought, a beverage best suited to the beach. But we know better. Today's best rosé makers are fastidious control freaks who are constantly fine-tuning throughout the growing and winemaking process, with an eye toward making a wine that's memorable, mouthfilling, and age-worthy.

So the next time someone you know mocks rosé for lacking character, bring them to the new neighborhood Indian-Italian fusion joint for dinner. And see if you aren't both absolutely salivating for a glass of rosato.

Kings and Queens of the South

In marketing vernacular, the concepts of "push" and "pull" don't merely represent supply and demand. Pushers are evangelists who must shake up the status quo to convince the industry that their products are relevant and important. Pullers are those prestige brands that enjoy buzz and "it" status, brands whose names propel people to open their wallets.

The zeitgeist has declared rosé to be a pink Cadillac moving at high speed. Wine marketers, wineries, wholesalers, and retailers are fueling the engine by pushing the juice.

Although they began by pushing harder than any of their peers, a few rosé producers now pull with powerful magnetism. The five producers, featured in the pages to follow, are the rosé royalty—the elite producers of the prestige pinks of the South of France.

"We probably carry about three times more selection than we've carried in previous years. Our rosé inventory still runs heavy with French wines, particularly from the Provence area," says Scott Beckerley, of the prominent California-based retail chain K&L

Wines. "Brad Pitt and Angelina Jolie's wine from Miraval Estate brought a lot of attention to rosé in recent years. And Domaines Ott has cult status these days."

Before pink was big, the drivers behind brands like Miraval and Ott were unwilling to accept the idea that rosé was a third-class wine. Partly by cult of personality and partly by headstrong determination, they have gilded their supply with mystique and glamour, building an unstoppable demand even while surmounting personal tragedies.

No other part of the world has so successfully linked pink wine with status in the way Southern France has. And no other lineup of labels has moved the rosé market so dramatically as the five you're about to meet.

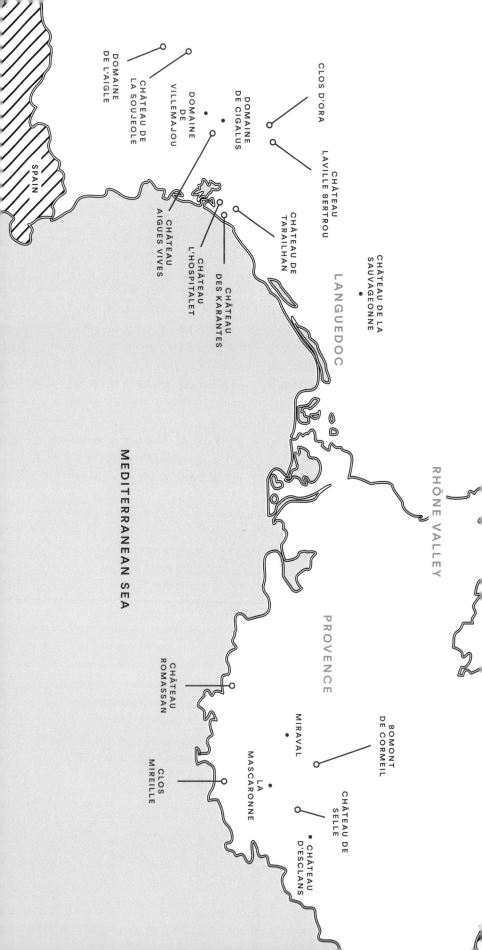

Angel in Ascension:
Château d'Esclans

"It all started with a Whisper . . . Now it's time to Rock!" So reads the advertising for Rock Angel, a rosé from Château d'Esclans.

If any single winery has provoked the recent rosé craze, it has been d'Esclans. In its first eight years, this upstart brand saw production skyrocket from 11,000 to 225,000 cases annually. In 2013, a *Wine Spectator*–affiliated trade journal reported that d'Esclans accounted for 20 percent of all the Côtes de Provence rosé wine sold in the United States,[53] and according to the winery's marketing director, d'Esclans owned even more of the market as of 2016.

The château is located on a rural stretch of road about an hour west of Cannes and just a few minutes south of Gorges de Pennafort, a chasm where pale turquoise waters roil over golden boulders. The viable land in this area is devoted to vineyards and olive groves, while the rest is forested hinterland accented by rocky outcroppings.

The winemaking operations have spilled out of the original winery facility. Despite a new lineup of massive steel fermentation tanks as tall as buildings, the winery is now in its fourth phase of expansion.

The château itself, obscured by the winemaking structures, is washed in a *stil-de-grain* shade of yellow suggestive of the most high-end d'Esclans wines. In the adjoining chapel is a bas-relief of two cherubs, their disembodied heads leaning toward each other as though in confidence. This same image is depicted on the label of the winery's entry-level pink wine, known in eighty different nations for its rose-petal hue, delicate finesse, and above all, its unforgettable name: Whispering Angel.

Château d'Esclans is the brainchild of Sacha Lichine, a globe-trotting bon vivant who grew up traveling between his father's Bordeaux estates and his Belgian-German mother's New York apartment. According to a 1991 account, "While still in his teens, he was shepherding rich Americans around France on custom-tailored tours that enabled them to gorge themselves at two

---

[53] "*Sacha Lichine Aiming to Make Provence the 'Champagne' of Rosé,*" Shanken News Daily, *2013.*

three-star restaurants a day."[54] Still in his twenties when his father died, Lichine was catapulted into a leading role in the wine business.

Lichine is a man who works all the angels, er, angles. In 2014, he brilliantly rebranded the basic Château d'Esclans estate-grown rosé[55] as "Rock Angel." Sure, this hand-harvested wine is a touch more fragrant and mouthfilling than the more quotidian Whispering Angel, but does it merit the extra $15? Or do consumers simply pay more to "Rock"?

Atypically for Provençal rosés, kosher wines are a key part of his business model, and the cellars of Château d'Esclans include a row of pristine Taransaud barrels stamped with the Hebraic date.

Thanks to its success, Whispering Angel has inspired its share of imitators and has driven competing wineries mad with jealousy. This was especially true in 2007, when this new brand, just one year in business, rolled out the unthinkable: a $100 still rosé.

The gamble worked, because Lichine had noticed something that few others had: Rosé has a lot in common with Champagne.[56] Most white and pink Champagnes are made from red grapes, just like rosé. The best-known southern French rosé producers aim to re-create a house style annually, in the same way that Grandes Marques Champagne strive for continuity in their signature cuvées.[57] And more and more, rosé is seen as luxurious and celebratory, thanks to its adoption by the yacht-dwelling species and aspiring masters of the universe. When the Louis Roederer Champagne house took controlling interest of Domaines Ott in 2004, Lichine was paying attention.

The Château d'Esclans hospitality showroom is a veritable museum of monumental glass, displaying formidable oversize bottles ranging from 1.5 to 6 liters. The plump glass vessels, each equivalent to two to eight bottles, resemble the prestige cuvées from

[54] *Prial*, New York Times, *1991.*

[55] *Three-quarters of the grapes for Whispering Angel are sourced from other vineyards in the immediate vicinity and machine-harvested at night, so Whispering Angel is not "estate-grown."*

[56] *"Sacha Lichine Aiming to Make Provence the 'Champagne' of Rosé,"* Shanken News Daily, *2013.*

[57] *It's increasingly chic among Provence's finer pink producers to offer a house-made* méthode traditionnelle *sparkling wine in the tasting room. This is no accident.*

Blending to Create Southern French Pinks

Some wine regions specialize in a single grape variety, but in Provence and the Languedoc, blending prevails. Different grape varieties tolerate different conditions and ripen at different times, providing an insurance policy against trying weather conditions. For example, in hot vintages, Cinsault's big berries can cool off a heady blend with their low sugar levels, which translate into lower alcohol levels.

For the rosé winemaker, blending is also the artistry of combining colors, aromas, and flavors. Cinsault brings a light cantaloupe tint to rosé blends. Heat-loving, drought-resistant Grenache Noir[58] makes fruity, apricot-hued juice that tastes fresh even if the acidity is low, due to its low potassium levels. Its cousin Grenache Gris renders a cloudy gold juice.

Syrah is spicy and aromatic; its black skins add bluish-lavender notes to a rosé blend. Mourvèdre brings depth as well as citrus and red-fruit flavors—think blood orange.

[58] *Typically referred to simply as "Grenache."*

Champagne houses like Laurent-Perrier and Ruinart.

Patrick Léon began working for Sacha's father, Alexis Lichine, in 1972 and went on to a glorious career, most notably serving as managing director for Baron Philippe de Rothschild. Léon is today a spry seventy-something globe-trotting "flying winemaker,"[60] retired on paper only, who is on his way to Russia to consult on a new wine-growing venture when I meet him.

His high-end rosés are as luxurious on the palate as they are in price point. "We are trying to make a soft wine, based not just on fruit and acidity but on complexity and suppleness—a fullness in the mouth," he says. Plush Grenache has the biggest presence on the 660-acre (267-ha) estate, where some of the vines are a century old. It's followed by Rolle (Vermentino).[61] Other grapes include Cinsault, Merlot, Mourvèdre, Syrah, and a couple of acres of the antique oddity Tibouren.

Léon, betraying his Bordeaux background, confides that he and Lichine like to think of the property as a future Cru Classé estate. After all, Domaine du Jas

What's in a Name

Sacha Lichine's name appears on all of his wines' labels, a gesture that might appear arrogant to those who don't know his family history. But Sacha's father, Alexis Lichine, was arguably the most influential figure in French and American viniculture from the 1950s through the seventies, known as "the pope of wine."

The Russian-American served as director for Château Haut-Brion, authored monumental books such as *Wines of France* and *Alexis Lichine's Encyclopedia of Wines and Spirits*, and owned two prestigious Bordeaux estates, Château Lascombes and Château Prieuré-Lichine.

The Lichine nomenclature is so powerful that a conglomerate that owned an "Alexis Lichine" négociant[59] brand sued young Sacha, early in his career, for doing business under his own name. That has been resolved, as Lichine now produces a trio of inexpensive négociant table wines under the Sacha Lichine label.

[59] *Négociants purchase excess juice and finished wines from other wineries to create their own cuvées. Négociant wines are typically bargain-priced.*

d'Esclans, another rosé-producing winery just down the road, has been deemed Cru Classé, and the soil isn't any different. Back in 2006, if he had voiced such a thought aloud, Léon's Bordelaise colleagues would have wondered if he had lost his mind. "Back then they said, 'Oh, Patrick, you are getting older, but you are still crazy,'" Léon chuckles. Today, the winemaker behind the world's priciest[62] still rosé is enjoying the last laugh.

Château d'Esclans "Les Clans" Côtes de Provence Rosé ($$$$)

This subtle blend of about three-quarters Grenache and one-quarter Rolle (Vermentino) is a ghostly faded-sunflower color due to the fact that it's mostly free-run juice[63] from the first gentle press. The nose is floral and the texture creamy and silky, enhanced by aging in temperature-controlled barrels. Some stone fruit on the palate is followed by a hit of white pepper and a botanical finish. It should be noted that the age-worthy Les Clans and Garrus (below) are in a different class entirely than the Whispering Angel, which should be drunk within one year of release.

Château d'Esclans "Garrus" Côtes de Provence Rosé ($$$$$)

Spicier, creamier, and slightly more orange in hue, representing the Provençal rosé ideal color of *pelure d'oignon*, or "onion skin," the Garrus has a higher percentage of Rolle. It is assembled from vines approximately eighty years old. Half the production stays in Provence and is consumed on the Riviera. Like a Marsanne from the northern Rhône, it is mouthfilling and satisfying. Whether it is worth the price is another matter altogether.

---

[60] This term refers to high-profile oenologists who travel around the world to consult for wineries.

[61] Many southern French rosés are cofermented white and red grapes. Rolle, known as Vermentino in Italy, is the predominant white grape used in Provençal rosés. Although it originated in Liguria, it has been in Provence since antiquity.

[62] That is, the most expensive widely distributed flat rosé.

[63] Again, here we have another Champagne-ism. In Champagne, the first bit of free-run juice is called the "cuvée," and the very best wine, made exclusively from this juice, is called tête de cuvée.

71

The Original: Domaines Ott*

When Marcel Ott registered the title of his company in 1935, he was informed by French bureaucrats that proper names couldn't be brands, never mind the fact that the Ott winery had already been in business for more than two decades. So, in a moment of desperation turned inspiration, he drew an asterisk after his name.

Domaines Ott*, as it is officially known, has been a star ever since.

Arriving in Provence in 1896, the Alsatian agronimist Ott found a recently poverty-ridden region that had emerged from a long downturn and was reinventing itself as a tourist destination. The seaside towns boasted new boardwalks and Belle Époque–style hotels. The colorful countryside attracted Impressionist and Post-impressionist painters.

The vineyards, however, were in shambles. The root louse phylloxera had made its first appearance near Avignon in the early 1860s, first ravaging the South of France, then moving north. Those Provençal landowners who could afford to regroup replanted hastily and carelessly, allowing many of the old indigenous strains to die out.

Ott was inspired by the landscape and the mild climate. He took over management of a vineyard in Cavalaire as a tenant farmer, first rebuilding the soil, then carefully replanting. By 1912, he had determined that this temperate seaside region could produce world-class rosé wines. He developed innovative wine-making methods, such as direct pressing, in his quest to create *grands vins de Provence*.

Ott was alone in his thinking. Rosé was, at the time, nothing more than a byproduct of red winemaking. It was for quenching the thirst, not contemplation. The idea of putting the name of a château on a bottle of rosé was laughable. Ott wanted to change that. In the wilds of the *département* of the Var,[64] halfway between the towns of Draguignan and Vidauban, he purchased Château de Selle, an estate on the edge of

dense forest in the middle of no-where. The Gare d'Aix-en-Provence train station, built in 1877, was some 70 miles (110 km) away.

In his remote surroundings, Ott got to work. He replaced fast-growing, prolific, and inexpensive grape varieties like Carignan—planted in haste post-phylloxera—with classics such as Grenache, Cinsault, and Syrah. He planted white grapes as well, to use as bargaining chips. "He said to the restaurant owners, 'OK, I'll sell you a cask of white, but only if you buy two casks of rosé,'" says his great-grandson, Jean-François Ott.

The haggling worked. As did the distinct bowling-pin-shaped bottles his son René designed and introduced in 1932. By 1938, the Otts were exporting their excep-tional pink wines to the United States. A photo from the Ott archives shows a New York City delivery car topped with a Château de Selle sign, next to a stack of twenty-five wooden wine cases, stamped with the name of the im-porter: "Bloomingdale Brothers."

Thanks to its history, the Ott brand needs no introduction, and the Ott family can stay under the radar. Clos Mireille is tucked into a sharp corner of a country road

---

[64] *A département is an administrative region, something like a county in the United States.*

outside La Londe-les-Maures. It's difficult to find and receives few visitors. The vineyards are flanked by forest on both sides and spill down to the sea. Trees hide the property from the view of passersby strolling down the beach or passing in boats.

"When I was in *lycée* [secondary school], I used to work driving a water taxi, ferrying people from their yachts to the harbor at Saint-Tropez," Ott recalls. "I would ask them, 'Do you want to go explore the islands?' But they never wanted to go outside of their comfort zone." Following his train of thought, I ask him if the motorboat I saw parked at the beach at Clos Mireille is for picking up VIP clients from their yachts, and he bursts out laughing. The neighbors, he tells me, use it for fishing. The Otts need not pander to the jet set.

In fact, Jean-François confesses to me that he is more than happy to leave marketing duties to Louis Roederer, the Champagne conglomerate that manages the Ott empire. This allows him—and his cousin Christian—to focus on what they love: vineyard and winery management. They prune their vines down for maximum structure and flavor. Whole bunches go into the press; after fermentation, the wines rest in neutral oak *foudres*, where they soften and stabilize naturally. The estate wines go through battonage (lees stirring) all winter long.

The Provence Cru Crew

In 1955, the Institut National de l'Origine et de la Qualité (INAO) singled out twenty-three outstanding Provençal winemaking estates as "Cru Classé," in the manner of Bordeaux. Château de Selle and Clos Mireille, both owned by Ott, earned the recognition. And as if owning not one but two of Provence's top properties weren't enough, René Ott purchased yet another estate the following year: the eighteenth-century Château Romassan in Bandol.

Provence has eighteen[65] Cru Classé, or classified estates, today. These single properties have been deemed superior to their peers in terms of quality, which, if you want to be crass about it, means that they can charge more for their wines.

---

[65] *Five properties have dropped off the list—snapped up by real-estate investors over the years, according to* Le Figaro Magazine.

From a business perspective, it's worth noting that Ott, a name that has been prominent for a century, isn't a large company—output is smaller than that of Château d'Esclans, which is just more than a decade old. As of 2015, production was approximately 57,000 cases annually of the single-estate wines, plus 6,500 in oversize formats. There was just enough Ott to go around without flooding the market. That said, the family with the most recognizable name in Provence wine isn't beyond capitalizing on the current rosé craze. By.Ott, a new brand that sells for $20 to $25 and partly sources fruit from neighboring growers, replaced Ott's previous estate-grown lower-priced line, Les Domaniers, in 2016. The spokeswoman I contacted was coy about production numbers.

....

Domaines Ott* "Clos Mireille" Côtes de Provence   ($$$)

Acquired by the Ott family in 1935, Mireille originally produced only white wine. Only in 2007 did the focus shift to estate rosé. A blend of 50 percent Grenache, plus Cinsault and Syrah, vinified in stainless-steel tanks, it's fresh on the nose, with notes of honeydew melon and a pleasantly bitter finish that screams "apéritif." The verve in the glass reflects the sea spray and breezes this waterfront estate enjoys.

....

Domaines Ott* Château de Selle Côtes de Provence   ($$$$)

This inland château, the original Ott estate, is located in Taradeau (just north of Vidauban and about an hour east of Cannes), where nearly half the soil is stone. The cuvée is Grenache, Cinsault, Syrah, and Cabernet Sauvignon. Bright, perky, and citrusy, despite a slightly lower total acidity level, the Château de Selle has a minerality that works well with seafood and spices. White pepper on the finish seals the deal.

....

Domaines Ott* Château Romassan Bandol   ($$$$)

In the Ott portfolio since 1956, the Romassan estate is planted mostly with Mourvèdre. This is the richest pink of the Otts (apologies), with the boldest fruit character, in keeping with the prized Bandol subappellation. The plushness of barrel aging is apparent on the nose and palate. This is one of those rosés that can power through a meal and will stand up to fish and meat admirably.

The Mastermind: La Mascaronne

Way back in 1994, when young Angelina Jolie's sole film credits were *Lookin' to Get Out* and *Cyborg 2*, the buzzing began among the French wine-erati. It was said that an American multimillionaire couple, living on a massive, isolated estate in the Var, was making a dry rosé that had enthralled the Parisian press and public.

Thomas and Jane Bove also produced excellent red and white wines under their Château Miraval label. But oh—that rosé! As *Le Monde* put it, "L'un des grands élégants de Provence, le Château Miraval . . . régulièrement récompensé dans les concours."[66] (Pardon my French, but I believe this translates as "One of the most elegant Provençal producers, Château Miraval . . . is regularly rewarded in competitions.")

The wines began to arrive on American soil in 1998. Chris Davis, an importer in Portland, Oregon, made a pilgrimage to visit the outlier Americans in 2001. The wines stayed with Davis, haunting him. Three years later, despite a weak market for dry rosé, he finally decided to pull the trigger and order a shipment of Miraval pink. "I have to say I was afraid to import that first vintage," Davis recalls now, shaking his head. "We only brought in twenty cases, but I didn't want to piss my boss off by tying up a bunch of cash. Twenty dollars retail was really expensive for rosé back then."

Davis now owns his own importing firm. Looking back at the pre–Château d'Esclans era, he remembers Miraval as the wine that moved the needle on the dry rosé market. Consumers were wary of pink juice, no matter how high the quality. But those oenophiles who had discovered Miraval were sucking it down. "It was the wine that walked on water," Davis recalls. "We brought in the rosé and it evaporated every year after that. Miraval put rosé on the map for a lot of drinkers."

When the Boves had purchased Miraval back in 1992, it was, as Tom Bove now describes it, "beautiful but in a deteriorating state." No wine had been produced for seven years; vast swaths of ailing vines had to be replanted. The couple stripped back layers of plaster to reveal original sixteenth-

and seventeenth-century façades in their painstaking renovation of the ten-bedroom château. They restored the vineyards to their former glory while pursuing organic certification.

Then, in 1998, tragedy struck. Swissair Flight 111, en route from New York to Geneva, crashed in the Atlantic Ocean, killing all 229 people onboard. Jane Bove was a passenger on that flight.

Tom Bove continued to rehabilitate Miraval alone, by all accounts throwing himself into the work. But in 1999, he purchased another property, approximately 30 miles (40 km) to the southeast: La Mascaronne. In 2008, he leased the Miraval château to Angelina Jolie and Brad Pitt.

When he finally sold the Miraval estate in 2012—for a reported $60 million—Bove retained a 250-acre (100-ha) parcel in the northwest corner. He continues to make wine from the property, under his Mira Luna label, and is rebuilding on

---

66 *Ribaut*, M: Le Magazine du Monde, *2007.*

the ruins of the old bastide and bergerie,[67] constructing an estate house and winery. Bove also owns an additional domaine, Bomont de Cormeil, about an hour north of La Mascaronne. At more than 1,640 feet (500 m) of elevation, it's on the edge of thickly forested truffle country on the outskirts of the commune of Fox-Amphoux.

But Bove's home and headquarters are at La Mascaronne, just outside the village of Le Luc. It's hidden in the foothills above another domaine, La Bernarde. The mile-long road is so wrecked that it's nearly impossible to coax a car up it. This feels like the land that time forgot.

Then, suddenly, improbably, one emerges from a stand of trees to arrive at a low-slung contemporary building, built from the pale gold limestone rocks that blanket the earth. Inside the minimalist space, sleek with floor-to-ceiling panels of glass, office workers tap quietly at keyboards.

At the back of the building, Tom Bove sits in his office, running, it would appear, the world. He's the founder and director of Rochem Group, a wastewater-treatment conglomerate based in Geneva but stretching its tentacles all over the globe.

White-haired, sharp-eyed, and immaculate, Bove speaks with a crisp, bluestocking diction that sounds like mainline Philadelphia or finishing school in Switzerland. He claims to have grown up in Indiana, the grandchild of Italian immigrants and home winemakers, before attending the United States Naval Academy in Annapolis, but he exudes the air of an international man of mystery.

I ask Bove if La Mascaronne ever gets visitors, given that it's so well hidden. "Well, we had a problem with the owners of La Bernarde," he admits. "The easement got complicated, so the road wasn't maintained." I ask him why he's speaking in the past tense. "Because I bought it," he answers casually, Gatsby-like. "Seemed like the easiest way to solve the problem." He isn't sure whether he'll continue to run La Bernarde as a winery, Bove adds. He may just smooth out the road and be done with it.

Then we hop into his black Land Rover to tour his estate. We loop around to the southwest-facing Othello vineyard, a 6-acre (2.5-ha) block offering the best views of the property. He named it after a favorite former dog, Othello, the offspring of a Parisienne Jack Russell terrier and a Français hound belonging to the recording studio manager at Miraval. "His claim to fame was that he bit Brad Pitt," Bove says with a quiet chuckle.

"When I bought this place, the whole thing was one big fissured rock," he tells me, waving an arm as we climb steep craggy slopes. Then, as an afterthought, he adds, "We had to crush the stones." That is, Bove brought in bulldozers, which pierced the rock with steel claws and ripped it apart. The result: Rows of vines that appear to be growing directly out of a forbidding bed of sharp-edged, fist-size limestone chunks.

Despite the apparent paucity of soft dirt, the estate is in conversion to organic when I visit. In some vineyard blocks, white-blossomed wild rocket (arugula) blooms between the rows, a gift from nature that fixes nitrogen in the stony chalk-and-clay soils. Bove has always been a believer in minimalist viticulture and wine-making. Ironically, the membrane technology that has made him so wealthy can be used to engineer wine: In Bordeaux and other regions, where it is permissible, wineries use "reverse osmosis" machines to minimize alcohol levels while concentrating flavor. But as an adherent of a less-interventionist style of wine-making, Bove doesn't use reverse osmosis in his own cellars.

Where Miraval's rosé is minimalist in character, Bove appears to strive for something bolder with his unabashedly barrel-aged La Mascaronne "Cuvée Guy da Nine." "I really wanted to do a rosé that would be different—good for dining," he tells me. "I thought, if I go with a tannic red grape, it will age." His Mourvèdre-based "Guy da Nine" cuvée is a rich, opulent treat that would fare well with a couple of years of bottle age. Aged in Burgundy barrels, it's smooth and spicy. It's a statement wine from someone who, years ago, made a statement about rosé.

....

La Mascaronne "Cuvée Guy da Nine" Côtes de Provence Rosé ($$$)

A rich barrel-fermented and aged wine, composed mostly of Mourvèdre, opulent with a creamy texture and a marzipan-accented palate. It's a step up from the estate's everyday offering, "Quat'Saisons," a perky, oak-free Grenache-Cinsault-Syrah designed to be drunk all four seasons of the year. And at around $32, it's slightly more affordable than a similarly sumptuous Mourvèdre-based rosé like the Domaines Ott* Château Romassan Bandol (approximately $42).

---

[67] *While bastide can mean "fortified town" and bergerie can mean "sheepfold" in French, these words have different meanings in Provence. Old stone farmhouses—once the homes of shepherds—are called bergeries, while bastides are country estate houses.*

The Anointed Ones:
Miraval

Upon its initial release in 2013, Miraval was, as we learned on page 14, a pink phenom that sold out in hours, throwing a spotlight on dry rosé. To the general public, the appeal was obvious: Anyone of drinking age could purchase something delicious, stunningly beautiful, and intoxicating, made at the French vacation home of Hollywood's brightest stars: elegant Angelina Jolie, ruggedly handsome Brad Pitt, and their six charming children.

To the oenophile community, Miraval boasted an additional pedigree. The Jolie-Pitts' partner in the winemaking venture was not, as is typical with celebrity-endorsed wines, a marketing outfit. It was the Perrin family, of Château de Beaucastel in the southern Rhône. Beaucastel is arguably the top producer in the

Châteauneuf-du-Pape appellation, and its "Hommage à Jacques Perrin" is typically priced at between $500 and $700 per bottle.

While they could have simply enjoyed their illustrious inheritance, the Perrins—brothers Jean-Pierre and François and their seven grown children—have expanded their holdings and wealth, launching an affordable Rhône range labeled Famille Perrin, the extremely popular négociant brand La Vieille Ferme, and Tablas Creek in Paso Robles.

The Perrins brought that business acumen to their Provençal enterprise. In the weeks just after harvest, 2015, I visited Miraval in the company of Marc Perrin, who has been the spokesperson for the label. The estate was a beehive of activity: The original winery was under renovation and an additional production facility was in the works. Fifty acres (20 ha) of new vineyards were being planted, with fifty more to be added in the near future. Craftsmen tightly wedged stones together to build flawless new terraces as a few donkeys wandered around dazedly.

Miraval had been a sleeper hit when it was under the direction of Tom Bove. But it grew rapidly under the new regime, from 15,000 cases of the 2012 vintage to 50,000 cases in 2015. To keep up with demand, the owners

sourced fruit from neighboring properties. The label lost its "bio," or certified-organic, status, and was forced to drop the "Château" (with its unspoken promise of estate-grown fruit) from its name.

While a portion of Miraval falls within the Coteaux Varois en Provence appellation, the wines are labeled "Côtes de Provence," suggesting a sun-soaked, lavender-covered hillside overlooking the sea. But the forested property is located in the wild north-central part of "the Var," as habitués call it, covering an astounding 1,600 acres (650 ha). Despite its remote location, an armed guard stands at attention at the gate.

The estate encompasses an ancient Roman burial ground, the crumbling evidence of former moats, olive groves, and a pond. Twenty original terraces date back to Roman times; they were rebuilt in 1822 by prisoners from Toulon. A mile up one southwestern-pointed forested road, a magnificent stone guest house is tucked into a hillside, surrounded by rows of baby hazelnut trees, their roots inoculated with French black truffle spores.

For Perrin, this remote corner of Provence feels as much like a frontier as Paso Robles did back in 1989, when his family had founded Tablas Creek. "There is a lot of raw potential here," he declared. "In the Rhône, everything that could have been planted has been planted. Here, there is great terroir that is still untouched."

Thanks to contemporary technology, such as tractors and stone crushers that can climb any slope, Perrin had his eye on mountainside vineyard terrain where he could grow Syrah and—surprisingly for Provence—Pinot Noir. "We found a three-hectare [7.4-acre] plot of limestone in the Peyrefuguède Valley at about five hundred meters [approximately 1,600 feet] altitude with the same geology as the Côte de Nuits," he confided. "This place is amazing."

I asked Perrin if he was concerned that this venture would be nothing more than a dalliance, the whim of a couple of Hollywood stars. He shook his head emphatically. "We got involved because we had the absolute certitude that this was a long-term project," he told me. "We—both families—share the ideal of quality, and we value the importance of family above everything else."

The look of the living quarters, at the time, confirmed Perrin's

---

Miraval's Miraculous Past

Château Miraval was famous long before the current owners took residence. It was once the home of the Orsini Prince of Naples. A nineteenth-century owner of the estate, Joseph-Louis Lambot, was a pioneer in the business of reinforced concrete, and the original winery, dating back to 1899, is an impressive piece of gravity-flow-designed oeno-architecture.

A subsequent owner, French jazz pianist Jacques Loussier, outfitted a curious-looking turreted outbuilding—a combination bergerie and water tower—as a recording studio in the mid-1970s. Pink Floyd recorded parts of *The Wall* here;[68] everyone from the Cranberries to Courtney Love to Steve Winwood to the Cure laid tracks as well, as evidenced by the names of famous musicians etched into the furniture and scribbled on the walls.[69] The recording equipment remains in the studio, undisturbed. Who wouldn't want to drink a wine with such a backstory?

---

[68] *The rosé produced by the previous owner was named "Pink Floyd" in honor of the thirtieth anniversary of the recording.*

[69] *In 2003, the English blues musician Chris Rea released a film,* Dancing Down the Stony Road, *which documents the process of recording an album at Miraval; portions of it are posted on YouTube.*

assertion. A small enclosure near the château housed lop-eared rabbits, chickens, and goats with curved horns. A soccer ball sat on the grand lawn. A sunlit corner of the performance space in the music building was outfitted with fuzzy rugs and colorful toys. A parade of tiny clay animals, displayed on a ledge, was clearly the work of small hands. "The decisions I make today may not benefit me in the near future, but they will impact my children," Perrin told me. "The owners feel the same way."

Perrin was clearly in love with the place, and from his offhand remarks, I got the impression that Pitt was, as well. According to Perrin, Pitt had a keen enthusiasm for viticulture and a fondness for exploring the rocky dirt roads and paths that wound up impossibly steep slopes into the forested hills.

When news broke of the divorce of Pitt and Jolie, wine lovers' thoughts turned to Miraval, the estate in the wilds of the Var with a fairy-tale name, a sumptuous palace and—until recently—a king and queen reigning over it. I called Hubert Fabre, executive vice president and sales manager for Vineyard Brands, the American importer of Miraval that's partly owned by the Perrins, and inquired what the fate of the rosé would be.

Fabre reminded me that the business partnership between the Perrins and the Jolie-Pitts was fifty-fifty: The Perrins managed viticulture, winemaking, packaging, and business, while the Jolie-Pitts provided the land and the vision. He speculated that the Perrins might consider buying the other half of the business. As this book went to press, Marc Perrin had been quoted by the website of the UK wine magazine, *Decanter*,[70] saying that he did not expect the estate to be sold.

"There is no plan to stop making the wine," Fabre assured me. "Nothing will change. It has been too successful to just stop. Absolutely not, oh no, no, no, no! That is not going to happen. All of us—the Perrins, especially—have worked too hard to make this brand."

And Miraval has done too much for rosé to go away.

....

Miraval Côtes de Provence Rosé   ($$$)

So subdued that it's almost fleeting, this is an apéritif that's technically perfect but perhaps lacks conviction—that said, I prefer it to Whispering Angel. A prickle of spritz on the minerally palate refreshes; the finish crackles a bit. The blend of grapes is Cinsault, Grenache, Syrah, and Rolle.

---

[70] *Anson,* Decanter, *2016.*

The Champion: Gérard Bertrand

While the Otts and the Perrins were upholding family tradition, and Sacha Lichine, Tom Bove, and the Jolie-Pitts were exercising their wealth and power, a lone wolf was fighting his way into the top echelon of rosé producers. And he wasn't even in Provence.

Gérard Bertrand's name is known throughout France. He was a sports star from 1984 through 1994. But back then, rugby players were just about as financially successful as minor-league baseball players are today. To make ends meet, they had to find other work.

Bertrand grew up in the village of Saint-André-de-Roquelongue, speaking Occitan, a traditional language of southern France and northern Spain. In 1970, his father, Georges, bought a small winery, Domaine de Villemajou, near the village of Corbières.

Young Gérard began assisting in the cellar and the vineyard, taking on more responsibility as he grew older—even after beginning his professional rugby career at the age of nineteen, while continuing his studies. Then, when Gérard was still just twenty-three, his father was killed in a car accident.

As with Sacha Lichine and Tom Bove, Bertrand's immersion into the work of winegrowing came about by tragic circumstance.

The young athlete found himself juggling two careers out of financial and familial necessity. It was only manageable because the rugby season ran November through May, while the winery was busiest June through October. During this period, Bertrand broke his nose three times. ("It is only bones," Bertrand demurs.) His ability to smell wine was not affected, he says.

Bertrand describes the first two decades of building a winery business as "a struggle." Only recently have the pieces fallen into place. Today, he owns nine estates, employs 250 people, sells his wine in more than 100 foreign markets, and drives a Tesla.

Tall and suave, Bertrand wears his thick, wavy hair slicked back. He speaks with the aphorisms of a champion: "If you want to have success, you need to think big. You need to do the best you can do." His tanned face appears on posters, video screens, and displays throughout Château

L'Hospitalet, a winery estate that includes a restaurant and hotel and regularly hosts concerts and events. His marketing team would, of course, be foolish not to make the most of the handsome visage of their sports-star boss.

Bertrand built his business by taking risks and believing in his homeland, the Languedoc. The windblown plains of southwest France have been largely overlooked by critics until recent years, but Bertrand always believed that the terroir here could be truly great.

To that end, since 2002 he has converted the majority of his 1,480 acres (600 ha) of vineyard land to biodynamic agriculture. A longtime adherent to homeopathic medicine, Bertrand says it was a "revelation" to discover that he could farm his vines in a similarly holistic manner.

"My father used to say that wine is made from a thousand and one details," Bertrand tells me. "If you want to make the best wine possible, you need to have the best grapes. You need a balanced, healthy vineyard. You need to respect nature. You need to reinforce the vitality of the vine."

Just as he found *biodynamie* early in the game,[71] Bertrand saw

---

[71] *"Biodynamics" became a buzzword in the wine world sometime around 2010.*

the rosé trend coming before anyone else did. And if anyone epitomizes the new congruence of masculinity and pink wine, it's the strapping former rugby star.

In 1990, the head sommelier of the Alain Ducasse restaurant group asked Bertrand if he would consider bottling his rosés in oversize formats, like magnums and jeroboams. The vigneron jumped at the opportunity, and has championed pink wine ever since. In 2005, he introduced "Gris Blanc," an immensely popular blend of Grenache and Grenache Gris that's so pale that it could pass as a plain old blanc.

Between 2010 and 2016, United States imports of Gérard Bertrand wines rose from 20,000 to 250,000 cases—a factor that the trade publication *Market Watch* attributes to the brand's strong rosé portfolio of twelve different pink wines, including a luxe $75 bottling.[72] Gérard Bertrand, it appears, is a contender with the best brands of Provence. When I ask the man about this, he shrugs. "I love the competition, because I was a sportsman," he says. "We like to challenge the Côtes de Provence. We think we can do the same level of quality and perhaps better. We have the diversity of grapes and diversity of terroir."

Gérard Bertrand Coteaux du Languedoc "Côte des Roses" Rosé ($$)

Fresh and bright, with a touch of spritz on the palate, this floral pink has a fresh-spring, scrubbed-clean character, washed over by sea foam and a hunger-inducing bitterness. The color leans toward raspberry.

Gérard Bertrand Château La Sauvageonne "La Villa" Coteaux du Languedoc Rosé ($$$$)

The blend is mostly Grenache, with Mourvédre and smaller amounts of Rolle and Viognier, sourced from a combination of biodynamically farmed mountain and valley vineyards. Aged in barrel seven months, it is smoky, rich, and earthy on the nose, powerfully engulfing the palate like a white from the northern Rhône (that Viognier is evident), while presenting floral, fresh, woodsy flavors. A candidate for cellar age. A second, more affordable rosé from this biodynamic estate is the "Volcanic" cuvée ($$).

---

[72] *"Rosé's Rise is Unstoppable,"* Market Watch, *2016.*

PRETTY AND PINK: SOUTHERN FRANCE

$$$$

Château d'Esclans
Les Clans

$$$$$

Château d'Esclans
Garrus

$$$

Château d'Esclans
Rock Angel

$$

Château d'Esclans
Whispering Angel

$$$

Domaines Ott*
Clos Mireille

$$$$

Domaines Ott*
Château de Selle

$$$$

Domaines Ott*
Château Romassan

$$$

La Mascaronne
Cuvée Guy da Nine

$$$

Miraval
Côtes de Provence Rosé

$$

Gérard Bertrand
Côte des Roses

$$$$

Gérard Bertrand
Château La Sauvageonne

More Southern French Rosé

The supermodel, chanteuse, and political consort Carla Bruni, raised Italian but a naturalized citizen of France, is fond of quoting the French novelist and filmmaker Jean Cocteau: "Un Français est un Italien de mauvaise humeur."[73] As far as pink wine is concerned, she's wrong: France is in a very, very good mood.

France and Italy have long been rivals, particularly in cultural contexts. In art, fashion, and cuisine, the two nations are, arguably, neck and neck. And in wine, too. France might harbor more recognizably elite châteaux, but Italy produces more volume.

In pink production, however, France leads the world. And because habitués (and tourists) suck down so much vin rosé inside the nation's borders, France is also the world's top rosé consumer.

Provence is, unsurprisingly, the most fecund of the rosé regions, accounting for 39 percent of all AOP, or high-quality, pink wines. And all the remaining AOP wine regions south of the forty-fifth parallel[74] make an additional 39

---

[73] *"A French person is an Italian in a foul mood."*

[74] *Just to clarify, the semi-official term Sud de France represents only the coastal southwestern zone known as the Languedoc-Roussillon. This chapter will, however, attempt to provide an overview of Provence, the Rhône Valley, and Languedoc.*

PROFILE

SOUTHERN FRENCH ROSÉ

COLOR
translucent seashell pink,
accents of cantaloupe
and clouds

PERSONALITY
stylish, worldly,
fond of salade Niçoise

AROMATICS
citrus, floral, stone fruit,
alcohol

GOES WELL WITH
sandals, a cigarette,
Serge Gainsbourg,
pommes frites

---

percent of France's fine rosés.[75] In this chapter, the first of this book's six regional roundups, we'll acquaint ourselves with Southern France's most prolific, promising, and quirky rosé production zones.

Provence, of course, is king. But Provençal winemakers face the danger of being blinded by their own success. Every year, certain bottles get more baroque, certain prices climb higher, and certain wines get less interesting. Beware the pursuit of pale color in favor of flavor, as discussed in Chapter 2 (page 41). Too many offerings in the $25-and-up range offer only a few nominal notes of flowers and citrus before fading away, leaving the lingering sensation of alcohol on the palate. The wineries

profiled in this chapter might not include every one of the best-known names—as there are enough to fill an entire book—but in my tasting lineups, their rosés stood out for their quality. And take note that IGP wines keep their tonier AOP[76] Provençal brethren honest, because the winemakers who fall outside the most prestigious winegrowing zones have something to prove.

---

[75] *In 2014, southern France produced 78 percent of fine (AOP) French rosé and 76 percent of all French rosé, per the CIVP.*

[76] *See pages 282–283 for an explanation of AOP, IGP, and other classifications.*

ITALY

RHÔNE VALLEY

PROVENCE

CÔTES DE PROVENCE

LA LONDE

SAINTE-VICTOIRE

COTEAUX VAROIS

BANDOL

VENTOUX

LUBERON

CASSIS

CÔTES DU RHÔNE

COTEAUX D'AIX

LIRAC

TAVEL

PALETTE

COSTIÈRES DE NÎMES

CAMARGUE

MEDITERRANEAN SEA

PIC SAINT LOUP

CÔTES DE THONGUE

PAYS D'HÉRAULT

LANGUEDOC

MINERVOIS

CORBIÈRES

CÔTES DU ROUSSILLON

CÔTES CATALANES

SPAIN

Provence

Don't confuse the Provence of vacation brochures with the wine-producing area, which spans approximately 64,000 acres (26,000 ha), from Avignon to Nice, forming an egg shape in the all-encompassing state of Provence-Alpes-Côte d'Azur. Within are the mountains, the sea, and everything in between.

CÔTES DE PROVENCE

The word "Provence" doesn't appear alone on wine labels. The best-known of the Provençal appellations is Côtes de Provence, which encompasses more than 75 percent of the region, some 50,000 diverse acres (20,000 ha), and churns out more than ten million cases of wine annually. Nearly all of the juice produced here is rosé, although red and white make occasional appearances.

The two subzone names that you might see appended to Côtes de Provence on wine labels are La Londe and Sainte-Victoire. But just because an estate does not fall into a noted subappellation does not necessarily mean its wines are anything to sniff at—as the four high-profile Côtes de Provence wineries in Chapter 3 (see pages 64–83) and the example below will attest.

....

Château Minuty "Rosé et Or" Côtes de Provence ($$$)

Minuty isn't merely a Cru Classé wine estate overlooking the bay of Saint-Tropez. It's a worldwide brand that received a sales bump in the United States recently when mega-goliath Treasury Wine Estates picked up its importing rights. Of three Minuty-branded rosé bottlings, this estate wine is most interesting, offering fresh fragrances of flowers, herbs, and ripe peaches, with white pepper and mint on the finish.

....

La Londe

The village of La Londe-les-Maures, in the foothills of the Maures mountains, looks out over Porquerolles Island, enjoying moderate temperatures and breezes from the sea. Tourists can escape the unrelenting sun by visiting Les Mines de l'Argentière—the old mines, formerly stocked with lead, zinc, and silver. For our purposes, the schisty soil is of more interest,

Clos Cibonne Stands Alone

Tucked into the hills above suburban Toulon, where it's girthed by palm trees and a deliciously overgrown garden, Clos Cibonne is a holdout. While its peers race to produce nearly translucent, diamond-sharp liquids, Clos Cibonne's wines are natural pearls: softer and more rounded, glowing with history and authenticity rather than attempting to dazzle.

The estate has been in the Roux/Deforges family since 1793, and its Cru Classé vineyard is of true historical importance. The gnarled, twisted vine trunks here are mostly Tibouren, an archaic red grape that's difficult to grow but makes a lip-smackingly herbaceous wine.[77]

After the nineteenth-century phylloxera epidemic, most Provençal estates decided against replanting the obscure and ornery Tibouren. It was only saved from extinction by Marius Roux and his son André, who replanted it at Clos Cibonne during the first decade of the twentieth century. Today, Clos Cibonne enjoys a special dispensation from the French authorities to name its cuvée after the rare grape.

Inside Clos Cibonne's cellar, a long row of century-old *foudres*, or massive ovular oak casks, stand at attention, stained mahogany by time. The wine's packaging is equally timeless: a simple moss-green bottle, shaped unconventionally in the sloped Burgundy style and topped with a label design that dates back to 1930.

....

Clos Cibonne "Cuvée Tradition"
Tibouren Cru Classé Côtes de Provence   ($$$)

Tibouren is a grape that does well with moderate oxidation, and at Clos Cibonne, it rests in not-quite-full barrels, where a thin layer of *fleurette*—yeast—is allowed to form on top. This results in a savory, nutty, sherry-like flavor, a tawny color, and a wine that ages beautifully for up to forty years. At the age of three, it's peachy-gold and scrubbed clean on the palate, with notes of almonds and fennel and a perception of sweetness. Note: Clos Cibonne also vinifies a simpler Cinsault-Grenache-Tibouren rosé, sourcing fruit from neighboring properties, called "Tentations" ($$).

---

[77] *It has a following among the lovers of the Ligurian reds of Dolceacqua, where it is called Rossese.*

however. Cinsault and Grenache are grown in it to make rosé and red wines that tend to muster a hard-edged minerality.

....

Domaine Saint-André de Figuière La Londe Côtes de Provence "Première de Figuière" Rosé ($$)

Patriarch Alain Combard learned his craft in Chablis and passed on to his children a Burgundian approach to rosé. The "Première" is more Meursault than Chablis, though: A supple, luxurious wine with a rich leesy mouthfeel and pleasingly chalky palate, accented by a lingering lemon finish. Save yourself the money and buy this silky beauty—from old-vine, organically farmed Mourvèdre, Cinsault, and Grenache—rather than the pricier "Confidentielle," a less-impressive cuvée from the same winery that's presented in a fatter, heavier bottle. Glass is expensive.

....

Château Les Valentínes La Londe Côtes de Provence Rosé ($$)

A blend of organically grown Grenache and Cinsault, this pale peach wine is perky and exhilarating, with notes of starfruit, nectarine, persimmon, and fennel pollen, finishing with earthy, rocky notes. Also worthy of your attention are the minerally "8" ($$$) and the frivolous, fun, pear-ginger "Le Caprice de Clémentine" ($) bottlings from the same winery.

....

Sainte-Victoire

For the final years of his life, the artist Paul Cézanne worked from a hillside studio with a view of Mont Sainte-Victoire. He painted the mountain some sixty times, exploring the texture of its foothills with his brush. These limestone-riddled hills make up the Sainte-Victoire subappellation, just east of Cézanne's childhood home in Aix-en-Provence. The artist's frequent use of a pink-orange brick color in his studies of the mountain evokes the high clay content in the soil, which brings out red-fruit flavors in the rosés.

....

Château Coussin "César à Sumeire" Sainte-Victoire Côtes de Provence ($$$$)

The Sumeires own three estates in Provence but have called the Mont Sainte-Victoire region home since the thirteenth century. Their showcase rosé is lush on the palate, with a touch of spritz, and ripe white peach and yellow plum notes progressing to honeycomb as the wine opens up. Layered and complex, it finishes minty. The New Realist French sculptor César, a friend of the family, signed his name to this label.

▬▬▬▬▬▬▬▬▬▬▬▬

BANDOL, CASSIS, AND PALETTE

It's best to arrive at the seaside towns of Bandol and Cassis by yacht, as there's nowhere to park your car. Bandol earns raves for its meaty, herbaceous Mourvèdre-based reds, and Cassis is famous for its whites, but both produce remarkable rosés as well.

While the wineries of Cassis are just outside the eponymous town, Bandol's top estates are high in the hills. As for Palette, it's one of France's tiniest appellations and consists of merely four producers, making red, white, and rosé just southeast of Aix.

Together, these three are the best-known of six lone-wolf appellations that are technically within Provence but stand apart. Bandol was declared an AOC[78] in 1941, making it one of France's oldest designated wine regions. So if

---

[78] *As discussed on pages 282–283, AOC is the equivalent of today's AOP.*

you're visiting, don't be so foolish as to say something like "Côtes de Provence Bandol." Because Bandol is better than that.

In beginning wine classes, Bandol is generally acknowledged as the "best" rosé region in France. Why? Price, perhaps: $25 to $50 is the typical per-bottle range at retail stores. That's pretty steep for rosé. For some wine insiders, this is perplexing, as Bandol pinks have a propensity to be "hot"— that is, relatively high in alcohol— rendering those of us possessing delicate palates overwhelmed and underimpressed. But tastes are subjective, and for many connoisseurs, Bandol is peerless among rosé regions.

....

Domaines Bunan "Château la Rouvière" Bandol Rosé ($$$)

The Bunan family, a major Bandol landholder, produces multiple cuvées of rosé, paying special attention to—geek alert!—the differences between specific clones (cultivars) within each grape variety. This substantial, spicy wine is sourced from the prized steep south-facing lime and sandstone slopes of a subterroir known as Rouvière. It's mostly old-vine Mourvèdre, with Cinsault and Grenache. While the other

Bunan cuvées are also excellent, this wine is so rich with Asian pear, bitter herbs, minerality, vanilla, and quinine that one could eat it for dinner.

....

Domaine du Gros 'Noré Bandol Rosé ($$$)

If you're of the camp that finds Bandol rosés to be high in alcohol at the expense of fruit, the Gros 'Noré might alter your thinking. It's deceptively pale and challenges the senses in its ability to combine finesse with lean muscularity— ironic, given the winery's name.[79] Most interesting is its inherent tension. Both Bunan and Gros 'Noré are on the same hillside road, overlooking the picturesque village of La Cadière D'Azur.

....

Domaine du Bagnol Cassis Rosé ($$)

Cassis is a microscopic appellation, so we'll take a look at two neighboring wineries to increase your chances of actually finding one in stock. Domaine du Bagnol (not to be confused with la ville de Bandol!) sits on the west side of town, a few minutes' walk from the beach. Fruity, floral, and salty, this wine delights with wild strawberry notes.

Clos Sainte Magdeleine
Cassis Rosé   ($$$)

Clos Sainte Magdeleine may well be France's most scenic winery, reposing over white cliffs on a promontory that juts out into the Mediterranean. A blend of Grenache, Cinsault, and Mourvèdre, this wine is clean and fresh, its briny aroma and flavor echoing the nearby sea.

Château Simone
Palette Rosé   ($$$$)

This *foudre*-fermented and aged rosé is mostly Grenache and Mourvèdre, with some tidbits of Syrah and oddball grapes like Castets and Manosquin, which could be characters in a Molière farce. The wine stays on the lees until spring, and if it's not too cold in the cellar, undergoes malolactic fermentation, then hangs out in bottle for a couple more years prior to release. In short, this pink has the finesse and longevity of the best whites and reds. Barely any is imported into the United States, so if you see a bottle, grab it and run.

COTEAUX VAROIS EN PROVENCE

Provence's wild frontier[80] is inland central Coteaux Varois en Provence. Up in the desolate, woodsy foothills of a mountaineering destination called the Sainte-Baume Massif, high-elevation limestone ridges are now accessible for planting thanks to some seriously bad-ass mechanical tilling technology.

---

[79] *The owner's father, Honoré, was known as "Big 'Noré" by the inhabitants of his village due to his, er, corpulence.*

[80] *Coteaux Varois was not declared a protected appellation until 1993.*

Boarish Behavior

One of the greatest dangers to the southern French vintner is the wild boar. These cantankerous swine dig under fences, feast on ripe grapes, then rudely scratch their backs on vine trunks, thoughtlessly snapping precious limbs. The best defense against them? Guard donkeys, which rear up on their hind legs and kick ferociously. It's difficult to believe this when you see a benign donkey slowly plodding alongside a vine row, chomping on grass, but you don't want to mess with old Eeyore.

Tempier Sets the Temperature

"The best rosé I ever had was Lucien Peyraud's," recalls Kermit Lynch, the Berkeley-based merchant and importer. "It must have been the 1972. It was fermented in *foudres*. It did its malo. Lucien added very little SO$_2$. That, to me, was the rosé of my dreams."

If Lynch had never tasted that wine, this book might not exist. Because Americans knew nothing of fine dry French rosé in the 1970s. But the charming Lucien and Lulu Tempier Peyraud took Lynch—along with restaurateur Alice Waters and expat painter-cum-food-writer Richard Olney—under their wing, serving the Americans fabulous al fresco meals over many summers at their large yellow farmhouse, Domaine Tempier.

In an era when Americans knew only Bordeaux and Burgundy, Waters initially had to convince a Berkeley veterinarian with an import license to supply her restaurant, Chez Panisse, with Domaine Tempier's Bandol wines.

Then Lynch turned up at Chez Panisse in 1974, and shortly thereafter made a pilgrimage to Provence guided by Olney. By 1976, Lynch had taken over for the veterinarian. He didn't have too much trouble selling Tempier's brooding Bandol red. But "rosés were frowned upon by the clientele I was dealing with," Lynch recalls. "People would not buy it. I said, 'OK, don't buy it. I'll give you a bottle.'" And the rest is history.

Today, Domaine Tempier is a Bandol icon. Progress has made its mark, filling the old winery with steel tanks and new ideas, but Domaine Tempier Bandol rosé is still capable of outliving most pink wines. A 1981, tasted at the ripe old age of thirty-four, was a golden honey color, mysterious, haunting. So if you buy a couple of bottles of Tempier today, drink one now, and put the other one away.

....

Domaine Tempier Bandol Rosé   ($$$)

In its youth, Tempier's rosé has an energetic quality that makes you sit up and take notice. It's bright and fragrant, layered with pineapple, blood orange, cherry, and white pepper. With cellar age, it takes on distinct notes of grapefruit pith, caramel, smoke, and salt. Winemaker Daniel Ravier unapologetically gets approximately 10 percent of his rosé juice from *saignée*—Bandol is, after all, a red-wine-making region, and its winemakers don't shy away from the practice. This juice brings a linear, mineral element to the blend. The rest is split between direct pressing and approximately eighteen hours of maceration prior to pressing.

The blazing daytime sun here delivers ripe fruit flavors, while chilly nights keep acidity high. Vinetenders just have to be vigilant about frost . . . and stray rock climbers in stinky spandex.

....

Châteɪu Margüi "Perle de Margüi" Côteaux Varois en Provence Rosé ($$)

Margüi is a certified organic (and biodynamic-leaning) estate just north of Miraval at the town of Châteauvert. Creamy marzipan notes are countered by crisp grapefruit and white peach in this delightful pink. It's a perfectly balanced blend of five grapes: Cinsault, Syrah, Cabernet Sauvignon, Clairette, and Rolle (Vermentino).

....

Château Routas "Rouvière" Coteaux Varois en Provence Rosé ($)

Formerly owned by the Bieler family—more on them in the California section (see page 232)—Routas has long been a go-to label for affordable, solidly high-quality pink wine. The current winemaker trained at Domaines Ott and continues the tradition, reliably turning out an easy-breezy blend of Cinsault, Grenache, and Syrah that's peachy and juicy.

COTEAUX D'AIX-EN-PROVENCE

This northwest-leaning fan-shaped appellation surrounds the city of Aix, where *soupe au pistou*, a summery fresh-basil soup, makes a mean match for the rosés of the region. It's a jumble of different soil types and terroirs, growing a jumble of different grape varieties, including Counoise, Bourboulenc, and Clairette. Releasing nearly two million cases of wine annually, Coteaux d'Aix-en-Provence is second only to Côtes de Provence in production volume. As it isn't in the forested highlands, like Coteaux Varois, and doesn't dip down into the Mediterranean as the other appellations listed previously do, Coteaux-d'Aix-en Provence rosés strike me as less interesting than their peers. Perhaps for this reason, I have found the wine-making here to rely a bit too heavily on interventions in the cellar.

AIX Coteaux d'Aix-en-Provence Rosé ($$)

In case there was any doubt, this wine's provenance is announced in exclamatory uppercase letters (a stylistic approach not advised when you are texting your ex). The winery is actually called Maison Saint Aix, but that wouldn't make for the marketing triumph that this package presents. Sure, it's overtly candied and perfumed on the nose (see my comment above regard-ing cellar interventions), but the combination of silk and spritz on the mouthfeel, plus the perky exotic flavors of pineapple, starfruit, ginger, and Thai basil, followed by beeswax, are just too much fun to pass up.

MEDITERRANÉE

This designation is an IGP. Gath-ering up Provence as well as a portion of the Rhône and many vine-growing islands off France,

it's the "everything-else" category for a grab bag of uncategorizable wines that either don't fall inside an official geographic winegrow-ing boundary or stray outside the list of grapes proscribed for the particular region they happen to hail from. Heck—they may also fall outside the space-time continuum for all we know.

Triennes Mediterranée Rosé ($$)

While the general populace goes wild for Whispering Angel and Miraval, wine insiders go gaga for Triennes. Sure, it's a pretty, delicate color. And its blend of Cinsault, Grenache, and Syrah with Merlot is tasty for the price. But the real allure is the owner-ship: a partnership between two Burgundian superstars, Jacques Seysses, of Domaine Dujac, and Aubert de Villaine of Domaine de la Romanée-Conti. Jacques's son Jeremy Seysses runs day-to-day operations. The estate vineyards are farmed organically and bio-dynamically, although the winery purchases fruit to keep up with demand. When I last checked, that demand was high: Rosé produc-tion was at nearly 46,000 cases annually and going strong.

The Rhône

The Rhône Valley produces world-class red and white wines celebrated for their power, spice, and perfume. While the quality-oriented communes, with familiar names like Hermitage, Côte-Rôtie, and Châteauneuf-du-Pape, do not produce pink wines, the overarching Côtes du Rhône appellation turns out well-priced rosés for everyday drinking. There are, however, a few subzones that have made a specialty of rosé.

Fine Rhône reds tend to have a ferocity to them, with notes of wild game and black pepper. One would expect the best pinks to be the same way, but I'm still looking for the Rhône rosé with that dangerously feral sense of frisson.

CÔTES DU RHÔNE

It's not difficult to find a Côtes du Rhône rosé—they're everywhere. But I'm not a huge fan of this overarching category because the wines tend to be the afterthoughts of producers who focus their high-quality winemaking on solid, spicy reds and whites. On the bright side, it's difficult to find a Côtes du Rhône pink for more than $15.

More Mordorée, S'il vous Plaît

Upholder of old-fashioned winemaking techniques and producer of multiple Tavel bottlings, Mordorée is a classic. The Delorme family employs horses to plow their vine rows and produces wines that become more mysterious and intoxicating with age. Three to ten years is the ideal window, but Mordorée still holds its own after decades in the cellar—a strength that can be attributed to the use of extended maceration in tank prior to fermentation.

In the summer of 2015, tragedy struck this estate when winemaker and Tavel booster Christophe Delorme died suddenly and far too young, of a heart attack. His bereft father, Francis, returned from retirement to oversee winemaking, while his brother Fabrice runs the business side. But Christophe left a legacy. His highly regarded red winemaking program resulted in the legendary Châteauneuf-du-Pape, "La Plume du Peintre," and the Lirac Rouge, "La Reine des Bois." And his Tavels are haunting. A 2007 "La Dame Rousse" was still a stunning cranberry color when I tasted it at eight years of age, with an alluring perfume and a piquant palate of dried cranberries, savory notes, and spice.

....

Domaine de la Mordorée "La Dame Rousse" Tavel ($$$)
Mordorée's limited-edition Tavel cuvées, "La Reine des Bois" ($$$$) and "Les Vestides" ($$$), are outstanding. But the six-grape, Grenache-based "La Dame Rousse" blend is a fine introduction to the label. The color is a gorgeous ruby, the aroma floral, the palate savory and spicy over a frame of fresh tart cranberry. The fruit is sourced exclusively from the old-vine, organically farmed estate—which is named after the woodcocks that populate the area.

Les Dauphins Côtes du Rhône Réserve Rosé ($)

At first glance, it's a cheap wine hiding behind a blindingly over-wrought label. The styling screams "circus tent." The color—and, it turns out, initial sniff—is cotton candy. But the thirteen-vineyard cooperative, Cellier des Dauphins, has achieved a balancing act that would please everyone under the Big Top. Pretense-free but fun to drink, this is a wine to pair with popcorn and a crowd. And I like that this isn't just another after-thought label from a big-name producer whose talents are better devoted to reds and whites.

TAVEL

The forward-thinking Union of Tavel Winery Owners, established in 1902, outlined the boundaries of its prized production zone in 1926 and earned its all-rosé AOC status in 1936, just a year after the governing body for wine appellations was formed. Today, the wines of Tavel are shockingly underpriced when one considers the fact that kings of previous epochs lusted after them.

The list of allowable grapes in Tavel is long: Grenache Noir, Gris, and Blanc; Cinsault; Bour-boulenc; Clairette Blanche and Rose; Mourvèdre; Picpoul Noir, Blanc, and Gris; Syrah; Carignan Blanc and Noir; and Calitor Noir, which I think might be the name of a planet in the *Star Wars* series. The wine from this southern Rhône town tends toward a bright water-melon color. The best Tavels can be stunning at six to ten years of age.

Lirac, Tavel's neighbor to the north, is the only other Cru—that is, top-tier—village in the Rhône that produces rosé. It tends to be similar in style to Tavel, but for your money, I'd recommend you go with A. J. Liebling on this: "Tavel has a rose-cerise robe, like a num-ber of well-known racing silks, but its taste is not thin or acidulous, as that of most of its mimics is."[81]

To get that racing-silk red, Tavel winemakers blend red, white, and "gray"[82] grapes together. (This is permissible so long as the colors are mixed prior to fermentation.) The grapes then macerate at a slightly warmer temperature than their Provençal brethren do, and even ferment together, which is unusual, since most rosés are pressed off their skins prior to fermentation. The reds imbue the finished wine

---

[81] *Liebling,* Just Enough Liebling: Classic Work by the Legendary *New Yorker* Writer, 46.

[82] *As discussed, "gris" grapes are actually pink- or lavender-skinned.*

with bold pigment while the white grapes brighten the blend.

"Tavel is different—we are about structure," Vincent de Bez, owner and winemaker at Château d'Aquéria, tells me. "It's a wine to eat with. The rosé that is clear? It's nice for sand and swimming, but for me, it's not a serious wine."

....

Château d'Aquéria
Tavel ($$)

Cranberry-colored and strawberry-mint-scented, with notes of chile pepper and thyme, this blend of eight grapes is tart and delicious. Some of the lots are allowed to go through spontaneous fermentation. The sandy soils of Aquéria's vineyards boil over with round rocks, which differ from the shards of calcareous stones that populate the west side of the appellation.

....

Domaine Lafond
Roc-Epine Tavel ($$)

Founded in 1780 by a governor of Tavel, this organically farmed estate is run by the Lafond family but gets its charming surname from a champion 1930s racehorse named Roquepine. The wine is tart, tangy, and zippy—dare I say racy?—with notes of red currant. And, yes, it's the color of red racing silks.

LUBERON

The southerly Ventoux, Luberon, and Costières de Nîmes are much larger and more laid-back than their northerly neighbors. Thanks to affordable land values, these Rhône subzones are attracting a new generation of ambitious young winemakers who offer bang-for-the-buck drinking experiences.

This wild region doesn't have much in common with the rest of the Rhône and wasn't declared to be the Luberon AOP until 1988. The landscape is dominated by the Luberon *massif*, a grouping of three small mountain ranges. Culturally, one could consider the Luberon to be in Provence. (Peter Mayle's first "Provençal" home, in fact, was in the Luberon village of Ménerbes.) More than half the wine produced here is rosé.

....

Château La Canorgue
Luberon Rosé ($)

La Canorgue was the setting for the charming (if poorly reviewed) Russell Crowe–Marion Cotillard vehicle *A Good Year*. Sourced from biodynamically and organically farmed Grenache, Syrah, and Mourvèdre, this wine is the dry, pale rosé version of *Glühwein*— think cherry, orange slices, star

anise, cinnamon sticks—if allowed to open up in the glass.

VENTOUX

Mont Ventoux, a UNESCO Biosphere Reserve, is noted for its abundance of plant and bird life as well as its godforsaken fourteen-mile-living-hell Tour de France ascent. Its foothills are the sun-soaked aromatic scrubland of the Ventoux AOP, directly east of Tavel and Châteauneuf-du-Pape, and just south of the dessert-wine-producing town of Beaumes-de-Venise. Chilly night-time temperatures here impart freshness to the rosés.

Anne Pichon
"Gris Montagne"
Ventoux Rosé ($)

On the eastern side of the town of Mormoiron, Domaine Le Murmurium releases two labels, one of which is called "Mur-mur-ium," raising the possibility that the entire place could be a figment of the imagination of Finnish author Tove Jansson.[83] However, Anne Pichon is Danish, not Finnish; she and her husband, Marc, keep things real by farming organically. The fetching label on Anne's wine is a reference to the archaic name of the estate, which is Latin for the "murmuring" sound made by bees. This pale pink blend of Syrah, Grenache, Cinsault, and old-vine Carignan is like a yellow-plum clafoutis in all the best ways— creamy and slightly exotic.

COSTIÈRES DE NÎMES

The southernmost section of the Rhône connects Provence with Languedoc and reaches all the way to the Mediterranean Sea. More than 40 percent of the wine produced is rosé of the standard Rhône-ish G-S-M[84] variety, sometimes with a few other grapes thrown in for flavor.

Terre des Chardons
"Rosée d'Été"
Costières de Nîmes Rosé ($$)

The "Land of Thistles," as it translates, is located just west of the town of Bellegarde and north of the marshy Camargue natural reserve and national park. The rock-ridden soil is biodynamically farmed, and fermentation is spontaneous. After an initial whiff of barnyard, the Grenache-Syrah "Summer Dew" (as Rosée d'Été translates) hits the palate with a smooth texture and an irresistible salted caramel effect.

---

[83] *Originator of the Moomins, who reside in Moominland.*

[84] *Grenache-Syrah-Mourvèdre is the standard Côtes du Rhône red-grape blend.*

Languedoc

Like its neighbor to the east, Provence, the Languedoc-Roussillon[85] enjoys a warm, dry climate and Mediterranean beaches, albeit with quieter and somewhat seedier resort towns.

There are nearly a hundred different winegrowing appellations in Languedoc, including plenty of AOPs and twenty-three recently redefined IGPs. Mourvèdre is the prestige variety, and it's often accompanied by Syrah, Grenache, or Cinsault.

While young matadors keep a dying tradition alive by fighting Camargue bulls in the villages of the Languedoc-Roussillon, young vignerons fight against old stereotypes in their efforts to redefine winemaking in this promising place. Vineyards here grow a full third of France's grapes and contributed much to Europe's "wine lake," the glut of mediocre juice that pooled when competition from inexpensive New World regions quashed demand for cheap French swill (see page 282).

Now that a chunk of lower-quality vineyard land has been converted to other crops and a generation of vinetenders have moved on, the next generation is nursing those ancient vines that remain in promising growing zones back to health with gentle, organic agricultural practices. They're also resurrecting the reputation of the formerly reviled Carignan variety with careful pruning and vinification.[86]

The landscape here buds the same wild aromatic shrubs—lavender, sage, rosemary, thyme, juniper—that make up the Provençal and southern Rhône *maquis*.[87] In these soils, the scrubland is called *garrigue*, and it's a common descriptor for the aromas and flavors of the region's herbaceous wines. As with Provence and the Rhône, limpidity seems to be valued, but in the best of the Languedoc rosés, those savage *garrigue* notes really come through with thorny, brambly complexity.

---

[85] *Today known simply as "Languedoc."*

[86] *My challenge to this new generation of winemakers: Take pity on English-speaking journalists and quit using the term "saignée" to describe quickly macerated rosés that are not a byproduct of red-wine production.*

[87] *In Languedoc, the word* maquis *is not just used to describe the Mediterranean brushlands. During World War II, the resistance fighters who hid in the high-ground wilderness of France's mountainous regions, including the Pyrénées, were called "Maquis." Today's Languedoc revolutionaries, it could be argued, are winemakers.*

Listel's Sand-Sown Vines

The bistros and bars of the South of France sell seas of rosé. But at the Salin d'Aigues Mortes, the sea itself is rosé. Precious *fleur de sel* has been hand-harvested from these flats for more than 2,000 years. Every summer, as the salt water evaporates in the heat, keratin-producing algae turn the water pink.

It's just one of the many curiosities of the Camargue, the marshy meeting place between the Rhône River and the evocatively named Gulf of Lion. The locals call the pink sea "dead water," but this saline environment and the nearby marshes attract thousands of species of flora and fauna.[88] These include an heirloom breed of free-range horse that's black-skinned and white-coated—like the mammalian embodiment of *vin gris*, its fur shimmers silver—and curious green succulents that sprout from windblown mounds of the very substance that kills just about everything else in the plant kingdom: salt.

Everything else except grapevines. Next to the salt farm, acres and acres of them desperately claw their way out of the ground like turgid lobsters. The growing conditions of the *vins de sable* of the Camargue are so unique and worthy of note that the region was awaiting the declaration of its own AOP status as I was researching this book.

Domaine Royal de Jarras[89] is the home base of Domaines Listel. Sure, the vines are self-rooted, having skipped the scourge of phylloxera.[90] But that's the only advantage to farming white, loose, dry, salty sand. It's so nutrient-poor that the grapes are barely able to produce pigment or tannin. Thus, Listel produces rosé.

A lot of rosé. As in more than two million cases annually, making Listel, founded in 1883, the market leader in pink-wine production and a name as ubiquitous and familiar as that of Coca-Cola in France. It's not easy keeping this volume of pink wine fresh as it sits on store shelves all over the planet, so the wines are flash-pasteurized for shelf stabilization, like so many French cheeses these days, negating the need to add stinky sulfur dioxide as a preservative.[91]

It was not until 1955 that Listel really came into its own, clearing its sandy domain of more than 25,000 leftover land mines and converting the World War II–scorched coastal land to viticulture. Today, Listel's holdings stretch over 11,000 acres (4,500 ha), from Montpellier to Marseilles, forming Europe's most massive vineyard, with 5,000 acres (2,000 ha) under vine. Each year, some 50,000 tourists take train rides through the Domaine Royale de Jarras property.

The battle against the elements is primordial at Listel. A 4-mile (6-km) stretch of gorgeous, empty coastline is perpetually blasted by gale-force winds. As the planet's average temperatures rise, that beach, and Listel's vines, are imperiled. At approximately 3 feet (1 m) of elevation, the vines are currently protected by dikes. The future may call for the construction of walls.

The farming method is largely organic by necessity, as chemical fertilizers would simply wash away. Grazing sheep keep the weeds down. Every acre of vines is surrounded by an acre and a half of natural buffer, housing beneficial insects and wildlife.

The most spectacular wild residents of Domaine Royal de Jarras are flamingoes with otherworldly black-edged fuchsia wings. Of Listel's many rosés, its most classic is the "Pink Flamingo" *gris de gris* cuvée, sourced entirely from this estate.

....

Listel "Grain de Gris" Sable de Camargue ($)

Pink Flamingo is a classic, but the Grain de Gris is easier to track down in US stores. It's a blend of Grenache, Cinsault, Merlot, and Cabernet Sauvignon juice; as winery director Martial Pelatan puts it, "We have one foot in Bordeaux and the other foot in Provence here." Seashell pink, it's cheerful and balanced and conveys a sense of place: notes of sea brine and sand are accented by ripe nectarine, grapefruit juice, and white pepper.

---

[88] *Much of the Camargue is a UNESCO-protected biosphere reserve.*

[89] *The "Royal" dates back to Louis IX, who used the neighboring town of Aigues-Mortes as home base for the seventh and eighth crusades. Aigues-Mortes, by the by, translates as "dead water." Could refer to the bloodbath of the crusades, or a famous nineteenth-century massacre of Italian salt workers here—but I'm told it refers to those marshy, salty waters.*

[90] *Sand is Kryptonite to phylloxera.*

[91] *Serious oenophiles pooh-pooh the bacteria-killing pasteurization process as the realm of boxed-wine and kosher-wine producers. I would argue that Listel rosé is a simple pleasure, not a serious wine, and I appreciate the lack of SO_2.*

PIC SAINT LOUP

In the hills behind the city of Montpellier, Pic Saint Loup is a group of villages shielded by the eponymous limestone outcropping. Its moist, cool nights make for racy, energetic rosés. Saint Loup, if you were wondering, was a crusader whose beloved died while he was off being knightly. He and his brothers all went to live as mountaintop hermits after that. One wonders if they were able to drown their sorrows in the local rosé.

....

Bergerie de L'Hortus Coteaux du Languedoc Rosé ($)

Domaine de l'Hortus, a rocky estate at the foot of Hortus mountain, makes very fine red and white wines from its high-elevation vineyard blocks and bottles its lowland grapes under the more affordable Bergerie de L'Hortus label. The "Coteaux du Languedoc" is in the process of phasing out, to be replaced by "Languedoc," and this pretty, raspberry-tinted blend of Mourvèdre, Grenache, and Syrah is more or less a Pic Saint Loup wine. It's sophisticated and sexy, with notes of blood orange, white pepper, bitter herbs, dried apricot, and quinine.

MINERVOIS

Moving southwest, the landscape of Minervois skirts the southern edge of the mountainous Massif Central and edges into the protected Parc Naturel Régional du Haut-Languedoc. Medieval villages sit atop precarious limestone cliffs and astride vine-covered hillsides; the climate is a combo of Mediterranean sun and mountain freshness. Tourists come to see prehistoric paintings in craggy caves as well as to drink the fruity, floral, spicy wines.

....

Château Coupe Roses "Frémillant" Minervois Rosé ($)

This château wins acclaim for its lip-smacking and affordable reds and gets its name from the local Coupe-Rose clay, historically used in brick making. The rosé is in short supply and high demand thanks to its nice price, liveliness and alluring aroma of—I swear I was not influenced by the label!—rose water. The vineyards inhabit rocky slopes reaching 1,300 feet (400 m) in elevation, which accounts for the bracing acidity in this blend of Grenache, Syrah, Cinsault, and Mourvèdre.

CÔTES DU ROUSSILLON

The lower third of the Languedoc-Roussillon wine region falls inside the Pyrénées-Orientales *département*, bordering Spain. It's best-known for the sweet fortified wines Rivesaltes, Muscat de Rivesaltes, and Banyuls. But the extreme conditions here can produce complex dry wines as well. The *tramontane*, an ever-present wind that can gust as high as 99 miles (160 km) per hour through the Pyrénées, the Massif Central, and the Albera Massif toward the sea, renders dry, thick-skinned grapes and leathery red wines. The vineyards at higher, sloping sites are able to designate their wines "Côtes du Roussillon Villages"[92] as a mark of quality.

Domaine Lafage "Miraflors" Côtes du Roussillon Rosé   ($–$$)

Winemaker Jean-Marc Lafage is a darling of the critics and has performed some sort of necromancy on the surly, hardscrabble fruit of the Roussillon. He presents his petal-pink "Miraflors" in an arcing frosted-glass bottle—a statement piece declaring this to be as fine a place as any for elegant rosé. The blend is Mourvèdre and Grenache

[92]   *In France, "Villages" in plural refers to a particularly good group of growing areas within a larger AOP.*

Gris, grown on the rocky slopes between the city of Perpignan and the Mediterranean.

CORBIÈRES

Just south of Minervois, Corbières makes inky, thorny red wines. The rosés can be just as serious, complex, and delightful. It's difficult to generalize about the diverse terrain, and there's hope that its tangle of micro-terroirs will be divided into subappellations in the near future.

Just to give you a snapshot, imagine grim-looking, masochistic cyclists grinding up perilously winding roads that climb steep knobby hills, traverse high plains, and skirt dramatic gorges. The payoff: gentle slopes stretching down toward the sea.

Domaine de Fontsainte "Gris de Gris" Corbières Rosé ($–$$)

The bestselling rosé in importer Kermit Lynch's catalog is a standby in restaurants all over the United States for good reason. Hardworking Bruno Laboucarié (a childhood friend and neighbor of Gérard Bertrand) tends sun-drenched vines chilled by winds channeled down the Pyrénées Mountains.

Among them is the Grenache Gris that dominates his fine rosé. Fermentation is slow and cold; Grenache Noir, Mourvèdre, and Carignan round out the cuvée.

CÔTES DE THONGUE

The watershed formed by the Thongue river basin, between the Saint-Chinian AOP and the sea, is a mere IGP but still manages to turn out some very nice wines thanks to gently sloping vineyards and sea breezes. So: Do these wines coat the tongue? The reds do, when sourced from parsimonious old vines, but the zippier pinks and whites from the Côtes de Thongue are just juicy.

Domaine Montrose Côtes de Thongue Rosé ($)

Fun fact: Back in 1701, Louis XIV granted owner Joseph Alazard his reptilian coat of arms because his name sounded a lot like "lézard." Today, Alazard's descendants bottle this outstanding rosé from Grenache, Cabernet Sauvignon, and Syrah at a picturesque family estate that's surrounded by pink-flowering almond trees, as well as quince, wild apple, juniper, strawberry trees, elderberry, laurel, and more.

Foncalieu Is on Cue

In centuries past, European family farms were polycultures. Wine grapes were grown alongside sheep, pigs, cattle, ducks, vegetables, fruit trees, olives, and so on, and rural dwellers spent their autumns making barrels of wine for family consumption. Over time, these small-scale vignerons began pooling their resources by purchasing larger viticultural equipment, sharing their grapes, and assigning cellar duties to fewer workers.

Winemaking cooperatives are a major industry these days, producing more than half the wine in France.[93] Much of that hails from the Languedoc, where, historically, the emphasis was on quantity rather than quality (see the discussion of the "wine lake," page 282). But that changed when the EU decided to crack down on the overproduction problem rather than subsidizing it.

Today's Languedoc cooperatives are working to overturn a besmirched reputation, offering sophisticated services like branding, marketing, and international sales to their members. Of these, no collective has arisen from the ashes of the EU overhaul as impressively as Vignobles Foncalieu, a direct descendent of Languedoc's first co-op, Maraussan, founded in 1901.

Today's Foncalieu is an über-cooperative composed of some 1,200 vineyard members, representing more than 12,000 acres (5,000 ha) of vines. Under various brands, Foncalieu releases more than 2.2 million cases of wine annually, totaling more than 1,200 distinct wines at four main winemaking facilities. It made me tired just to type that.

Despite the breathtaking quantity, the emphasis here is on quality. The group releases an "Atelier Prestige" line of high-end reds from single terroirs and vinifies well-regarded estate wines and Corbières at its flagship estate, Château Haut-Gléon. But as far as I'm concerned, what's most exciting about this conglomerate is its focus on elevating the conversation about affordable Languedoc pink wine.

Les Vignobles Foncalieu Coteaux d'Ensérune Piquepoul Rosé ($)

One of the thirteen permitted varieties in Châteauneuf-du-Pape, Piquepoul Noir is the red version of the grape behind the alternately spelled Picpoul de Pinet white wine. Floral and low in tannins, Piquepoul Noir makes a low-alcohol, pale red wine, but is ideal for rosé. This one has notes of crushed rose petals and mint leaves, finishing with lemon. The smart packaging (see page 118) is more than just a "critter label," as the industry dubs anything animalian. The name "piquepoul" comes from *les poules picorer*, because this variety has a tendency to drop its ripe grapes to the ground, where hens peck at it. The IGP territory of Coteaux d'Ensérune is just south of the Saint-Chinian AOP, known for its southern Rhône–style reds and rosés.

Les Vignobles Foncalieu "Le Versant" Pays d'Oc Grenache Rosé ($)

A stylishly understated wine that doesn't fall down the Grenache trap of overripe berry notes, instead tending toward strawberry leaf, fresh wild strawberry, and green apple. Lees stirring during the wine's three-month rest in stainless-steel vats brings a slight smoothness to the otherwise-crisp character. Also worthy of note: Foncalieu's "Griset,"[94] a *gris de gris* made from Sauvignon Gris, a pink-skinned variation of Sauvignon Blanc that's rarely seen outside of Chile, the Loire Valley, and Bordeaux.

---

[93] *Fifty-one percent of the total wine, although just 43 percent if you discount the wine turned into brandy in the Charentes region, according to the Vignerons Coopérateurs de France.*

[94] *Not available in the United States at press time.*

PAYS D'OC

It's not possible to make any sort
of generalization about the terroirs
or wines of this catchall IGP
appellation. It encompasses
almost all of the Languedoc and
thirty-six different grape varieties,
selling some fifty-four million
cases of wine annually. So, yeah.

When dealing with a region so
vast, I look for the outliers: wineries working with very old vines,
vinifying a single grape variety
that's rarely allowed to shine on
its own, farming biodynamically,
or reviving old-fashioned cellar
techniques to make something
that's unique.

Domaine de Malavieille "Charmille" Pays d'Oc Rosé ($–$$)

A native-yeast-fermented blend
of Syrah, Cinsault, Mourvèdre,
and Grenache, from low-yielding,
biodynamically certified vineyards
in and near the Terrasses du
Larzac subregion of Languedoc.
Spontaneous, native-yeast fermentation might account for the
feistiness of this raspberry-tinted
pink. Cherries, cola, black olives,
and quinine bring to mind cocktail
hour, but this is a sharp-angled
wine that will slice through food.

Villa des Anges "Old Vines" Pays d'Oc Rosé ($)

Espitalet des Anges has been so
named for at least a century, long
before Whispering Angel was even
a whisper of an idea. As for the
wine: Made entirely from Cinsault,
it undergoes malolactic fermentation, an unusual move for a rosé[95]
fermented and aged in stainless
steel. The payoff is a dreamy,
creamy, pillowy texture, recall-
ing the region's sweet nougat de
Montélimar (almonds, egg whites,
maybe lavender honey). The color
is pale; the palate charms with
fresh tangerine, tarragon, and a
prickle of acidity.

PAYS D'HÉRAULT

Another all-encompassing IGP,
covering the entire Hérault
département, this designation is
about grape, not place. It allows
vignerons to experiment with
varietals outside the traditional
Languedoc lineup, such as
Cabernet Sauvignon and Merlot,
to make more complex, higher-
quality reds. However, the rosés
are light and simple. The name to
know here is Gassac.

Moulin de Gassac "Guilhem" Pays d'Hérault Rosé ($)

Le Mas de Daumas Gassac has turned the heads of critics with its expressive Cabs and its collection of rare vines culled from all over the world. Owner Aimé Guibert holds hero status among wine geeks thanks to his star turn, in the 2005 documentary *Mondovino*, as a leader of the resistance against the Californian Mondavi empire, which had proposed to develop vineyards and a winery in the Languedoc. The Grenache-Carignan rosé under his second-tier Moulin de Gassac label, named after local patron Saint Guilhem, shows no signs of irrev-erence, however. It's all softness and delicacy, rose hips, white tea, and Meyer lemon.

CÔTES CATALANES

You know you're getting close to Spain when the wine country goes by the name "Catalan Coast." This IGP covers the Roussillon end of the Languedoc-Roussillon, as well as grapes and winemaking techniques that don't adhere to the rules for the AOPs in the area. Of most interest viticulturally are the high-elevation foothills of the Pyrénées, the Fenouillèdes, where the Occitan language is spoken (in addition to French and Catalan), and the slopes of the Agly River Valley channel the *tramontane* effect.

Le Cirque Côtes Catalanes Rosé ($)

The *commune* (village) of Tautavel is surrounded by rocky cliffs and river gorges and is home to the 450,000-year-old Tautavel Man and the European Centre for Pre-historic Research. Oh, and there's a wine cooperative, too. The color of this Grenache-Syrah-Mourvèdre leans toward red. *Garrigue*, espe-cially *fenouil* (fennel), plus orange blossoms, green olives, and sea salt make a rosé as lean and rangy as a *Homo erectus* prowling the foothills of the Pyrénées on a hunt for reindeer and chamois. Serve it with musk ox, spit-roasted over an open fire, accompanied by grunt-ing sounds.

---

[95] *Malolactic fermentation is more often associated with oak fermentation and élevage than with stainless steel. It's also highly unusual with rosé . . . I just happen to have sniffed out as many malo-fermented wines as I possibly could for inclusion in this book.*

PRETTY AND PINK

$$$

Provence

**Château
Minuty**

$$$

Provence

**Clos
Cibonne**

$$$$

Provence

**Château
Coussin**

$$

Provence

**Château
Margüi**

$$

Provence

AIX

$$

Provence

Triennes

$

Languedoc

**Château
Coupe Roses**

$

Languedoc

Foncalieu

$–$$

Languedoc

**Domaine de
Malavieille**

SOUTHERN FRANCE

$$$

Provence

**Domaine du
Gros 'Noré**

$$$$

Provence

**Château
Simone**

$$$

Provence

**Domaine
Tempier**

$

Rhône

Anne Pichon

$$$

Rhône

**Domaine de
la Mordorée**

$

Languedoc

**Bergerie de
L'Hortus**

$

Languedoc

**Villa des
Anges**

$

Languedoc

**Moulin de
Gassac**

$

Languedoc

Le Cirque

Rosato d'Italia

Italia wins the size prize in global output of vino. And while its volume of pink-wine production isn't as massive as that of Spain or the United States,[96] the diversity, quality, and history of its rosati is unparalleled. Plus, Italy's enthusiasm for rosato is infectious.

The city of Lecce, in Apulia, hosts an annual international pink-wine summit and celebration called Roséxpo. And in 2012,

the Puglians rolled out the world's first national pink-wine competition. That same year, the international Vinitaly trade show sponsored an unprecedented panel discussion entitled, "Il futuro è rosa . . . anzi rosato."[96]

[96] *More does not necessarily mean better. Spain takes the world trophy for bulk (as in factory-made) wine production; and the United States churns out oceans of "blush" wines, including White Zinfandel, that are sold by the box or jug on the bottom shelf of your supermarket.*

[97] *"The future is rosy . . . in fact, it's rosé."*

PROFILE

ITALIAN ROSATO

COLOR
from strawberry gelato to
San Marzano tomato

AROMATICS
cherries, radicchio,
orange blossoms

PERSONALITY
stalwart, unflinching, uses
expansive hand gestures

GOES WELL WITH
Persols, Vespa,
spaghetti ai frutti di mare

In this chapter, we'll travel throughout the nation, discovering the distinct styles that are emerging in Italy's most prominent winegrowing regions.

Abruzzo, the Veneto, and Puglia are Italy's rosato powerhouses, each specializing in its own signature style of pink. Abruzzo's joyful Cerasuolo wines look like liquid Red Hots and smell like bowls of cherries. Chiaretto from the Veneto and Lombardy can be anywhere from petal-to-lychee pink and lends itself to lakeside sipping. Both of these appellations—Cerasuolo and Chiaretto— are DOPs specific to rosé and no other style of wine.

Puglia squeezes out seas of rosato. There isn't a particular pink-specific appellation here like Cerasuolo and Chiaretto in the aforementioned regions, but in the Salento subzone, the rustic Negroamaro grape certainly pulls its weight, making wines of lustrous color and irrepressible exuberance.

Italy's openness to exploration in the realm of rosé can surprise and delight. In staid Piemonte, time-worn Tuscany, or sanguine Emilia-Romagna, one stumbles across curious rosati that veer wildly from their archetypical red counterparts. Fragrant of balsamic vinegar or fresh basil leaves, ranging from shimmering gold to popsicle-pink, these are the wines of a people always eager to celebrate something—especially food.

Trentino-Alto Adige

Let's begin our exploration high in the snow-peaked Dolomites, just across the border from Austria and Switzerland. Many of the grapes in Germanophone Alto Adige have names like Gewürztraminer and Müller-Thurgau and self-identify as Teutonic, so one might expect crisp, snowy-pale rosés.

But Alto Adige wines tend to be hearty and packed with pigment, as though the fruit was flushed from the pleasurable exertion of growing on those precariously steep, craggy mountainsides.

Down south in Trentino, the elevations are lower, Italian is the dominant language, and the winemakers specialize in Pinot Grigio and Chardonnay as well as intense Bordeaux-style red blends. For our purposes, the subzone of Trento is of most interest, as it produces lovely Champagne-style sparkling wines for competitive prices.

ALTO ADIGE/SÜDTIROL

Tyrol was a part of the Hapsburg Empire until the conclusion of World War I, when Italy grabbed it. So on the *süd* side the local delicacies are smoked speck and beef *gulasch* (that is, pork fat and the German variation of *goulash*); and the landscape looks like the set of *The Sound of Music*. Cue the cowbells.

Even though the vineyards perch on snow-dusted mountainsides, it can get roasting hot here when the sun reflects off the gray rock cliffs and beats down on the Adige Valley. So it's possible to ripen a wide variety of grapes, of which Lagrein is the local luminary. It makes plummy, opaque red wines and guilelessly juicy, fiery red-currant-hued rosati that don't ask too much of the drinker. Those Dolomite mountains are so multi-dimensional that it's grounding to drink something so firmly rooted.

Kellerei Cantina Terlan Sudtirol Alto Adige Lagrein Rosé ($$)

You know you're in Alto Adige when the word "winery" appears twice on a label, in both German (*kellerei*) and Italian (*cantina*). The plum and black-huckleberry notes of the Lagrein shine through this peppy pink. Enlivened by spritz, exhilarating acidity, and bracing light tannins, it conveys the sense of climbing a mountain and breathing in Alpine air. *Ahhhh.*

DOLOMITI

Vigneti delle Dolomiti (aka Weinberg Dolomiten) are Alto Adige IGP wines. As with other IGP designations, winemakers can choose from a grab bag of grapes, ranging from traditional local varieties such as Kerner and Schiava to oddball expatriates like Carménère and Petit Verdot.

Mezzacorona Dolomiti Rosé ($)

Gruppo Mezzacorona is a giganto-size agricultural cooperative; its flagship winery, "Cittadella del Vino," is an architectural showstopper sandwiched between the Adige River and a tributary that feeds into Lago di Santa Giustina. This rosé of Lagrein is delicate and dry, with a creamy texture and a nice spicy finish of ginger, starfruit, and Asian pear. Plus—bargain alert!—it was all of $8 last time I checked.

TRENTO

Trento is the name of the capital city of Trentino as well as a DOP for sparkling wines made in the style of Champagne.[98] From the village of Salorno (famous for the ruined Haderburg Castle, which balances precariously atop a rocky pinnacle), this winegrowing zone follows the path of the Adige River

---

[98] *This is the* metodo classico, *aka* méthode Champenoise, *technique, whereby a carefully attended secondary fermentation in the bottle makes for a creamy, luxuriant sparkling wine.*

south to the town of Borghetto sull'Adige, enjoying mountain breezes and stunning backdrops the whole way. Most of the high-elevation vineyards employ a traditional pergola style of vine-training, which creates lush canopies of green in the summer-time. For elegance and creamy luxuriance, I might choose the more obscure sparkling wines of Franciacorta (see opposite page) first. But Trento delivers reliable quality, and Ferrari, Trento's flag-ship brand, is widely available.

....

Ferrari Trento Metodo Classico Rosé ($$)

Giulio Ferrari established Trento as a sparkling-wine center back in 1902, and his successors, the

Lunellis, continue to make out-standing wines. Visitors to Italy enjoy visiting their Ferrari Spazio Bollicine ("Ferrari Bubble Room") wine bars. This rose-gold blend of 60 percent Pinot Nero (Noir) and 40 percent Chardonnay has a soft, yeasty aroma and delivers the total package—assertive bubbles, minerality, raspberry, white tea, and lime—for an extremely reasonable price. This is a non-vintage-designated bottling, as is typical for basic Champagne-style wines. Unsurprisingly, given its name,[99] Ferrari bubbly tends to turn up on the finish lines of Formula One races.

_____

[99] *"Ferrari" means "blacksmith" and is a common surname in Italy.*

Lombardy

Even though its winemakers are permitted to produce Chiaretto and Lambrusco (two wines you'll meet in the Veneto and Emilia-Romagna sections of this chapter), rustic, simple wines just aren't Lombardy's jam. This is the most populous and wealthiest region in Italy, so the sig-nature vino has to be chic enough to be served at Milan Fashion Week

and in the bustling restaurants of Brescia. It's Franciacorta, a very sexy sparkling wine made—as in Trento—in the Champenoise manner. Here in the United States, Franciacorta is more expensive and rare than Trento bubbly, but in my experience, it's silkier and more luscious, justifying the extra effort required to find and pay for a bottle.

FRANCIACORTA

It's said that, as far back as 1570, a doctor in Brescia published a book about the frothy wines of a small growing zone called Franciacorta. These DOCG-level bubblies still aren't widely known to us, however, because most of them are consumed inside Italia, and they are pricey in comparison with those of Trento. Franciacorta country is at the top of the Po Valley at the south end of Lago d'Iseo, which funnels cold mountain air down from the glacial peaks of the Stelvio National Park. The nippy nighttime temperatures here give the sparkling wines their bite.

Barone Pizzini
Franciacorta Rosé ($$$$)

Getting back to the close association between sparkling wine and Formula One drivers, here's a story for you: During World War I, the Baron Edoardo Pizzini Piomarta Delle Porte sketched an iconic *cavallino rampante* (bucking horse)[100] on a letter to his friend Francesco Baracca, the celebrated Italian aviator and national hero known as the "Ace of Aces." Baracca was so taken with the image that he had it painted on his plane. Later, Baracca's mother, a countess, attended a Grand Prix race, where she met Enzo Ferrari and convinced the champion race-car driver to adopt the prancing equine as his mascot, in honor of her fallen son. This vintage bubbly from the Barone Pizzini cantina is, appropriately, zippy, with notes of tart Ferrari-red huckleberries and fresh-cut flower stalks. The organic-certified estate is next to a nature preserve at the southern shore of the lake; the Pizzini empire also includes *poderi* (wine estates) in Tuscany and Marche.

Ferghettina
Franciacorta Rosé ($$$$)

A decadent powder puff of a gold-tinted pink wine for fat cats, made by the Gatti family. (Yes, that's right, the "Cats" family, in *Inglese*.) This crème brûlée of a vintage rosé is a "*milledi*," meaning it spent 1,000 days on the lees.[101] Matteo Gatti designed the showpiece flat-sided bottle to increase the creamy effect of lees contact. Because cats like cream.

---

[100] *The sketch resembles the bucking horse on the coat of arms of the Pinerolo cavalry school, which Pizzini commanded and Baracca had attended.*

[101] *Standard Franciacorta must spend a minimum of 540 days on the lees. Vintage wines must spend 900 days on the lees.*

Veneto

Shielded from extreme weather by the Dolomites and the inlet of the Adriatic Sea, hilly Veneto is a wine-producing powerhouse boasting the most DOPs in the nation. If you live on alcohol-loving planet Earth, you know about Pinot Grigio, Prosecco, Valpolicella, and maybe Soave and Amarone, too. In Venice's canal-front bistros and at the bars surrounding Verona's Piazza Brà, these wines are guzzled in great quantities alongside buckwheat pasta, white asparagus risotto, radicchio salad, and fresh seafood from the Venice lagoon. But diners who have tired of the same old, same old are increasingly asking for another Veneto wine: light, refreshing Chiaretto.

CHIARETTO

In high season, the shores of Lago di Garda are a farrago of tour buses and sailboats. Sightseers cram into lakefront bars and cool off with the light, fresh, local pink. This wine style, called Chiaretto,[102] is produced on the east, south, and west sides of the lake, in the Veneto as well as in Lombardy. Although producers in both regions claim their own Chiaretto to be far superior to the stuff that's vinified on the opposite shore, the casual onlooker needn't choose sides. Overall, Chiaretto is a simple summer pleasure, typically pink with a lychee-fruit tint to it.[103]

It has a light, salty character thanks to the glacially deposited soils that encircle the lake, making it an ideal match for seafood.

The key subzone to know on the eastern Veneto shore of the lake is Bardolino. As with Valpolicella and Amarone, the main grapes here are juicy Corvina and herbaceous Rondinella. The western Lombardy side, by contrast, favors the Gropello grape, which brings a black-cherry character to the wines.

The official viticultural title for Lombardy Chiaretto country is Riviera del Garda Bresciano. This includes the smaller subzones Garda Classico and Valtènesi in the northwest, and Lugana on the southern shore.

Vigneti Villabella Bardolino Chiaretto Classico ($–$$)

Villa Cordevigo is a beautiful resort in the Bardolino region on the Veneto side of the lake. It also

happens to be the estate vine-yard of Villabella, a prominent Bardolino producer. The basic Chiaretto is yellow-tinted, with an enticing pastry aroma. On the palate, there's nectarine pit, lemon, and an acidity that stings the lips, it's so thrilling. The estate Chiaretto, "Villa Cordevigo Bio-logico" ($$), which also happens to be organic, offers a more comprehensive experience, with solid minerality and added aromatic components of cypress (think woodsy sage) and a Meyer lemon finish that keeps creeping back for encore performances.

Zeni 1870 "Vigne Alte" Bardolino Classico Chiaretto ($)

This family winery, well known for its Soave and Valpolicella, dates back to—you guessed it—1870. The cantina, a stone's throw from the

---

[102] *Chiaretto translates as "claret."*

[103] *Aesthetic note: The Bardolino consortium has consulted with the Centre du Rosé in Provence to improve the quality of its pinks, and has declared "lychee" to be the most desirable hue. That said, the spectrum runs from very pale to very bold.*

shore in the town of Bardolino, includes a museum displaying old winemaking implements that vaguely resemble torture devices. Better to grab a beach blanket and a bottle of this smooth, gold-tinted liquid, replete with aromas of ripe peaches and flowers, fresh acidity, and a long finish of nectarine, lemon curd, white pepper, and minerality. The blend is Corvina and Rondinella with a bit of Molinara, and the word "Classico" signifies that the grapes were grown in the lakeside heart of Bardolino.

Bertani "Bertarose" Veneto Chiaretto ($–$$)

Bertani's pale blend is a super-approachable introduction to Chiaretto. It's three-quarters Molinara that did a short *macerazione* (maceration) stint plus one-quarter direct-press Merlot. The result: minerality, white peaches, melon, white pepper, some fresh pea shoots . . . is it time for lunch yet?

Cà Maiol Garda Classico Chiaretto ($)

Cà Maiol (formerly known as Provenza) runs a sleek tasting room just south of Sirmione, the famous fortified spit that juts northward from the south shore of the lake. Celebrity oenologist Michel Rolland oversees the high-end reds here, but this inexpensive pink has a character all its own: Scrubbed clean, with notes of white peach, cranberry, and tarragon, it's a difficult glass to put down. The blend is equal parts Gropello, Marzemino, Barbera, and Sangiovese. Also, look for the Cà Maiol "Roseri" Valtenesi Chiaretto ($–$$) from the Valtenesi subappellation. A higher proportion of Gropello in the blend makes for a more saturated color and floral aroma, with a juicy palate of cherry flesh, strawberry seed, and nectarine.

Comincioli "Diamante" Riviera del Garda Bresciano Chiaretto ($$)

On the lake's western shore, in the province of Brescia, the Comincioli cantina is tucked into the foothills of the Parco Regionale dell'Alto Garda Bresciano, which offers stunning clifftop and mountaintop views of the lake. This bottle, alas, is needlessly heavy. However, the Chiaretto, which looks like it's tinted with beet juice, has a bouncy red-wine personality: juicy red apple, cinnamon stick, fig, pepper, light tannins. Serve alongside *bresaola*.

Piemonte

Piemonte is renowned for its truffles, its Michelin-starred restaurants, and its Nebbiolo-based collector's trophies, Barolo and Barbaresco. It also does very well, thank you, with its frothy sweet Moscato, its sturdy reds, Barbera and Dolcetto, and its curious dry whites, Arneis and Gavi. So what role does rosé have to play here?

It's a distraction. Which is why rosato producers in Piemonte feel free to take artistic license and push boundaries. The wines described below are from cantinas located outside of the primary winegrowing zones. Here, DOP rules are less stringent, so winemakers have more grapes and techniques to experiment with. And because land isn't so expensive, they have less to lose by trying something new. These are the quirky wines to slurp while participating in the "Battaglia delle Arance," the annual orange-throwing melée in Ivrea, when the juice runs orangish pink in the streets.

....

Valli Unite "Rosatea"
Piemonte Rosato   ($)

A four-family cooperative in the village of Costa Vescovato, south of Tortona on the eastern edge of Piemonte, Valli Unite is an organic farmstead with a homey little eatery and a tendency to fundraise for the causes of solidarity and social change. This cloudy orange, spontaneously fermented blend of Moscato d'Amburgo (Black Muscat) and Barbera, plus some Malvasia Bianca and juicy red Brachetto, is a throwback to the days of yore. It's vinified with a *pied de cuvée* yeast[104] and has an untamed quality. If your bottle is stinky, leave it open for an hour or two. Then return to it to experience this wine's cotton-candy texture and its notes of dried orange peel, radicchio, almond pastry, and ginger. Imperfection can be a whole lot of fun.

COSTE DELLA SESIA

In Alto Piemonte—the mountainous, forested far north—Coste della Sesia is a subzone that's west of the Sesia River and at the foot of Monte Rosa, where the Matterhorn is just as close as Barbaresco. High, dry, and sunny, it gets wicked cold at night thanks to those nearby snowy mountaintops, and the sandy, acidic soils seal in freshness and minerality. There's a small rosato movement happening here among producers who can't ripen their Nebbiolo grapes to Barolo or Barbaresco standards. If you're a fan of the lively reds of this neighborhood—notably Gattinara and Ghemme—give these shimmering rosati a try.

Le Pianelle "Al Posto dei Fiori" Coste della Sesia Rosato ($$)

Bring this punch-bowl-pink wine "instead of flowers" to the hostess and you'll be the hit of the evening. This spicy, mouthfilling wine with its relaxing, sunbaked quality feels like it was made for long, meandering conversations. It's nearly all Nebbiolo—also called "Spanna" in these parts. There's also a teensy bit of the pigment-rich blending grape Croatina in the blend, as well as Vespolina, which guest stars in the deliciously humble DOCG-classed reds of Gattinara and Ghemme.

Proprietà Sperino "Rosa del Rosa" Piemonte Rosato ($$)

Chianti Classico fans know and love the De Marchi family's Isole e Olena estate, but few Italophiles realize that the De Marchis originally hail from Lessona in Alto Piemonte. (Their rosato has, in the past, been labeled Coste della Sesia, so I've classified this wine as such.) Again, this blend is mostly Nebbiolo, with the addition of some Vespolina. Smoky, meaty, and savory, with blood orange on the finish, this hearty rosato keeps the palate engaged with an alternately tannic and smooth texture that's a bit like sliding your foot back and forth along a tiled shower floor.

---

[104] *The French term for a starter yeast cultivated from an earlier natural fermentation.*

Liguria

Most Europhiles are familiar with the five villages of the Cinque Terre, but how many of us can name a Ligurian wine? Viticulture is scarce on the Italian Riviera, where the terraced slopes overlooking the sea are precariously steep and the arable land very precious.

The whites tend to be acid-driven, zesty, and seafood-friendly. The region is also known for its dessert wines, and for beguiling sour-cherry reds made from the Rossese grape, as well as the midnight-skinned Piemontese Dolcetto and the Tuscan Ciliegiolo. Given that Rossese is genetically identical to Provence's Tibouren, one would think the Ligurians would make more rosato, but there just isn't much to go around. This seems wrong given that the Ligurian color palette is cantaloupe, coral, and pink sand.

PORTOFINO [105]

Ahoy there, Elizabeth Taylor and Richard Burton! Once you and your 1960s celebrity friends have parked your yachts in Portofino's protected harbor, go ashore and track down a bottle of pink.

Because this is one of the few places in Liguria where you can find rosato.

....

Bisson Portofino Ciliegiolo Rosé ($$)

The blue-skinned Ciliegiolo grape gets its name from the Italian word for "cherry" and is a specialty of Portofino. This wine doesn't disappoint with its cherry color and scent. It's also delicately floral and wonderfully juicy, finishing with a suggestion of dried leaves, like the gentle resurfacing of a long-forgotten memory. The ghost of Maria Callas, strolling the streets of Portofino, perhaps.

---

[105] The DOP also goes by "Golfo del Tigullio-Portofino."

Emilia-Romagna

Gorgeous sea views, bracing high mountains, rugged terrain . . . Emilia-Romagna hasn't got those things. Instead, it has Modena, Bologna, Parma, and balsamic vinegar, fresh pasta, mortadella, prosciutto di Parma, Parmigiano-Reggiano cheese, and I could go on. Happily, the Lambrusco grape, one of Italy's oldest varieties, thrives on Emilia-Romagna's flat plains and makes a

light, bubbly, dry red that has been enjoying a revival in US restaurants. Now, let's meet its pink side.

LAMBRUSCO DI SORBARA

Sorbara, 10 miles (16 km) northeast of Modena, is home to a charming balsamic vinegar farm and an eponymous variety of Lambrusco. This thin-skinned grape makes a wine that isn't red but a deep Gerbera-daisy pink (confusingly, some labels state otherwise, but there's no mistaking the color when it hits the glass). The best Lambruschi di Sorbara are fresh, floral, fully sparkling DOP wines that are often described as smelling like violets. Lambrusco is a wine that has a reputation for taking a backseat to food, but this wine is no shrinking violet; to me, it's bottled happiness.

Cleto Chiarli e Figli "Vecchia Modena-Premium" Lambrusco di Sorbara ($)

Modena osteria proprietor Cleto Chiarli opened the first commercial Lambrusco winery in 1860; the label for today's "Vecchia Modena-Premium" dates back to the 1890s. Fermented in a sealed tank to capture fresh fruit flavor—along with carbon dioxide, which expresses itself as bubbles in the wine—it's aromatic with raspberries and strawberries. I also love Cleto Chiarli's "del Fondatore" Lambrusco di Sorbara ($$), which is fermented in the bottle in the old *metodo ancestrale*[106] manner and topped with a *spago*.[107] It's the color of pink grapefruit juice, with cloudy sediment and the

aroma of melon sorbet; on the palate, it's fresh and satisfying, with a bite of white pepper at the finish. Cleto Chiarli also makes a chic Champagne-style Brut de Noir Rosé from the Lambrusco Grasparossa clone and Pinot Nero (aka Noir). It's a confection of black-cherry kirsch, lime peel, rose water, honey, and marzipan, with a dry steely finish.

Villa di Corlo "Primevo" Lambrusco di Sorbara ($)

At the seventeenth-century Villa di Corlo, just southwest of Modena, traditional balsamic vinegar is produced in the attic; the cantina also makes *metodo classico*–style[108] sparkling wines. The Sorbara grapes in this cuvée are supplemented by the addition of Lambrusco Salamino. Aromas of pastry crust, peonies, and watermelon candies are joined on the palate by notes of blueberry and lemon. The Lambruschi are held at 32°F (0°C) until just before bottling, so each release is as fresh as possible.

[106] *This archaic winemaking technique results in a slightly sweet sparkling wine. To learn more, see page 183.*

[107] *A string tied to the top of the bottle to prevent the cork from popping out.*

[108] *Bottle fermented in the style of Champagne—see page 183.*

Lambrusco Rosato
for the *Fantasy Island* Generation

The skiers are partying slopeside. The romantic couple wanders through an ersatz Venice. The happy picnickers play baseball and scarf down hot dogs. And in come those violins and that disco-dance-hall voice, with its flirtatious trill: "Ree-yoo-nee-tee on ice, Ree-yoo-nee-tee so nice, Ree-yoo-nee-tee!"

Riunite, the brand behind those cheesy commercials, came in red, white, and pink, but just one color lingers in our hazy recollections: Riunite rosé in an ice bucket. Or—why not?—poured over ice in a glass. As the tagline went, "Riunite on ice—that's nice!"

For baby boomers, Riunite—produced in Emilia-Romagna and marketed specifically to Americans—was Lambrusco. And Lambrusco was sweet. And often pink. From the early 1970s through the mid-1980s, Riunite was the top-selling European imported wine in the United States, and pink Riunite was the only image Americans could conjure up of Italian rosato.[109] It was the European counterpart to White Zin, the pink wine for the Grey Poupon set who liked to purchase items with foreign-sounding labels. It was Italian wine culture as though viewed through the lens of a Disney camera.

We couldn't have been blamed for our ignorance. Back then, few Americans were aware of the existence of European dry rosé. Today, Riunite produces a range of five dreadfully, treacly sweet rosati. Fortunately, we have many more rosati—and Lambrusco wines—to choose from.

---

[109]   *I'm embarrassed to admit that I was obsessed with wine advertisements as a preschooler.*

Tuscany

Tuscany gets a lot of things right: Florence, the picturesque country-side, the artwork, the cuisine. And the wines: Chianti, so-called "Super Tuscans," and Vin Santo.[110] But beware the cheapie Toscana rosato. It's likely to stink of sulfur and lack personality because the winemaker had better things to do, like make savory red Chianti, and phoned it in. (A similar problem crops up with cheapie Tuscan grappas, which are distilled outside of the region and trucked back in to be sold as "estate-grown" to unsuspecting tourists.) All that said, there are a few standouts that make the most of Toscana's sweet-and-sour Sangiovese grape.

Rocca di Montegrossi
Toscana Rosato   ($$)

Winemaker/proprietor Marco Ricasoli-Firidolfi is the great-great-great-great-grandson of Bettino Ricasoli, the iron baron who was the first prime minister of the Italian Republic and established Chianti's reputation as a fine winemaking region. In the shadow of a seventh-century ruined fortress—the rocca of Montegrossi

in Chianti Classico, the heart of Chianti—Ricasoli-Firidolfi farms certified-organic, high-elevation vineyards. His pale-peach rosato is Sangiovese with the addition of some Canaiolo, a traditional black-skinned Tuscan grape. Tropical fruit aromas and flavors—mangosteen, pineapple—enliven this silky, spritzy wine.

La Spinetta
"Il Rosé di Casanova"
Toscana Rosato   ($$)

The label is a print that Albrecht Dürer rendered from a written description of a rhinoceros, having never seen the animal. La Spinetta's Tuscan property, Casanova, has a similar story. The Rivetti family is deeply immersed in Piemonte, where it produced the first-ever single-vineyard Italian Moscato in 1978 and runs three separate estates producing everything from Barolo to bubbles to bitters. When winemaker Giorgio Rivetti bad-

---

[110] *"Super Tuscans" are powerhouse reds, often made from French grapes like Cabernet Sauvignon and Merlot, that fall outside the zone and/or DOP rules for Chianti. Vin Santo is a dessert wine made from dried grapes.*

mouthed the "Super Tuscan" trend of ripping out Sangiovese and replanting with French varieties like Merlot and Cabernet Sauvignon, a smackdown ensued, and Rivetti accepted a dare to vinify Sangiovese in Tuscany. Thanks to this hotheaded Italian, we have not only an array of Sangiovese-based reds and a popular, piney Vermentino (white), but also this cool rosato. The fermentation is spontaneous and the grape makeup is half standard Sangiovese, half Prugnolo Gentile clone (the type of Sangiovese that goes into Vino Nobile di Montepulciano). It's minerally and mouthfilling, with some stray notes of wild greenery.

....

Biondi-Santi "Tenuta Greppo" Toscana Rosato ($$$$$)

Tuscany's most legendary pink wine comes from the historic

tenuta (estate) that put Brunello di Montalcino—Italy's finest Sangiovese appellation—on the map. Since 1927, Biondi-Santi has, as the best Bordeaux châteaux do, topped off and recorked collectors' old bottles.[111] In keeping with this respect for history, the rosato ages in steel vats for eighteen months prior to release and improves with additional cellar age. Greppo, Biondi-Santi's hilltop vineyard, rises above 1,600 feet (500 m) of elevation; its youngest vines provide the fruit for the rosato. This wine is heady, often getting close to 14 percent alcohol, and is the color of tomato preserves. Alas, it's almost impossible to find in the United States. But one can always dream.

---

[111] *Minute amounts of wine evaporate through the cork over time; the oxygen that seeps in endangers the longevity of the wine. Biondi-Santi keeps a library of old wines so that it can top off the depleted bottle with the identical vintage.*

Lazio

The wine region surrounding Rome is overshadowed by its better-known neighbors, which include Tuscany and Abruzzo. It didn't help that for much of the twentieth century, Lazio was written off as a mass producer of white wines. However, in recent decades, winemakers have rediscovered the region's endemic grapes and worked to revive the region's reputation. They're experi-

menting with obscure varieties like Cesanese and Aleatico, so I'm not quite ready to make any sweeping statements about the new wave of rosato production here, other than: Watch this space.

....

Andrea Occhipinti "Alea Rosa" Italy Vino Rosato ($$)

The red Aleatico grape is transformed into a sweet wine on the northern shore of Lago di Bolsena and, incidentally, on the Isle of Elba. But maverick vintner Andrea Occhipinti vinifies Aleatico as a dry wine—by all reports, he was the first in Italy to do so. He macerates the grapes for one night, allows spontaneous fermentation to take over, then continues to age the wine in open-topped cement vats. The color of this oxygen-rich rosato borders on pumpkin, the texture is matte, and the aroma, at first whiff, is suspiciously like vinaigrette. But allow the wine to sit in the glass and warm up to room temperature. Time introduces an aroma of apricot and flavors of black currant, worn leather, gentle spice, and a finish that's like opening a door at the end of a dim hallway and seeing sunlight.

Abruzzo

The expansive hillsides of Abruzzo rise above the bustling city of Pescara and the sparkling Adriatic, overlooked by the craggy massifs of Gran Sasso and Majella. The richly pigmented Montepulciano[112] grape makes savory, lip-smacking red wines, but the impatient *viticoltori*[113] of the region like to release an early Montepulciano every spring, when the wild asparagus starts poking out of the ground. This is Cerasuolo, named in the Abruzzo dialect for its ripe-cherry color and flavor. This fuchsia-hued beverage is sometimes labeled as a "dry red wine" as a matter of pride by Abruzzi, who take offense at the idea of their flavorful Cerasuolo being classed alongside those flimsy ciphers that are sipped at the beach.[114] And indeed, it's a substantive wine, with a tart balsamic-vinegar quality that stands up to the mutton dishes, piquant pepperoncini peppers, and sharp sheep's milk cheeses of the region.

Valentini Cerasuolo d'Abruzzo ($$$$$)

Take one vaunted noble vinetending family, add one enigmatic winemaker, and you've got a cult label. A bottle of Valentini's red Montepulciano will put you back $300 to $1,000, depending on the vintage; the Cerasuolo is a bit more affordable in the $90 range. It's said that the reclusive Edoardo Valentini used ancient Greek texts as farming manuals. Since Edoardo's death in 2006, his son Francesco has let it slip that he barrel-ages his Cerasuolo and holds it back for a year and a half prior to release. Most of Valentini's fruit is sold; Francesco keeps only a fraction of it, in the best vintages, to make wine from. So you won't get a chance to taste this spicy, ripe, viscous oddity unless you're very, very lucky.

Cataldi Madonna Cerasuolo d'Abruzzo ($$)

Luigi Cataldi Madonna, a philosophy professor at the University of

---

[112] *Montepulciano is a grape. It is not to be confused with the hilltown near Siena by the same name, where the Tuscan wine Vino Nobile di Montepulciano is made.*

[113] *Winegrowers.*

[114] *The Consorzio Tutela Vini d'Abruzzo describes Cerasuolo as "a charming rosé" on its website, which no doubt infuriates these vintners, but justifies our inclusion of it in this book.*

La Valentina's Valentine to Soave

Two of Abruzzo's most prominent producers have names to match the valentine-red-or-pink color of the Montepulciano wines. We've already met mystique-heavy Valentini (see opposite). By contrast, La Valentina is simply a well-run family *fattoria*[115] that produces very nice wines and sells them at affordable prices.

But La Valentina has its own mystique-laden Cerasuolo project: Binomio, or "two names." It's a partnership between La Valentina's Sabatino Di Properzio and winemaker Stefano Inama, one of the Veneto producers credited with resurrecting Soave's sullied reputation from dull, mass-produced plonk to dynamite white. The two men shared the idea that Abruzzo Montepulciano had been similarly misjudged by the wine-erati and could be great if farmed and vinified with care.

Their south-facing Binomio vineyard, located at the edge of the Parco Nazionale della Majella, is planted with an archaic cultivar of Montepulciano that's now known as the Africa-Binomio clone.[116] The old vines are trained in the traditional *pergola Abruzzese* manner, creating green canopies, or *tendoni*, that protect the fruit from sunburn. They're extremely low-yielding, but the small amount of fruit they produce each year crackles with character.

....

La Valentina Cerasuolo d'Abruzzo ($)

A classic Cerasuolo with an heirloom tomato color, a perfumed nose of cherries and gardenia, and juicy notes of sour cherry and pomegranate on the palate. As with so many of Abruzzo's vineyards, these grapes, too, are trellised in the *pergola Abruzzese* style.

....

Binomio Cerasuolo d'Abruzzo Superiore ($$)

Dry and luxuriant, with notes of hazelnuts, roasted game, and salty, bitter olive pit, this Cerasuolo feels more like a fine, well-aged red wine than a rosato. The color is dark papaya and the finish is layered with spice. The alcohol tends to be on the high side—in the 14-percent range—but the wine stays balanced. This is not your usual tutti-frutti summer pink; rather, it's a wine meant to be aged or paired with hearty foods. A steal at approximately $20.

---

[115] *Farm. Many Italian wine estates have "fattoria" in their names.*

[116] *Formerly just the "Africa" clone. Its new name honors the Binomio vineyard's role in reviving it.*

L'Aquila, made a name for his family *tenuta* by championing Pecorino, an autochthonous white grape that's scarce outside of Abruzzo and Marche.

Today, joined by his nephew and daughter, Cataldi Madonna makes a pomegranate-tinted Cerasuolo with notes of cranberry skin and sour cherry, accented by clove. The winery also produces an ultra-pale rosé called "Cataldino." The estate is tucked high in the Apennine foothills, surrounded by a national park, where it enjoys cool breezes off Il Calderone, Europe's southernmost glacier (which, unfortunately, is doomed to disappear soon).

Torre dei Beati "rosa-ae" Cerasuolo d'Abruzzo   ($$)

The winery is named after a tower, depicted in a fourteenth-century fresco in a nearby church, that guides blessed souls to heaven on Judgment Day, and this wine's scent of incense elicits a feeling of either damnation or sanctity, depending on how your day is going. It's fragrant with cinnamon, clove, slate, sage, and almond skin in addition to the more recognizable red cherries. Wisely, the winery suggests to its customers that they serve the "rosa-ae" with *brodetto alla Vastese*, Abruzzo's cioppino-style seafood stew.

Puglia

Humble, agrarian Puglia is known for its menhirs[117] dating back to god knows when and its odd little farmers' huts, called *trulli*, that could be from the set of *The Wizard of Oz*.

Puglia is also a winemaking machine, third in Italy in total production volume and churning out 40 percent of all the pink in the nation. Yes, that is a lot of rosato. But the Puglian industry is built on the bulk-wine business, so one must remember that quite a bit of that juice is sold off to be repackaged as supermarket plonk.

Happily, we can buy high-quality Puglian pinks at ridiculously affordable prices, so let's skip the plonk and focus on deliciousness. Negroamaro (translation: "black bitter") is the star of the Puglian rosato scene. Vinified as a red, it's juicy and leathery and tastes like tobacco, coffee, and licorice. As a rosato it has all that, but more of a sour Morello cherry character and an underlying note of bitterness— this is the vegetable-loving land of broccoli rabe, wild arugula, and dandelion greens, after all. It tastes best when one is relaxing at one of the region's many white-washed stone *masserie*, or country estates that have been converted into inns.

SALENTO

There are many small DOC appellations in Puglia turning out rosato, but you're most likely to see wines labeled with the IGP of Salento, as these have the greatest distribution here in the States. This is the stiletto heel part of the Italian boot and it's daaang hot. Fortunately, the copper-colored chalky-clay soil retains moisture, and the vineyards tend to be on flat land, so those few drops of precious rain don't go running off. Salento bills itself as Italy's rosato heartland, and winemakers here claim that Salento rosato was once as important to Italy as *clairet* was to France. If not my favorite wine,[118] the "Five Roses" from Leone de Castris is said to have been the first rosato bottled in Italy, and it was exported to the United States as early as 1943.

Arcangelo Salento Negroamaro Rosato ($)

A side project from the Palamà family, whose patriarch was the magnificently eponymous Arcangelo and whose busy winemaker, Ninì Palamà, vinifies at least sixteen different wines under the family label. The thick-skinned Negroamaro grape makes this purplish-tinted rosato. This is more Dr Pepper than 7Up, so don't try to match it with summer salad or fresh herbs. Its notes of maple, black cherries, and brine beg to be tasted alongside salty soppressata.

Cantele Salento Negroamaro Rosato ($)

The Cantele family is a prominent part of the Salento success story,[119] with their chic tasting room and "synesthetic laboratory" called iSensi, where cooking classes and wine-pairing meals are curated to stimulate the eyes, the ears, the nose, and the tongue. This

---

[117]   *For those who were not raised by the Asterix comic books, menhirs are historically significant standing stones, similar to obelisks.*

[118]   *With apologies to its many fans, I find it to be simperingly floral.*

[119]   *That is, the recent shift from bulk-wine production to fine estate-grown wines.*

devilish-red rosato was certainly made for food. The Negroamaro grape skins give it tart astringency and a botanical aroma that beg for a pairing with peppery arugula.

....

Li Veli "Primerose" Salento Negroamaro Rosato ($)

There's something meditative about visiting Li Veli, and I'm not just referring to the cool, pristine winery with its vaulted stone ceiling. It's the vineyard. At Li Veli, the vines are pruned like trees, and are aligned no matter which way you look. This is the *settonce* system, a hexagonal layout developed by Roman military engineers. Cool stuff. Anyway, Li Veli's zippy, 1980s-neon wine lives up to its name: It's quite li-vely.

Campania

Before those Elena Ferrante novels made us all so curious about messy, glorious, stratified Naples, Campania was known for its stunning Amalfi Coast, its idyllic island of Capri, and its remnants of antiquity—most notably, the lava-encased cities of Pompeii and Herculaneum and the temples at Paestum. For oenophiles, Campania offers a vinous history lesson: The wines are still made from ancient grapes such as the bluish-black Aglianico.

As with Negroamaro, Aglianico and its kin can make strong, dark reds, redolent of charcoal, tobacco, leather, and dark chocolate. And they can reach high alcohol levels—not very refreshing in the southern Italian heat, and not what you want to be drinking alongside the sea-food and light pizzas of Naples. Rosato to the rescue. Winemakers here manage to coax a surprisingly brisk, fruity pink wine out of the ornery old grape varieties.

IRPINIA

Campania's top wines come from the province of Avellino, where the Irpinia DOP encircles three DOCG-level subzones—Taurasi, Fiano di Avellino, and Greco di Tufo—in an embrace. If you can believe it, there's a ski resort this far south (yes, it does employ snowmaking machines) in the Apennine Mountains. Further downhill, slopeside vineyards enjoy day-to-night temperature swings that their flatland neighbors would kill for, making for equal abundance of ripeness and acidity in the wines. The rosati here tend to have a honeycomb undercurrent.

....

Terredora Dipaolo "RosaeNovae" Irpinia Rosato ($$)

The Mastroberardino clan traces its Irpinian wine-trade roots back to 1878. In the mid-1990s, Walter Mastroberardino broke away from the family company and named his own label Terredora Dipaolo, after his wife. This rosato of Aglianico is sourced from vineyards grown in volcanic soil on windy hillsides at between 1,300 and 2,000 feet (400 and 600 m) of elevation. It comes in an unconscionably heavy bottle, but thanks to its subtle notes of kiwi, fennel, persimmon, and beeswax, you'll keep lifting it up for another pour.

TERRE DEL VOLTURNO

One of ten IGPs in Campania, Terre del Volturno follows the serpentine path of the Volturno River, an important military prize for leaders from Hannibal to Garibaldi. It touches the coast just northwest of Naples and stretches north to the Parco Regionale del Matese, known for its limestone mountains and pristine lakes. The indigenous grape names to know here are the rare, archaic Pallagrello Nero and Casavecchia. In Pallagrello Nero we once again have a grape that makes a dense, tobacco-redolent red; Casavecchia is more herbaceous. In a rosato, that translates into pleasant sour-cherry and spring-garden notes—fitting, since the Campanian economy relies on its floral greenhouses.

....

Terre del Principe "Roseto del Volturno" Terre del Volturno Rosato ($$–$$$)

There's nothing archaic about this raspberry-colored blend of equal parts organically grown Pallagrello Nero and Casavecchia. It's got palate-scrubbing acidity, a floral fragrance, a hit of spritz, juiciness, and a lime twist. Try it with the regional specialty, *mozzarella di bufala*.

Calabria

Yeah, yeah: The grimy toe of the Italian boot is stuck in a previous decade, if not century. But Calabria is beautiful in its decay, a mess of crumbling clifftop towns, laid-back beaches, and unexplored mountainous national parks. The red wines of the local Gaglioppo grape are fragrant but can pack the double punch of high alcohol and chunky tannins on the palate. Gaglioppo also has a tendency toward a weak, orangey color, which has driven some producers to blend this grape with other varieties, like Cabernet Sauvignon. An alternative and, I think, better solution: Simply lighten up a bit on the maceration time and make a knockout rosato.

CIRÒ

Of Calabria's twelve DOCs, the most respected for Gaglioppo-based wines is Cirò. It occupies the notch on the Ionian coast where the toe (of that boot) arches. Old bush-trained[120] vines descend from the humble namesake hilltown down to the sea, and the soil is, unsurprisingly, an oceanic calcareous marl. The Gaglioppo reds of Cirò can be wonderfully aromatic, with floral and red-berry notes, and the rosati follow suit.

Librandi Cirò Rosato ($)

Calling all red-wine lovers: Try a Cirò before you write off rosato. Librandi's has the glow of a lit paper lantern and an uplifting cherry-pie nose. Earthiness, ripe red-cherry and blackberry flavors, and a mouth-coating richness make this a candidate for pairing with spicy foods.

---

[120] *Bush-trained, or head-trained, vines grow in the shape of a shrub rather than relying on the support of a trellis. The bush shape shields the fruit from sunburn in hot growing regions.*

Sicily

Save the sweet Marsala for drinking alongside Sicily's famous cakes and sweets. Dry rosato made from the blue-skinned Nero d'Avola

Planeta's Universe

Diego Planeta had the crazy idea to plant French varieties in Sicily. He won international attention for his inaugural vintage of an . . . oaky Chardonnay. Today, the Planeta family runs a solar system of estates, with each planet (er, winery) specializing in a different terroir and style of wine.

Here on the banks of Lago Arancio,[121] on the southwest outskirts of the village of Sambuca di Sicilia in northwestern Sicily, the soil is riddled with rocks, making for minerally wines. The rosato described below hails from a farm owned by the Planeta family since the 1600s.

....

Planeta Sicilia Rosé   ($)

This blend of Nero d'Avola and Syrah is a pale apricot color, and remarkably light and refreshing, considering that this winery made its name with blockbuster reds and whites. The nose is light citrus, the mouthfeel is supple, and the palate is pineapple and clove, suggesting the exotic flavor combinations that pervade Sicilian cuisine.

---

[121] *As noted on page 148, orange trees are ubiquitous in Sicily. They even name bodies of water after them.*

grape is the perfect fit for Sicily's Arabian- and North African–influenced cuisine, with its nutmeg, pine nuts, and pistachios. These wines seem to be imbued with the unforgettable scent of orange blossoms and pith that floats through the thick Sicilian air.

The landscape of the Mediterranean's largest island has been shaped by volcanoes and seismic activity, as evidenced by the trail of fiery lava that's always trickling down the side of Mount Etna. Likewise, Italy's third-most-productive wine region is erupting these days. For one thing, it's a font of ridiculously inexpensive, ridiculously tasty table wines. For another, it's home to an exciting new crop of experimental winemakers.

···

Stemmari Sicilia Rosé   ($)

Remember traveling around Sicily in a beat-up rental car and slurping down four-euro wines without ever having to think about them? This is that kinda wine. Stemmari is a sister brand of Sicily's well-known Feudo Arancio and part of the massive Italian agricultural cooperative Gruppo Mezzacorona. This attractive, perky, gold-tinted rosé is from Nero d'Avola grown in the Ragusa province in the southern part of the island. For all of ten bucks a bottle, it's a delightful nectarine-kissed quaffer that puts other supermarket brands to shame.

···

**Murgo Sicilia
Brut Rosé**   ($$$)

The thin-skinned Nerello Mascalese grape, grown on the volcanic slopes of Mount Etna, makes a quirky, enchanting sparkling wine when it is harvested young, getting its bubbles via *metodo classico*.[122] There's plenty of mountainside minerality in this glass, along with caramelized strawberries, a hint of drinking vinegar, an assertive fizziness, and a spicy kick to the finish. Ideally it should be consumed at an al fresco bar in the stunning cliffside resort town of Taormina.

---

[122]   *See page 183.*

Pro or Con Cornelissen?

Existence is perilous for the vines that grow on the crunchy basalt-and-powdered-pumice slopes of Mount Etna. But renegade Belgian-born winemaker Frank Cornelissen refuses to spray anything on his vines—even organic or biodynamic treatments—unless it's a life-or-death situation. One of his plots predates phylloxera, and thus the vines grow from their own roots;[123] the newer blocks are *selezione massale*[124] plantings sourced from the best of these very old vines.

In the winery, Cornelissen never adds sulfur and uses fiberglass tanks or epoxy-lined amphorae so his wine won't be affected by the flavor of steel or wood. His murky, unfiltered, raspberry-jam-meets-tomato-paste-colored rosato could pass as a red thanks to forty-five days—no, not hours—of maceration. But it's a co-fermentation of white and red grapes: Malvasia, Moscadella, Insolia, and Nerello Mascalese. It goes through malolactic fermentation, but of course.

Cornelissen's die-hard supporters tend to be geeky sommeliers and wine retailers who will tell you to decant Susucaru® for a few hours before getting near it, to give the truly weird initial aromas a chance to dissipate. Depending on your perspective, it's all very earnest, or else very precious. I mean, the guy trademarks the names of his wines. Who does that? (*Susucaru* means "swallowed" or "stolen" in the local dialect, Catanian, so it's not exactly original.)

....

Frank Cornelissen "Susucaru®"
Terre Siciliane Rosato   ($$$)

Susucaru® has intense concentration thanks to seriously low grape yields[125] and zesty acidity due to the cold nights on Mount Etna. There's also a homemade pomegranate cider character that you'd be hard-pressed to find in any other wine. Love it or hate it, Susucaru® is, at the very least, one of a kind.

---

[123] *The majority of the world's wine-grape vines are grafted onto American rootstock because it is resistant to phylloxera. Own-rooted vines are a prized rarity; they can survive on Etna because the root lice don't like the sandy, ashy soil.*

[124] *This is a time-honored practice (known as* sélection massale *in French) whereby the vinetender clips branches from the strongest vines in the vineyard.*

[125] *Cornelissen prunes his vines relentlessly to get the most flavor from every grape.*

PRETTY AND PINK

DENOMINAZIONE DI ORIGINE CONTROLLATA

$$

Trentino-Alto Adige

Terlan

$$$$

Lombardy

Barone Pizzini

$$$$

Lombardy

Ferghettina

$

Emilia-Romagna

Cleto Chiarli

$$

Tuscany

Rocca di Montegrossi

$$

Tuscany

La Spinetta

$$

Abruzzo

Binomio

$

Puglia

Arcangelo

$

Puglia

Li Veli

ITALY

$–$$

Veneto

Villabella

$$

Veneto

Comincioli

$$

Piemonte

Proprietà Sperino

$$

Abruzzo

Cataldi Madonna

$$

Abruzzo

Torre dei Beati

$

Abruzzo

La Valentina

$

Calabria

Librandi

$

Sicily

Planeta

$

Sicily

Stemmari

Rosado on the Iberian Peninsula

Winemaking on the Iberian Peninsula dates back 3,000 years or more, prior to the arrival of the Phoenicians. It survived the destruction wreaked by the Visigoths and even the anti-alcohol sentiments of the Moors.

But fortified—and thus seaworthy—Port, Sherry, and Madeira were the only wines of note to be exported over the centuries. The enterprise of dry table wines stayed localized and agrarian until the later 1800s. Then, when phylloxera wiped out French vineyards, a sudden, urgent demand for wine in northern Europe led to the founding of commercial bodegas (wineries) in Iberia. That window closed when the nasty little buggers marched south, but by then the seeds had been planted for a formalized industry.

Thus, lacking the formalities of the posh French châteaux or the entrenched opinions of the Italian marchesi,[126] the rosado makers of Spain and Portugal do not make arrogant claims of distinction. Their pink wines are ridiculously inexpensive and comfortably pleasurable, made for casual, flavorful foods and lazy afternoons. A siesta is always optional.

---

[126] *The aristocratic pride of the French and Italian wine scenes is evidenced by the many winery titles that begin with words like "Château," "Castello," "Villa," and "Marchesi" (marquis). In Spain, most winery titles begin with the humble "Bodega," meaning "cellar."*

PROFILE

SPANISH ROSADO

COLOR
bold as a bullfighter's
cape [127]

AROMATICS
strawberries, paprika,
saffron, roasted peppers

PERSONALITY
spicy, funky, meaty,
flamboyant

GOES WELL WITH
Almodóvar, gypsy rock,
chorizo, paella

Red: It's on the national flag and everyone's tush on New Year's Eve.[128] It's also nearly synonymous with Spanish dry table wine. While only about 4 percent of Spanish vinous exports are flat rosado, a full 54 percent are *tinto* (red). That said, Spain is legendary for its uniquely bold and long-lived pink wines.

Rosado, then, is a strong side plot in the Spanish wine story; you just have to know how to read between the lines.

If you've lived in Spain, you probably know that a *gorrilla* is a hustler who finds you a parking spot, and a *butanero* is the burly guy who replaces the gas canister under your stove. And there is a difference between a pintxo bar and a tapas bar, people. (You can drink Txakolí[129] in one and Cava in the other.) Likewise, there's an insider's idiom for pink wines—words like *clarete* and *lágrima*, which differentiate one style from the next. So let's pretend like we're locals and visit the hottest spots in Spain for rosado production. If you're paying attention, you'll pick up some insider's lingo along the way.

---

[127]   *In the annual running of the bulls in Pamplona, a few people are gored, a few hundred people are injured, and dozens of bulls are tortured and killed. But, on the bright side, thousands of spectators swarm the streets and get drunk, mostly on Navarra rosado, since it's July.*

[128]   *It's a thing to wear red underwear on December 31 in Spain.*

[129]   *In a pintxo bar, the bartender holds the Txakolí bottle overhead and pours it into a tall cylindrical glass, for an impressive frothing effect.*

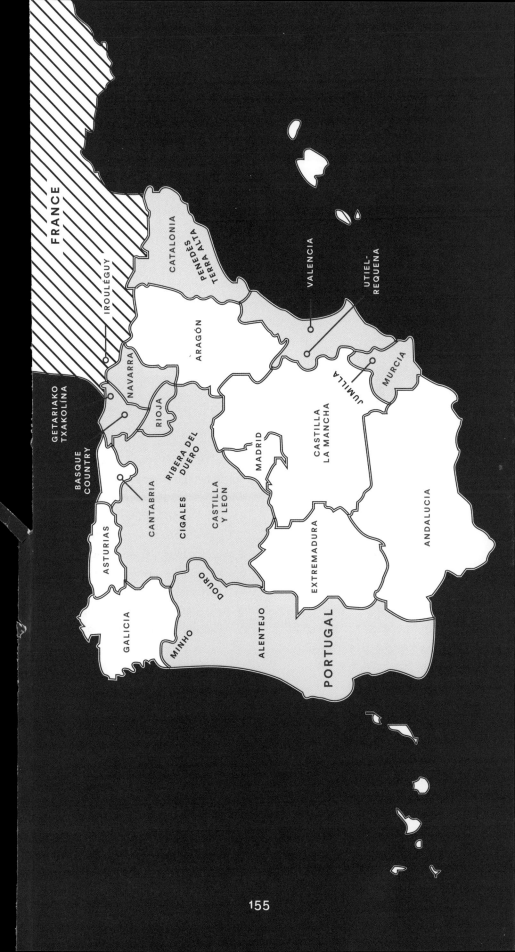

FRANCE

IROULÉGUY

GETARIAKO
TXAKOLÍNA

BASQUE
COUNTRY

CATALONIA

PENEDÈS
TERRA ALTA

VALENCIA

UTIEL-
REQUENA

NAVARRA

ARAGÓN

MURCIA

JUMILLA

RIOJA

RIBERA DEL
DUERO

MADRID

CASTILLA
LA MANCHA

ASTURIAS

CANTABRIA

CIGALES

CASTILLA
Y LEON

ANDALUCIA

GALICIA

DOURO

EXTREMADURA

MINHO

ALENTEJO

PORTUGAL

Basque Country

We'll commence in the far north. In Euskadi—which is the Basque name for Basque Country—the people aren't the only separatists. The wine, too, stands apart: Txakolí[130] is bone-dry and fizzy, with razor-wire lean acidity and an alcohol level that lends itself to noontime drinking. It's fermented in stainless steel and bottled young to capture natural effervescence. The wines are so popular in Bilbao, San Sebastián, and overseas markets (most notably, the United States) that the few commercial *upeltegiak* (bodegas) have trouble keeping up with demand.

GETARIAKO TXAKOLÍNA

The three Txakolí-producing DOPs all helpfully have names that end in "Txakolína." (Very roughly, Txakolí means "wine village," and Txakolína means "from a wine village.") For our purposes, Getariako Txakolína is the most important, as it produces the most pink.

While the primary Basque grape is the white Hondarrabi Zuri,[131] purists claim that the red Hondarrabi Beltza grape is the only true Basque native. In fact, even though most of the production is white today, traditional Basque wines were pink field blends of white and red grapes. So don't let anyone rib you for drinking pink Txakolí.

White Txakolí can hit the palate like a dry gin and tonic: frothy, slightly bitter, citrusy, restrained. Pink Txakolí is, in my experience, more forgiving, with mellower fruit and floral notes.

....

Zudugarai "Amats" Getariako Txakolína ($)

Zudugarai's sandy-soiled vineyards are on breezy hillsides west of San Sebastián on the Gipuzkoa Coast, near the mouth of the Oria River. With its lilting, alluring aroma, this pink is a delightful surprise for anyone accustomed to the briny, unripe-green-apple-y Txakolína whites. It's a very pale peach color, with the perfume of a spring flower garden, and ultra-dry and refreshing on the palate.

---

[130] *Chacolí in Spanish. Pronounced "CHALK-oh-LEE."*

[131] *Basque is just a lot more fun than other languages, isn't it?*

Ameztoi "Rubentis" Getariako Txakolína Rosé ($$)

Seventh-generation winemaker Ignacio Ameztoi makes vibrant young wines from vines that are up to a century and a half old. His "Rubentis" smells like barnacles and sea stones at first; on a return sniff, it unfurls nutmeg, clove, and cardamom. The palate is brisk and spritzy with fresh-cut starfruit, white pepper, and lemon chiffon. The winery also releases a fully sparkling brut version, "Hijo de Rubentis" ($$$), that makes a person salivate for Idiazabal sheep's milk cheese.

Irouléguy—Why?

País Vasco (that's Spanish for Basque Country) is shaped like a hen. It borders the Bay of Biscay, and its Atlantic Ocean–influenced climate is dominated by the *txirimiri*, a chilly—or should I spell it *txilly?*—mist.

But there's another dollop of Pays Basque, as the French call it, to the east: teeny-tiny Irouléguy.

Yes, we're in France now. And yes, this is still the Spanish chapter of this book. But if you're Basque, you aren't much concerned about the location of the French-Spanish border.

Irouléguy's green-terraced vineyards hug the sides of extraordinarily steep foothills of the Pyrénées, and its clay-based soils are excellent for the favored red-wine grape, spicy Tannat. Since it's inland, the climate is more continental, allowing for a richer style of wine. The rosés here are deeply saturated, with a grainy texture. They're so satisfying that to drink a glass is to feel as though you have eaten a small meal. (PS: "Why" doesn't rhyme with "guy" if you're in France.)

Domaine Ilarria Irouléguy Rosé ($$)

A softer, gentler version of your favorite red wine. It's a pale garnet color, with ripe blueberries and vanilla bean on the nose and palate, topped off with bitter wild rosemary. Drink now or in a couple of years.

Clarifying *Clarete*

Yes, rosado is the Spanish way to say rosé. But if you get into a conversation about the finer points of vinification with a Spanish winemaker, you'll hear them call their pink wines by different names.

First things first: You can't tell what type of rosado you're looking at by color alone. Color is determined, case by case, by both the grape makeup and the vinification technique. Second: Many Spanish wineries just go with the French "rosé" on their labels, because everyone understands it, and because knowledge of contemporary rosé winemaking came from France to Spain in the late nineteenth century. Third: None of the following terms are officially recognized by the European Union in the way that, say, "Chiaretto"[132] is. But you will still see these words on wine labels, simply used as descriptors:

Clarete: Like the Medieval French *clairet*, this is a co-vinification of red and white grapes most commonly found in Rioja. It needn't, as some have suggested, be dark in color. In fact, there are very pale *claretes* composed mostly of white grapes, and very dark *claretes* composed mostly of red grapes. The difference between a southern French comacerated rosé and a Spanish comacerated *clarete* is that the Spanish winemaker does not separate the juice from the skins until about halfway through the fermentation process, while most rosés are pressed off their skins prior to fermentation.[133] Thanks to the tannins from that skin contact, a good oak-aged *clarete* will cellar beautifully for years, even decades. The self-proclaimed "cradle of *clarete*" is the Rioja town of San Asensio, which gets awfully sticky each July when everyone sprays each other with pink wine—from bottles, jugs, balloons, water guns, and hoses—in the annual *Clarete* Battle.

Ojo de Gallo: This term is often thrown around interchangeably with *clarete*. It means "eye of the rooster," and here's the problem: The eyelids of a rooster are a bold lychee-red color, just like the comb. But the actual eyeball of the rooster is pinky-gold. So it's best to just ignore this phrase, because Riojans seem to use it in conflicting ways, depending on how up-close-and-personal they have gotten with a rooster, I suppose.

Vino de Lágrima: "Wine from tears." How sad. Actually, it's just wine made from free-run[134] juice . . . that is, the juice that flows out of the press before any pressure is applied. The mere weight

of the grapes splits the skins and sends the juice flowing like tears. *Waaah!* Free-run juice is thought to be less astringent than juice from crushed or pressed grapes because it hasn't spent time in contact with the bitter skins.

Rosado: Some Spanish wine insiders might insist that *clarete* and rosado are two entirely different things. But guess what? No one aside from Spanish wine critics and winemakers really cares which term you use. So you can just call it all "rosado." Or "rosé." Or "Bourbon," as long as you keep it to yourself.

---

[132] *Chiaretto translates as* "claret" *or . . .* "clarete."

[133] *Exception: In Tavel, too, winemakers allow their red and white grapes to begin fermenting together on their skins.*

[134] *See pages 49 and 51 for more on pressing.*

Rioja

Celebrated for its soft, spicy reds, Rioja is as renowned as Bordeaux or Burgundy. But while a fine château or domaine would never stoop to release a rosé, there's nothing dishonorable about a top bodega producing an easy, affordable pink wine alongside its world-renowned *tintos*.

Rioja's vineyards fall into three unofficial subzones and specialize in three indigenous grapes (although more are grown as well). For reds, lowland Rioja Baja is warmer and does better growing strawberry-scented Garnacha,[135] while Rioja Alavesa and Rioja Alta are high-elevation and do better with leathery, plummy Tempranillo. Viura (aka Macabeo in other parts of the nation) grows throughout. It makes an almond-scented white wine that gets waxy and even more nutty when it luxuriates in oak barrels, as is typically the case in Rioja. Accordingly, the rosados of Rioja can be spicy and leathery, cherry-strawberry juicy, coconut-oily, or a combination of all of the above.

In Rioja's wine capital, Haro, the Barrio de la Estación (railway station quarter) is a precursor to today's urban winery districts.[136] This cluster of bodegas popped up around the train tracks when phylloxera knocked out France's supply of *vin*.

....

Rio Madre Rioja Graciano Rosado ($)

It's not often that one comes across a 100-percent Graciano red, let alone pink. In Rioja, vine-tenders call this indigenous grape variety "Gracias, no," because it's so fickle in the vineyard and

---

[135] *The same thing as the French Grenache.*

[136] *The most condensed urban winery districts in the United States tend to be in wine towns, such as Paso Robles, Santa Barbara, or Lompoc, California; Walla Walla, Washington; or McMinn-ville, Oregon.*

Heredia Stands for Heritage

The grande dame of the Barrio de La Estación is R. López de Heredia, one of the oldest family-owned bodegas in all of Spain. Its winery complex covers a staggering 200,000-plus square feet (20,000 m²). In lingua Americana, that's a Home Depot and a Costco combined. It has been dubbed Haro's "cathedral to wine" due to the imposing masonry, the lacily ornate rooflines, and the fact that construction is never quite complete.

López de Heredia clings steadfastly to the winemaking traditions of centuries past. It's one of the world's few wineries with its own barrel-making shop, staffed by three master coopers. And it ages some 40 percent of its wines in casks that are already a decade old to achieve a well-mellowed effect: The rosados and the whites smell and taste sherry-like thanks to the ultra-oxidative vinification and aging regime.

The cellars may be blanketed with dust bunnies and cobwebs (a point of pride), but the stunning tasting room was designed by architectural superstar Zaha Hadid. Tilted and angular, it encases an elaborate fin de siècle wine pavilion that looks like a hand-carved wooden carousel. The overall effect is something like a circus tent inside a white spaceship.

Due to the winery's exacting standards (the rosé is only produced every decade or so) and lengthy barrel-aging regime, this is an extrem rare wine. Fewer than 1,200 cases of the '08 are scheduled to h the market . . . in 2018. The last vintage I was lucky enough to taste was the 2000.

....

R. López de Heredia "Viña Tondonia" Rioja Gran Reserva Rosado ($$$)

Thanks to a minimum of four years spent in barrel, this single-vineyard *clarete* is the color of marigolds or Scotch whiskey, gold rather than pink. It's a blend of Garnacha with Tempranillo plus some Viura (aka Macabeo) to round out the white part of the equation. Sensually speaking, it's a tour of the souks of Marrakesh: soft leather and faded Berber carpets; dried figs, dates, and apricots; almonds and walnuts; saffron and cardamom. Its aroma is nutty and sherry-like, with dried flower notes—as the *Wine Advocate* so aptly puts it, "decayed rose petal and hints of nougat."[137] It's a wine for fans of Miss Havisham, and I say that in a strictly complimentary sense.

---

[137] *Martin,* Robert Parker's Wine Advocate 202.

yields so little fruit. This unusual hibiscus-colored quaffer, a collaboration between Bodegas y Viñedos Ilurce and wine importer Jorge Ordoñez,[138] has a nose of dark-crushed berries and jasmine and a juicy palate that surprises with ripe passion-fruit flavor and white-pepper spice.

....

Zinio Rioja Rosado ($)

In the high-elevation Rioja Alta (an unofficial subzone), Bodegas Patrocinio is the cooperative of the village of Uruñuela, where stone-studded slopes overlook the Najerilla River and serve up striking views of the Cantabrian and Sierra de la Demanda mountain ranges. Zinio is one of four brands produced by the Bodegas. This pale-raspberry-colored rendition of Tempranillo has a lilting softness to it. It dreamily delivers notes of strawberry and dried cherries, then a one-two punch of vanilla extract and Valencia orange at the finish.

---

[138] *Massachusetts-based Ordoñez frequently partners with bodegas to create his own blends.*

Navarra

The wine region of Navarra, formerly part of France, occupies the southern half of the kite-shaped political province of the same name. Its cool, damp northern half is Basque; the south is dry and continental, with hot summers and cold winters. It shares with neighboring Rioja the *cierzo*, a cold dry wind from the north that makes for frisky, assertive fruit. It's no wonder that these two regions take first and second place, respectively, as Spain's top rosado exporters.

Prior to the 1980s, nearly all Navarra vineyards were planted with Garnacha that was vinified into cheap, fruity rosados. Vine acreage has dropped significantly since then, and pink now accounts for only a quarter of Navarra's production. Vineyards have been replanted with Tempranillo as well as French varieties like Cabernet Sauvignon and Merlot, but for rosado production, old-vine Garnacha is ideal.

It makes reliably inexpensive watermelon-punch-colored wines with lip-smacking red fruit notes that are ideal for barbecue season.

Cool Moves at Cune and Muga

Two neighbors of López de Heredia in Barrio de La Estación make noteworthy, if decidedly more modern, pink wines. Cune has been around since 1879; the remarkable steel-trussed ceiling of the bodega's barrel warehouse was designed by Alexandre-Gustave Eiffel of Eiffel Tower fame. (Just for the record, the official business name is CVNE, for Compañía Vinícola del Norte del España. But everyone calls it "KOO-nay," so that's how it's spelled on the label.)

Not to be outdone by López de Heredia, Muga employs a master cooper and three in-house barrel-makers. Its energetic rosado is a contender for the title of official summer weekend beverage of the restaurant industry—a demographic of refined palates and small pocketbooks. I can't tell you how many times I've seen mags of Muga in sommeliers' social media feeds. Fortunately for all of us, the bodega produces approximately 20,000 cases of this wine annually.

Cune Rioja Rosado ($)

This drinks like a young red—think Beaujolais. The nose is watermelon candy and strawberry jam. On the palate, in addition to that fruit, there's green olive, savory-sweet roasted red peppers, and sage, with spice and fullness to the finish. This expression of the Tempranillo grape is so robust that a higher alcohol level (it tends to hit 14 percent) isn't noticeable. Cune also owns the Viña Real bodega in Rioja Alavesa, which produces a pale 85-percent Viura *clarete*-style rosé, but I prefer this full-throttle rosado.

Muga Rioja Rosé ($)

Third-generation winemaker Jorge Muga favors ultra-slow, spontaneous fermentations, and ferments and ages his rosé in large wooden vats. That time on the lees in soft wood lends comforting yeasty notes to the wine. The color is pale. The blend is dominated by Garnacha, followed by Viura,[139] topped off with Tempranillo. The fragrance is floral and plummy, and the acidity is phenomenal, thanks to careful cultivation of rosé-destined vines on north-facing slopes in the foothills of the Obarenes Mountains. Flavor—pineapple, earth, spice—spills over the sides of the tongue, lingering on the finish.

---

[139] *Viura, a white grape, goes by the names Macabeo and Macabeu in other parts of Spain.*

Bodegas Lezaun Navarra Rosado ($)

The Yerri Valley *pueblo* (village) of Lácar[140] is home to this charming bodega in the foothills of the Urbasa-Andia ranges. The stone winery dates back to 1780 and offers tours of the organic vineyard by horse-drawn wagon . . . or Segway. As for the rosado, it's all Garnacha and a bold cranberry color. The nose is floral and fragrant with crushed red berries; on the palate there are red cherries, pimiento pepper, brine, and juicy acidity.

Aliaga Navarra Lágrima de Garnacha ($)

Navarra rosado works at room temperature, so if you get a sulfur-stinky bottle, like I did, leave it open on the counter for a couple of hours or aerate it in a decanter. Then . . . Clove and cardamom. Cinnamon. Tart cherry and earth. Old-vine Garnacha. The winery, Bodegas Camino del Villar (the family name is Aliaga) is on the west side of the town of Corella, in the little finger of Navarra's Ribera Baja that joins Rioja Baja.

Enanzo Navarra Garnacha Rosado ($)

Navarra's massive co-op controls more than 3,700 acres (1,500 ha) of vineyards and was a pioneer in the campaign to replant with Tempranillo and Bordeaux varieties. But old-vine Garnacha still remains, thank goodness. This singular rosado smells like strawberries roasted in a wood-fired brick oven with rhubarb pie, and Red Hots. Guzzle it alongside chorizo.

Señorío de Sarría Navarra Garnacha Rosado ($)

Señorío de Sarría, part of a family of wineries, owns more than 500 acres (210 ha) of vineyard in hilly Valdizarbe, an unofficial subzone of Navarra. The two paths of Spain's famous Camino de Santiago pilgrimage route meet quite close to the winery, on the Río Arga in the medieval town of Puente la Reina. This jewel-bright, cranberry-flavored rosado is floral, spicy, and pleasantly bitter, with some *agua fresca de jamaica* notes adding nuance. It may not be sexy, but it could surely revive tired souls.

---

140 *The label is printed with the Basque spelling: Lakar, in the Deirri Valley.*

Cigales

The Cigales wine region follows the path of the Pisuerga River northeast from the busy city of Valladolid through the town of Cigales and beyond. It's a flat but fairly high-flying landscape—every time I read "see-GAH-less," I think "seagulls"—with an average vineyard elevation of nearly 2,500 feet (750 m). The gravelly soils are porous and poor, the summers are hot and dry, and the winters feature frost and whipping winds. And then there's the fog. One wonders why so many castles were built here. Those medievals were masochists.

Cheap, easygoing rosado was Cigales's calling card for decades. That changed in the 1980s, when winemakers began aiming to produce high-quality reds and whites from Tempranillo (called Tinta del País here)[141] and French varieties. Today, 70 percent of Cigales wines are consumed within Spain, and the majority of those imported in the United States are red, so we don't hear much about the region's much-improved rosados. These eminently food-friendly wines exude the unabashed glee of Garnacha: that irrepressible aroma of dripping-ripe strawberries and cherries. At the same time, the new, more refined rosado style incorporates sophisticated sour and bitter notes that match beautifully with food.

Sinfo Cigales Rosado ($)

This wine looks like a Japanese maple in full autumnal brilliance. The nose is all cherries and the palate is like a knockout Negroni, flipping from sweet fruit to wickedly satisfying Campari bitters. Sinfo's gnarly old vines are planted in plots around the town of Mucientes. The grapes—mostly Tinta del País (Tempranillo), plus white Verdejo and Albillo for fruit aromas and brightness—are interplanted in the vineyard, and are picked, crushed, and vinified together. The bodega is co-owned by the three Vaquero brothers, who also produce a limited-edition rosado that's fermented in small American oak barrels, then aged in small French oak barrels.

---

[141]   *Tempranillo goes by a number of different names. Some of its best-known aliases are Tinta del País, Cencibel, Aragonez, and Tinta Roriz.*

Ribera del Duero

The Ribera del Duero follows the path of the Duero River in north-central Spain. Its emblematic castillo, Peñafiel, houses a wine museum; as you will often see in Spain, incongruous *Lord of the Rings*–ian chimneys rise out of the hillside below the castle, to ventilate and light the massive underground cellar. In short, Ribera del Duero is dead serious about its wines. Like Rioja, the specialty is fine barrel-aged Tempranillo. Unlike Rioja, it's unusual to see an inexpensive rosado under the label of a top-notch bodega here.

In fact, rosado accounts for a teeny tiny fraction of overall production, so we won't devote too much time to it. Rioja does rosado so well, after all. And again, there's not much point in a top-notch red-wine region churning out inexpensive pink that might risk diluting its strong high-end brand.

But if you are a real fan of Ribera del Duero reds, you'll want to delve into its rosés simply out of curiosity. Just as Ribera del Duero's reds tend to be all gristle and black coffee, its rosados are tougher and more menacing than the soft, juicy pinks of Rioja. *Grrr!*

Cepa 21 "Hito" Ribera del Duero Tempranillo   ($$)

Bodegas Emilio Moro is one of those wineries that needn't bother with rosado. It makes dense reds that score big with the critics, and its top wine sells for well more than $100 per bottle. But its low-key little sibling winery, Cepa 21, isn't under pressure to deliver power wines. Which is good news for us, because we get this savory rosado that's fragrant of Fernet Branca and tastes a bit like Amaro (think Dr Pepper, only completely dry). It has a leathery, Don Quixote feeling about it, with some nice plum on the finish.

Catalonia

Catalonia can, as so many European regions do, trace its vinous history back to Roman times, but it wasn't declared a DO until 2001. There was that rough period of Visigoth invasions and border disputes between the Islamic Emirate of Córdoba and the Frankish Carolingian Empire. But wine production bounced back in the late ninth century AD under the benevolent reign of a Barcelonan count, Guifré (aka Wilfred) "the Hairy," who ought to be resurrected as a Muppet with that name.

The foreign occupiers are gone, but the state remains a conflicted place. We know it as Catalonia, the Spaniards call it Cataluña, the Occitan speakers spell it Catalonha, and to the Catalans, it's Catalunya. The wine region by the same name is similarly smorgasbord-like, allowing thirty-five different grape varieties. These include a number of indigenous strains that appear most prominently in Cava, the Champagne-style sparkling wine so adored by the Barcelonans.

Cava is Catalonia's best-known wine.[142] We'll spend most of this section luxuriating in its rosé bubbles, but first let's check in quickly to take the temperature of the next generation of Catalonian winemakers.

TERRA ALTA

In the late nineteenth and early twentieth centuries, Catalonia just so happened to be crawling with young acolytes of the great architect Antoni Gaudí. They all designed slightly sinister-looking wineries featuring skeletal arches, now collectively called the "Catedrales del Vino." The most notable of the designers was Cèsar Martinell, and his two masterpieces are located in high and dry Terra Alta. So visit the cooperatives at El Pinell de Brai and Gandeza. And look up. Do you see what I see? Pink ceilings. That guy must have been a rosado drinker.

As for the wines, we're just learning about the possibilities of this region, Terra Alta ("high ground"), because it's rugged, rocky, forested, mountainous, and somewhat remote—ideal for Picasso to paint, but not so much for competing with wine regions located much closer to Tarragona and Barcelona. (Martinell's cooperatives made wines for the locals,

---

[142] *Cava can be made in other regions as well, but Catalonia is the center of production.*

not for shipping overseas.) Some pundits compare its reds to those of the Rhône, so it follows that its rosados should have meaty and herbaceous notes.

Clua "El Solà d'en Pol" Terra Alta Rosat ($)

For generations, the Clua family grew grapes as a commodity and churned out wine in bulk. Today, the family's high-elevation vineyard holdings around the village of Vilalba dels Arcs are getting personalized attention from husband-and-wife winemakers Xavier Clua and Rosa Domenech. Their intellectual, affordable Celler Xavier Clua Coma (or simply "Clua") wines exemplify the new Catalonia. This blend of mostly Garnatxa (aka Garnacha) Negra,[143] with some Syrah (sounds like the Rhône, *non*?), is agreeably untamed, with just the faintest whiff of raw meat and kimchi. On the palate, there's baked sweet potato, blood orange, and a razor-wire ferocity.

PENEDÈS

Yes, flat Penedès rosados do exist, but sparkling Cava, Spain's most exported wine, is the star here. It's made by *méthode traditionnelle*,[144] but it comes across the palate (and in the pocketbook) as loose and informal: If Champagne is the blazer you pull out of your closet semi-regularly, Cava is the jean jacket you wear every day. And the Barcelonans do just this, sipping Cava without compunction.

Oeno pundits blame Cava's rustic personality on the presence of home-team grapes like Macabeu (aka Macabeo aka Viura), Parellada, and Xarel·lo.[145] Today, an increasing number of producers are switching over to classier French varieties (and charging more for their wine), and many Cavas are blends of the old white grapes with their cool new friends. Rosé Cavas range in color from pink to red and in flavor from fruity to nutty. Don't hold me to this, but with their fierce bubbles and juicy pigment, the darker ones might actually cure the common cold.

Jaume Serra "Cristalino" Brut Rosé Cava ($)

One of the seven wonders of the wine world, Jaume Serra Cristalino is always dirt cheap, in good supply, and really quite nice, outperforming more expensive peers in blind taste tests. This brick-tinted bubbly has some yeastiness to the nose, dry red currant and nougat on the

palate, and lime peel/grapefruit pith on the finish. After a little trademark tussle with Louis Roederer, Jaume Serra was forced to change its bottle design and print a disclaimer just in case anyone should confuse a sub-$10 Cava with $200-plus Cristal Champagne.

··

Marques de la Concordia "Reserva de la Familia" Brut Millésime Rosé   ($–$$)

This vintage-designated blend of 70 percent Pinot Noir and 30 percent Monastrell (aka Mourvèdre) cellar-ages for forty (!) months prior to release. The first bottle I opened was excessively sulfurous, but a second held a crisp and pleasing peach-colored bubbly. Fierce, tiny bubbles release a botanical aroma; the palate is tart raspberry-and-citrus-driven, finishing with a nice touch of sea salt.

··

Avinyó Reserva Brut Rosé Cava   ($$–$$$)

This one is a bit pricey because it's all "free-run"[146] Pinot Noir juice, cellar-aged twelve months. The color verges on coral, and the bubbles are potent and persistent. I always find an undercurrent of old library in Avinyó's Cavas, as though each bubble contains a long-forgotten story. If there's fruit here, it gets lost between the pages. The dry palate evokes salted walnuts.

---

[143] *Garnacha Blanca is a specialty in Terra Alta, so the "negra" is added here to differentiate the two.*

[144] *The sparkling winemaking method, in which a secondary fermentation is carried out inside the bottle, that's used in Champagne. See page 183.*

[145] *Xarel·lo is Catalan, thus the interpunct, and the "x" is pronounced like "sh" or "ch."*

[146] *As you might recall, the very sad Spanish term for free-run juice is* vino de lágrima. *See page 158.*

169

Valencia

Valencia is a striking seaside metropolis—the third largest in Spain. It's also the name of the Spanish state known for its warm white-sand beaches and its hiking trails along the old Roman road, Vía Augusta. Last but not least, it's a DOP producing a wide variety of wines. A buffer zone of natural parkland separates the sea from many of Valencia's best winegrowing subzones.

UTIEL-REQUENA

Many wines labeled "Valencia" are pumped up with juice from the many, many vineyards surrounding the two towns of Utiel and Requena. U-R mostly vinifies just one red grape, the indigenous Bobal, known for its fecundity and uneven ripening. Because so much Bobal is used for bulk wine, we're just beginning to get a sense of its potential, but a new generation of producers are pruning its finest old vines down for quality, to glean dense, chocolatey red wines from the loam-limestone soils.

The region's red winemaking technique, called *doble pasta*, is enriched by rosé winemaking:[147] The skins left over after the juice has been squeezed for pink production are scooped out of the press and added to red-wine vats to intensify the aromas, colors, flavors, and tannins of the darker wines.

Tarantas Spain Rosado ($)

Bodegas Iranzo bills itself as Spain's oldest estate winery, tracing its roots back to 1335. Tarantas is a bargain-label side project, produced solely for export (the Utiel-Requena DOP is not printed on the bottle for administrative reasons). However, the grapes are farmed organically and are non-GMO certified. This 100-percent Bobal bottling is rustic, not refined. Closer to brick than pink, it's all cinnamon, berry, and almond pastry on the nose, with caramelized strawberries and savory tomato on the palate. Is it a little burnt? A little raw? Sure, but it's a little unusual and a lot affordable (usually around $9). There's also an equally affordable sparkling version of this wine.

---

[147]   *Unlike* saignée, *which is a red-winemaking process that results in a rosé and a red,* doble pasta *is a process whereby red wine is enhanced by the leftovers from rosé production.*

Murcia

Valencia's southern neighbor doesn't look like the ideal place to grow grapes. It's hot and arid—except for the occasional torrential downpour—and follows the Segura River Valley through scrubby, cave-ridden cliffs and hills. But the Moors, who founded the city of Murcia way back in 825, installed impressive irrigation systems, and thanks to these, the region is known throughout Europe for its oranges and lemons. And grapes.

JUMILLA

"Murcia" is a table-wine designation, but within its borders are three quality DOPs. Of these, northern Jumilla—which spills over into the *comunidad autónoma*[148] border into Castilla-La Mancha—turns out crazily underpriced wines from crazily old vines. The sandy soil here kept that icky phylloxera bug at bay, which means that there are numerous old, ungrafted Monastrell vineyards. This variety—the same as France's Mourvèdre—makes heady, earthy, and inexpensive red wines in Jumilla's dry heat. The rosados, likewise, aren't about precision but oomph. They tend toward a baked-tomato color and red-fruit jam and rhubarb pie flavors.

....

Olivares Jumilla Rosado ($)

On the western side of the Sierra del Carche at above 2,700 feet (825 m) of elevation, Olivares is renowned for two things: its remarkable late-harvest dessert wines, and the Finca Hoya de Santa Ana, an impressively large, old-vine, self-rooted vineyard in sandy, chalky soil. This rosado was until recently like its peers—Monastrell-based and like reduced fruit punch in color and aromatics. But the winemaking style has gone in a lighter direction recently, perhaps marking a new era for Jumilla rosado as a whole, and the flavor profile leans more toward fresh than overripe. The blend is now dominated by Garnacha, with Monastrell in the minority.

---

[148]   *Like an American state.*

PROFILE

PORTUGUESE ROSÉ

COLOR
ranging from almond
blossom to piri piri sauce

AROMATICS
crushed cockles,
sopa de tomate

PERSONALITY
eclectic, casual,
mysterious

GOES WELL WITH
cavaquinho[149] music,
cod fritters

Portuguese rosés are few and far between. Even the Portuguese don't drink much pink. But that's changing. There are *espumante* —sparkling—wines in pink, and increasingly, red-wine regions are exploring rosé production.

The United States has been slow to see Portuguese rosé imports for linguistic and historic reasons. Brazil and Angola are often the first two markets to receive Portuguese wines, because there is no language barrier and the trade routes were established long ago. But watch this space: New Portuguese pinks appear on American store shelves every year.

MINHO/VINHO VERDE

Let's begin our exploration of Portugal in the cool, damp northwest. It can be difficult to ripen grapes here, but the winemakers make the most of their challenging circumstances by producing delightfully light, slightly fizzy, lower-alcohol wines with bright acidity. The Minho IGP[150] is Portugal's largest winegrowing region, delineated by the Minho River and the Spanish border on its north side. Within Minho, the Vinho Verde title is applied to young, "green"—*verde*— low-alcohol wines made from an approved list of native grapes.

The Vinho Verdes we see here in the States are nearly always

white. But it turns out that quite a bit of Vinho Verde red wine is made and consumed in Portugal. The top red grape, blue-skinned Vinhão, is unusual in that its flesh is red, so extracting pigment is a piece of cake. The red wines are purple-colored, which might lead one to expect dense tannins and fruit, yet they're light-bodied and fresh. The rosés, likewise, can have a boiled-lobster-shell color but—surprise!—light citrusy flavors.

In keeping with the *verde* theme, the *Game of Thrones*–ian landscape here is electric green. Portugal's only national park, the Parque Nacional da Peneda-Gerês, is a stunning hiking destination where former shepherds' trails wind up to granite peaks past the requisite ruins and castles. If you go, pack a sweater and a rain slicker and leave room for a bottle of pink wine.

....

Broadbent Vinho Verde Rosé ($)

Bartholomew Broadbent, son of the famed wine auctioneer and

---

[149]   *Similar to a ukulele.*

[150]   *Indicação Geográfica Protegida.*

authority Michael Broadbent, is an importer and négociant. His take on Vinho Verde is gorgeously perfumed with flowers and fruit; the palate progresses from peach to salty olive and back.

....

Nortico Vinho Minho Dry Rosé ($)

This wine qualifies as a Vinho Verde, but the label is printed with the larger Minho designation for administrative reasons. It's a drink-in-your-underpants blend of the local grapes Alvarelhão, Pedral, and Vinhão, ethereally light and prickly with acidity, with a long finish of crushed seashells and lemons. Good morning!

DOURO

The Douro River Valley produces much more than Port and Mateus. Lately, the region's spicy, savory dry red wines have garnered an onslaught of favorable attention from critics, and with table wine on the table, some estates are branching out into dry pink territory. While the red Douro style is leathery, herbaceous, and dense with sun-ripened blackberry characteristics, the rosés can range from light and spritzy to fuller-bodied and bold with red berry notes, a style

that feels more closely related to Douro's dense, heady Port.

The same grapes that go into Port also make the red and pink blends. Typical varieties include tobacco-and-leather Tinta Roriz;[151] floral Tinto Cão; brambly Touriga Franca; and the king of all Portuguese grapes, plummy, licorice-y Touriga Nacional.

The steep slopes on both sides of the Douro River are covered with terraced vine rows. The soils are unwelcoming flaky schist and the summers are scalding hot, but somehow the vines manage to pull through every year. A white-Port-and-tonic on ice offers respite from the sizzling heat, but so, too, these days, does dry pink Douro.

....

Quinta do Romeu Douro Vinho Rosé Seco ($)

The Menéres family has been in business since 1874 and controls a massive certified-organic estate that includes cork forests. Its location some 40 miles (65 km) north of the Douro River isn't ideal for Port production, but it's a perfectly fine place to grow grapes for dry wines. This pink is a blend of some of the usual

---

[151]   *Called Aragonez in other parts of Portugal, this is the same thing as the Spanish Tempranillo grape.*

Mateus + Lancers: Made to Last?

During World War II, the market for Portugal's best-known fortified wine, Port, crashed. The landowners in the Douro River Valley, where Port grapes are grown, found themselves holding the hot potato.

Two new brands rose phoenix-like from the ashes. Mateus and Lancers both proffered fun, fizzy pink wines to the war-weary masses. The UK and the US markets lapped them up. But after peaking in popularity in the 1970s and eighties, the two brands are now merely footnotes. Once found on every supermarket store shelf, they can now be difficult to track down (I had to special order my bottle of Mateus).

Other Portuguese rosés may have surpassed these two pioneers in terms of quality, but Mateus and Lancers will always occupy a special place in the hearts of those who drank wine to the soothing sounds of Barry Manilow and Barbra Streisand back in the day. You know who you are, people.

Lancers Portugal Rosé   ($)
The earthenware carafe is gone, replaced by a glass bottle that takes the same shape. Which means you get a clear view of the baked-cherry-tomato color of this wine. On first sniff, it emits a head-spinning dose of sulfur. Returning for more, one gets bone-dry, flavorless, generic liquid, made from "native Portuguese grape varieties," according to the back label.

Mateus "The Original" Portugal Rosé   ($)
Another throwback bottle shape, this one designed to suggest the shape of a World War I soldier's flask. The glass is green, so the nectarine color of the wine comes as a surprise. On the nose, there's an attractive strawberry-juice fragrance that follows through on the spritzy, slightly sweet palate. This is the totally innocuous wine equivalent of a fruit-flavored soda pop. In a pinch, I'd buy it again.

suspects of the Douro: Tinta Roriz, Tinto Cão, and Touriga Nacional. It has a bluish tint, a nose of fresh plums and pastry crust, and a palate that's softened by lees stirring. Bonus points to the estate for maintaining a "Museum of Curiosities."

ALENTEJO

Alentejo falls within the borders of the cultural region[152] of the same name that accounts for a massive hunk of eastern Portugal. It's an all-encompassing IGP[153] designation surrounding eight DOP sub-zones. The IGP wines are labeled as "Alentejano" or "Vinho Regional Alentejano."

The climate here is hot and dry in the summer, cold in the winter. The economy is agricultural, and cork trees are a key crop. Until recent decades, the wineries here were largely co-ops, in keeping with the farming lifestyle. Portugal's admission into the EU in 1986 brought investment into the relatively remote Alentejo and eased the journeys of aspiring young winemakers to other nations, such as France, to study oenology and viticulture. They returned determined to make rich, flavorful wines, and have succeeded in building a reputation for Alentejo as a heavy-hitting region for powerful reds.

Tinta Roriz (Tempranillo in Spain) is important for quality red winemaking—it goes by the name Aragonez here. The juicy Periquita ("parakeet") is another key player. French varieties such as Cabernet Sauvignon and Syrah are also grown. The few rosés I have come across have been hearty, close to a red bell pepper in color, and somewhat tannic, like the little siblings of those burly reds.

Defesa Alentejano Aragonez Syrah Rosé   ($)

The seriously old-time Herdade do Esporão estate, near the watershed of Lake Alqueva, dates back to 1267 and boasts its own Neolithic archaeological site. Defesa is one of many labels produced by the Esporão company, which also owns a historica *quinta* (vineyard property) in the Douro. This blend is tomato-tinted, with licorice and spice on the nose, chunky red-wine texture on the palate, crushed-gravel notes on the finish, and a weightier body than you get from those wimpy Vinho Verdes.

---

[152]   *Something like New England.*

[153]   *As is the case in so many other parts of Europe, the Portuguese have been slow to adopt the EU's IGP classification, so you are likely to see "VR," or "Vinho Regional," on labels at present.*

PRETTY AND PINK: THE IBERIAN PENINSULA

$$

Basque Country
Ameztoi

$

Rioja
Zinio

$

Rioja
Cune

$

Navarra
**Señorío de
Sarría**

$$

Ribera del Duero
**Cepa
21**

$$–$$$

Catalonia
Avinyó

$

Valencia
Tarantas

$

Vinho Verde
Broadbent

$

Minho
Nortico

$

Douro
**Quinta do
Romeu**

Pink Traditions of Northern Europe

When we think rosé, we think beaches and hot sun. But from a farming perspective, it makes sense that the north should produce pale wines. Where the temperatures are cooler, the grapes struggle to ripen and tend to have lower pigment and tannin levels and more acidity than their southern brethren.

The winemaking nations of northern Europe harbor a surprisingly complex array of rosé traditions, most of which you can't experience unless you visit. For example, consider the best-known of Switzerland's many regional rosés. *Oeil de perdrix,*[154] or "eye of the partridge," is a blushing apricot-colored wine that primarily hails from the Neuchâtel appellation. It's made from Pinot Noir and is said to be the color of a dead partridge's eyes.[155] I know, appetizing, right?

In addition to Switzerland, Germany, Austria, and England all have thriving rosé-making scenes. I'll try not to delve too deep into obscurity in this chapter, because it won't do any of us any good to focus on wines that never make it past their own nation's borders. Instead, we'll hop around some of the most interesting and prominent cool-climate growing regions in Europe and sample pink wines that you should be able to find here, perhaps with a bit of digging.

Of course, this chapter also includes northern France. Because we're not done with France yet. And we need to spend some time lapping in the Loire and taking some brisk hikes through Alsace and the Jura. But first, let's luxuriate in Champagne.

---

[154]   *The Latin name for the genus is "perdix"—the French add an R.*

[155]   *If you're an upland hunter or bird watcher, you'll find this confusing since partridge eyes are brown, and many partridge species have eyelids as hot pink as a Crayola marker. However, I believe that this term refers to the Hungarian Partridge, or Hun, which has flesh-colored eyelids and tends to close them peacefully when shot.*

PROFILE

NORTHERN FRENCH ROSÉ

COLOR
Normandy cider as
reinterpreted by Lancôme

PERSONALITY
jet-setting, cheese-loving,
outdoorsy

AROMATICS
honeycomb, zesty herbs,
baking bread

GOES WELL WITH
limousine interiors, Moncler
jackets, Bresse chicken

After southern France, the north feels like an entirely different nation. There's a completely new set of grapes and a dissimilar perspective on rosé. For example, quite a few of the wines in this section are so dark that they could pass as reds—a rare sight down south, where it's all about the absence of color. (Oh, the irony: Down south, where the red wines are nearly black, they make the palest pinks possible. Up north, where the reds are light ruby, they make the darkest rosés they possibly can.) And there's no shame in employing the *saignée* method, as there is in Provence. In Champagne, in fact, the term *"saignée"* has a different connotation. We'll get to this in a minute.

Speaking of bubbles, there are at least five popular songs by North American musicians entitled "Pink Champagne." It has become a compulsory cultural ritual to pop the cork on a bottle of pink bubbly every Valentine's Day.

And in the decade between 2004 and 2014, Champagne exports to the United States fell by more than 5 percent while the percentage of rosé Champagne exports to the US increased by 66 percent.

In short, if you haven't sipped a glass of rosé Champagne or pink Crémant over the past year, you'd better be working at an Antarctic research station. So let's start there. No—not in Antarctica, silly!

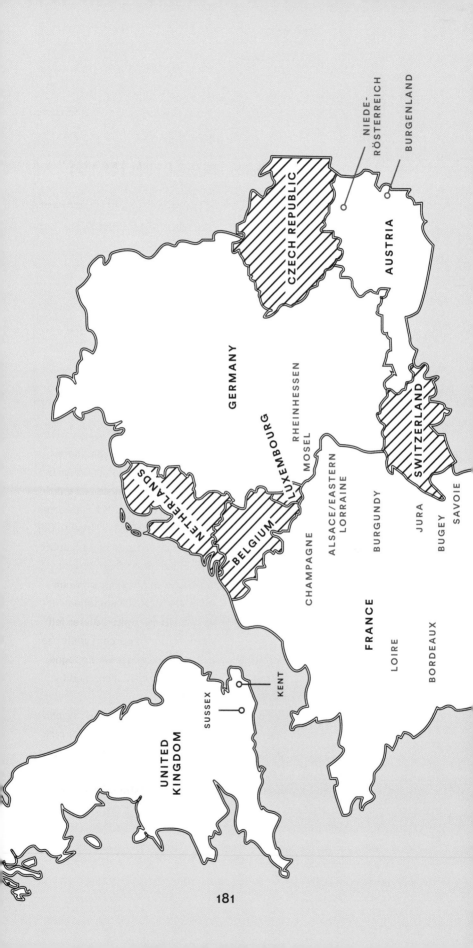

Champagne

All Champagne except *blanc de blancs*[156] is, in a sense, rosé, because it's made from the juice of dark-skinned Pinot Noir and Pinot Meunier, directly pressed with no maceration. Ruinart, "la plus ancienne maison de Champagne," claims to have made the first pink Champagne in this manner. They called it *oeil de perdrix* because they're just as sick and twisted as the Swiss are.

By 1818, however, Veuve Clicquot had developed the method most widely used today to color Champagne, a method that's absolutely verboten everywhere else in France: A small amount of red wine is added to a white wine. *Mon Dieu!* It's a cheap way to make rosé if you're just blending any old white and red wine—and if you try it at home, you'll find that many combinations are dreadful. But if you're carefully adding red Pinot Noir juice to white Pinot Noir juice, the result is more refined. All the same, it took some time for oenophiles to grow accustomed to color-blended rosé Champagne. Writing in 1851, Cyrus Redding described color-blended Champagne as "of the second quality," adding, "both the taste and quality of the wine are injured by this mix-

ture."[157] Today, it's the predominant style, prized for its delicate honey and fresh-raspberry notes. If you don't see the word *saignée* on a bottle of pink Champers, you can bet it's a blend of white and red.

Saignée Champagnes are rarer. Despite what the term implies, their vinification does not result in a pale rosé and a second red wine. Rather, the *saignée* wine itself tends to be ruddy-colored, earthy, slightly tannic, and redolent of dark red fruit. All the grapes are simply crushed and allowed to macerate for a day or two prior to vinification; two days gets you into almost-beet-red territory, aesthetically speaking. If you're a red-wine lover, more likely to go for Lambrusco than Champagne, this is your wine. And even if you're a sucker for the creamy delicacy of a *blanc de blancs* Champagne, consider putting a *saignée* rosé on the table when you're serving hearty foods.

---

[156]   *Champagne vinified solely from white grapes. Most* blanc de blancs *is Chardonnay.*

[157]   *Redding,* A History and Description of Modern Wines, *113–14.*

THREE WAYS TO MAKE PINK BUBBLY

1. MÉTHODE TRADITIONNELLE

aka *Méthode Champenoise*; *Metodo Classico*; *Méthode Cap Classique*; Traditional Method. Makes Cava; Champagne; Crémant; Franciacorta.

For saignée Champagne, grapes are crushed and macerated. Juice is dark.

For blended Champagne, grapes are pressed. Juice is clear.

Then red wine is added for color.

ABV 11–13%

| Initial complete fermentation makes a flat wine. | Wine is blended in bottle with sugar and yeast. | 2nd fermentation traps effervescence. Bottle is slowly rotated, to capture yeast. | Neck of bottle is frozen, yeast pops out. | Wine/juice added to make bone-dry wine more approachable. | Strong bottle and cork due to high pressure. Small, intense bubbles. |

....

2. MÉTHODE ANCESTRALE

aka Ancestral Method. Makes Pétillant Naturel; "Pét Nat"; Pétillant Originel.

ABV 6–10%

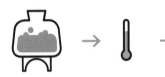

| Grapes are crushed & macerate for a few hours. Juice is pink to raspberry. | Fermentation halts in response to chilling. Only partially completes. | Completion of initial fermentation in bottle. There is no 2nd fermentation. | Bottle is slowly rotated, to capture yeast. Neck is frozen, yeast pops out. | Light bottle; thinner cork or crown cap (like beer). Large, soft, frothy bubbles. |

....

3. CHARMAT METHOD

aka Tank Method; *Cuve Close*; *Metodo Italiano*. Makes most Lambrusco; Mousseux; Prosecco.

ABV 10–12%

| Short maceration for pink color. 1st fermentation makes a flat wine. | Add sugar and yeast. 2nd fermentation in airtight tank. | Filtration. | Juice added. | Light bottle; thinner cork or crown cap. "Frizzante" = large bubbles. |

Note: Fizzy rosé wines, like Txakolí, are "spritzy," not "sparkling," and only undergo a single fermentation in a sealed tank.

Savart "Bulle" Premier Cru Rosé Champagne ($$$$)

Let's begin with a minimalist color-blended Champagne that's on the pale-and-pretty end of the spectrum. Mostly Pinot Noir, with 10 percent Chardonnay, it's a bright, weightless wine that's delicate and ethereal. Frédéric Savart is based in Écueil, a few minutes southwest of the city of Reims, and is making a name for himself as a precise, detail-oriented winemaker. A "Premier Cru" vineyard has been deemed by the authorities to be excellent, one notch below Grand Cru.

Taittinger "Comtes de Champagne" Rosé Champagne ($$$$$)

This squat bottle of vintage Champagne will put you back more than $250 but will impress your friends to no end. Taittinger is one of the "Grandes Marques" houses—the big boys.[158] The maison, in Reims, is built over miles of *caves*, which include Roman-era chalk quarries (bring a thick sweater if you go for the tour). "Comtes de Champagne" is a "prestige cuvée," or special bottling sourced from Grand Cru vineyards, and it's released only every few years. A decade past its vintage date, this color-blended wine is a very pale copper hue and presents notes of red cherry, raspberry, vanilla, nectarine pit, and lavender that will continue to evolve for years to come.

Camille Savès Grand Cru Cuvée Rosé Champagne ($$$$)

The Savès clan has been making bubbly and flat *rouge* in Bouzy since the late nineteenth century. This village, about 16 miles (27 km) south of Reims, is known for producing still Pinot Noir wines similar to red Burgundies. This blend of 60 percent Grand Cru Chardonnay with still and sparkling Grand Cru Pinot Noir serves up cherry and raspberry notes that persist well into the finish. The bubbles are precise and the aromatics include lilies and caramel.

Pierre Gerbais Rosé de Saignée Champagne ($$$$)

And now, let's meet a rosé that is not a blend of finished wines. Pierre Gerbais is located in the *département* of the Aube, in far southern Champagne. Here, the vines on the sunny slopes of the

---

[158]   As opposed to small independent "grower" Champagne producers.

Ource Valley render riper fruit; this dark pink wine is a rosé Champagne for red-wine drinkers, with a pomegranate-juice color, a nose of candied raspberries and red currants, and a palate of tart cherries, gravel, cranberries, and clove.

Geoffroy Champagne Premier Cru Brut Rosé de Saignée ($$$$)

This bruiser of a bubbly creeps toward that beet-red end of the

---

Giraud and the Days of Old

Claude Giraud is an iconoclast among Champagne winemakers. Where it's standard practice to harvest early so the grapes are lean and acidic, Giraud lets his fruit hang on the vine until it's ripe. He does a long "cold soak" prior to fermentation, which is unusual. And a portion of his red wine chills out in terra-cotta amphorae prior to *assemblage* (blending).

Since World War II, most Champenois have vinified their wines in stainless steel tanks. The few who use barrels source them from elsewhere; the Champagne tradition of barrel-making is dead. But Giraud, who can trace his family's vinetending heritage in Champagne back to 1625, has become a connoisseur of the oak trees of the Argonne forest (coincidentally, a historic Argonne oak tree has been known in the region by the name of "Giraud" since Napoléonic days—which must be a sign that Claude is onto something). His custom-made barrels are distinctly fine-grained and give his wines a distinguished character.

Henri Giraud "Fût de Chêne" Aÿ Grand Cru Brut Rosé ($$$$$)
The Grand Cru vineyards of Aÿ (ah-yee), surrounding the town of Aÿ-Champagne, were made famous as far back as the eleventh century by Pope Urban II, who was a big fan. This special, salmon-colored cuvée, resplendent with notes of yeast, papaya, and cinnamon, is called *fût de chêne* (oak barrel) in honor of the oak barrels that it spends a year mellowing in. It's the Champagne equivalent of a pair of Hermès loafers: elegant, comfortable, timeless, and held together by an attractive brass bit. When you see it, you'll know what I mean (page 212).

color spectrum. And the palate comes on strong. I couldn't kick the mental image of a barfly smoking a cigarette as I tasted it, but it was a positive image, I swear. There's something rough, unpredictable, and deliciously dangerous about this *saignée*; it will forever change your image of rosé Champagne. (Note: Both Gerbais and Geoffroy make more than one rosé Champagne; I've just written up the *saignées*.)

ROSÉ DES RICEYS

In the Côte des Bar, the far southern outpost of Champagne on the Burgundy border, Les Riceys are a trio of tiny villages that produce red, white, and rosé still wines under the Coteaux Champenois AOP. The more specialized Rosé des

Riceys is a particular rosé of Pinot Noir. It has a sugar-coated aroma thanks to partial carbonic maceration[159] and a luxuriant ruby color.

Jean-Jacques Lamoureux Recoltant Manipulant[160] Rosé des Riceys   ($$$)

Smoky, sultry candied rose petals on the nose, and roses, sea salt, raspberries, green stems, and brambles on the palate. This admittedly strange translucent red-velvet-colored wine isn't welcoming in its youth but will reward cellar age and curiosity.

[159] *Whole, uncrushed clusters are placed in a sealed tank and fermentation happens inside each intact grape.*

[160] *The mark of a vigneron who grows his or her own grapes, as opposed to purchasing them, as many large Champagne houses do.*

Alsace/Eastern Lorraine

The boomerang-shaped hunk of land between the Vosges Mountains and the Rhine River has been a disputed border for centuries. So Alsatians and residents of eastern Lorraine often speak German and a local dialect as well as French. There are scores of half-timbered gingerbread houses, and the most

relevant grapes are the German top-hits list: Riesling, Pinot Blanc, Gewürztraminer, Pinot Gris, Pinot Noir, Sylvaner, and Muscat. The Alsatians even use tall, narrow green wine bottles, labeled by grape variety, as the Germans do.

Truly fine, transcendent rosé—whether sparkling or still

and dry—is a way for this part of eastern France to declare its independence, because the pink wines of Alsace and Lorraine are unique. Baden, on the other side of the Rhine in Germany, vinifies some cheap Pinot Noir rosé (called Spätburgunder Weißherbst), but the industry here is dominated by co-ops, and the wines aren't made for export. Alsace sparkling rosé, on the other hand, is beloved worldwide. And Côtes de Toul rosé is poised to be the next obsession of the oeno-geek squad.

ALSACE

Crémant is sparkling wine made via *méthode traditionnelle*, aka *méthode Champenoise*, aka the labor-intensive dual-fermentation technique used in Champagne. But Alsatian bubblies are oh so much more affordable. Sadly, more than three-quarters of the wines produced in Alsace are sold in France, and most of the rest go to nearby nations, namely Belgium. (One can't blame them—I mean, pink French bubbly with Belgian frites? To die for.)

Long, skinny Alsace sidles up to the Rhine River and Germany's Black Forest, protected from incoming Atlantic storms by the Vosges Mountains. While aromatic white grapes bask on sunny slopeside vineyards, vines for sparkling wines grow in the cool, shady lower elevations of the Rhine Valley. While there are numerous soil types, the Alsatians are proud of a particular *grès de Vosges* sandstone subsoil that's purpley-pink.

In your wineglass, that *grès de Vosges* makes for a subtly delicious sparkling wine with fine minerality. The word most often used to describe the color of the rosés is "salmon," although the hue depends on the maceration time. And yes, this rosé is made via what the Champenois would call *saignée*. I find it interesting, however, that on the nose and palate, the best Crémants d'Alsace are difficult to differentiate from color-blended rosé Champagnes with their delicate fruit and floral notes. What do you think?

....

Dopff & Irion Crémant d'Alsace Brut Rosé   ($$)

Silky and sexy, perfumed with freesia and lilies, creamy and delicately fruity, this wine makes a girl want to slip into an elegant party dress and go someplace fancy. Like, say, the Château de Riquewihr, to hang out with one of the princes of Wurtemberg. (These days, said château is home to the Dopff & Irion winery.) Kiwi, pear, and lemon curd, along with

reams of tiny, persistent bubbles, make for a mouthfilling mousse that's irresistible.

....

Jean-Baptiste Adam Crémant d'Alsace Brut Rosé ($$)

Jean-Baptiste Adam began blending wine back in 1614; things at his namesake family winery in Ammerschwihr haven't changed much over the past four centuries.

The timber-beamed cellar is outfitted with wonderfully worn *foudres*; and the vineyards are farmed biodynamically. This Crémant has a delicious yeasty nose and a color that verges on mango. The palate is dry, creamy, and mineral-driven until the finish, when fresh orange, apple, and caramel creep in. Serve it with *grès de Vosges*, which isn't just a soil type . . . it's also a fragrant Alsatian cheese.

Willm Crémant d'Alsace Rosé ($$)

Relative newcomer Maison Willm has only been around since 1896, but founder Emile Willm made up for his late start by getting in on the US market the moment Prohibition ended. Located in Barr, about 20 miles (32 km) south of Strasbourg, Willm makes eaux-de-vie[161] from its own orchard fruits in a traditional copper still, in addition to its range of wines. This apéritif-style sparkler is subtle, with hints of vanilla bean, lemon, and white pepper, a floral nose, and tiny but persistent bubbles.

CÔTES DE TOUL

The Lorraine plateau has the unfortunate honor of occupying the side of the Vosges Mountains that collects all the rain. The French tend to dismiss all the wines from this area as *vins de l'est*, as in "wines of the east."

That said, Lorraine was highly regarded from the fifteenth through nineteenth centuries, when delicate reds were in fashion. Today, with rosés and lighter reds coming back into vogue, it's time for a Lorraine wine revival.

The Moselle River—same thing as Germany's Mosel—carves out the Moselle AOP, a path of good vineyard sites near the city of Metz that crosses the border into Luxembourg. Côtes de Toul, the only other AOP in Lorraine, has been generating buzz recently for its *vin gris*. Gamay and Pinot Noir are the majority grapes, with Aubin Blanc,[162] Auxerrois Blanc, and Pinot Meunier as the minority blending partners. The straw-colored dry wine is the ideal match for quiche Lorraine, with its delicate spices and perky acidity. Here's hoping that US importers bring in more of this delicious wine—I know of only three Côtes de Toul labels available here at present.

Domaine Régina Côtes de Toul Gris "Vieilles Vignes" Rosé ($)

A delicious surprise from an unheard-of appellation. The aroma evokes fresh hay, the mouthfeel is creamy, and the flavors range from lemon cream to fresh orange juice to ginger. Mostly Gamay grapes, with some Pinot Noir, are pressed immediately without macerating, resulting in a wine that's pale, with a golden tint.

---

[161]   *Clear brandy.*

[162]   *A cross between two other grapes you have never heard of, Gouais Blanc and Savagnin, Aubin Blanc is unique to Côtes de Toul.*

Jura/Savoie/Bugey

Three small winemaking appellations in the foothills of the Alps curl around the spot where Lake Geneva pokes into France, crossing through three *départements:* Jura, Ain, and Haute-Savoie. To give you a sense of the atmosphere here, the Ain River (on Bugey's west side) is a favorite of fly-fishers, Les 3 Vallées in Haute-Savoie bills itself as the world's largest ski area, and hikers flock to the section of the "Grande Randonnée" network that skirts the Jura Mountains. The wines are, likewise, bracing.

JURA ARBOIS

The Jura is an oeno-region of the absurd, best known for Vin Jaune, a highlighter-yellow, sherry-like liquid made from the Savagnin

grape. In Arbois, the northern-most subzone of the Jura, the red wines are tart, light, and one of a kind. The grapes, sour-cherry Trousseau[163] and floral Poulsard,[164] don't have much pigment to speak of, making haunting translucent wines that fade significantly with age. I know of at least one winery intentionally producing a still rosé, but more interesting to me are the simple, fruity, unintentionally pink "red" wines of this region. They're a window into a chillier, simpler past, when so many of Europe's wines were pigment-challenged.

Domaine de la Tournelle "L'Uva Arbosiana" Jura Arbois ($$$)

Vignerons Evelyne and Pascal Clairet make a fresh, unfiltered wine that's a deep, cloudy pink. Their organically farmed Poulsard grapes go through carbonic maceration—whole-berry fermentation, which results in low tannins and Juicy Fruit flavors—then cellar the wine in enamel-lined tanks for nine months. The result is something like an artisanal Kool-Aid, flavored with strawberry, watermelon, and lavender. One can only imagine how delicious this wine must be when consumed at the Clairet's riverside garden eatery, Le Bistrot de la Tournelle.

SAVOIE

The crisp, citrusy wines of Savoie, aka Savoy, are tailor-made for the end of a day spent hiking or skiing. I used to grab the easy-breezy whites made from the unassuming Jacquère grape in the subzones of Apremont and Abymes for about $11 off the bottom shelf of my local gourmet grocery. Those days are over; Savoie has been discovered. Drat.

The rosés are equally weightless and refreshing, with more floral notes. They're the perfect apéritif or lunch wines—they fill you up with delight without weighing you down in alcohol.

Les Rocailles Vin de Savoie Rosé   ($)

Don't tell anyone about this wild-rose-petal-pink rendition of Gamay, OK? The vines grow under the protruding shoulder of Mont Granier, and drinking it is like hiking through a high alpine field on a sunny day: wildflowers, crushed herbs, and invigorating mountain air. *Ahhhhhh.*

BUGEY CERDON

Within Bugey, the term "Cerdon" is devoted to the electric boogaloo of wines: a semisweet, funky, frothy pink frippery. It's made possible by the chilly autumns in the storybook village by the same name. Red Gamay and Poulsard grapes, harvested from the steep mountainside vineyards, start to ferment in Cerdon's cellars, but the process stops when the outside temperature drops. The semisweet *méthode ancestrale* wine that results is like liquefied Strawberry Shortcake cartoons.

---

163 *Its name suggests elegant clothing in French; but in Portugal, where it goes into Port, it's called Bastardo.*

164 *Sometimes spelled "Ploussard."*

....

**Renardat-Fache
Bugey Cerdon** ($$)

**Bottex "La Cueille"
Bugey Cerdon** ($$)

Organically farmed Gamay and
Poulsard unleash intense aromas
of ripe strawberries, raspberries,
and crabapples. As is typical with
méthode ancestrale, the bubbles
are soft and foamy rather than
pinprick-sharp, and the alcohol is
low, around 7 to 8 percent. Drink
with dessert . . . or breakfast.

Strawberry shortcake. Not the
cartoon, but the dessert. Only
better. The sweetness of this
Gamay-heavy fizz fest isn't cloying,
mind you. It's counterbalanced by
fresh fruit flavor, upright acidity,
and a touch of spice. A glass of
this would absolutely kill with
French toast and bacon.

Loire

The Loire Valley wins the award
for best fairy-tale châteaux. Case
in point: Château de Chambord.
But while the castles are grand,
the wine scene is low-key.
Oeno-geeks like to think of the
dry and sweet whites made from
Chenin Blanc and Sauvignon
Blanc, and the reds, of Cabernet
Franc, Gamay, and Pinot Noir, as
their little secret.

In summer, the Loire River
enjoys a delicious breeze that keeps
châteaux-goers—and grapes—from
burning up. The resulting wines
emphasize delicate, fragrant fruit
and zippy acidity, so it should come
as no surprise that more than 30
percent of the vins[165] here are rosé.

TOURAINE

Red, white, rosé, sparkling—you
name it, Touraine makes it. This
catchall wine region grabs hold of
the Loire River's hand as it branches
out into fingerlike tributaries:
the Vienne, the Indre, the Cher,
the Beuvron, and the confusingly
named Loir (because the river is
bigger than the stream, it gets
more letters, one supposes).
Overall, Touraine's most prized red

[165] *And possibly more, since sparkling
wines and rosés are tallied separately
in the annual report issued by the Loire
wine trade association.*

grape is Cabernet Franc. Gamay is far more prolific, and it's the favored variety for rosé thanks to its fresh wild strawberry character. After these two, the native Grolleau is the third-most-planted red grape in the Loire; it's favored for rosés due to its bright acidity.

I'm going to go rogue with my next two recommendations, however, and highlight a couple of producers who are seeking out the potential of alternate grape varieties, most notably elegant Pinot Noir.

Domaine des Corbillières Touraine Rosé   ($$)

Mostly Pinot Noir, with a hearty dollop of Pineau d'Aunis, a grape that brings a white pepper note and pleasingly low alcohol levels to blends when farmed attentively. This charismatic rosé has so much going on: white peach, raspberry, stones, spritz, length, Red Hots, bitter herbs, thyme, sage, grapefruit pith, and did I mention the mint on the finish?

Sparkling Saumur

Loire bubbly offers elegance at a moderate price tag—it's really best enjoyed at a *guinguette*, or open-air riverside bar and eatery where the reedy sound of an accordion can often be heard. In the central section of the valley, the heart of sparkling-wine production is Saumur, an appellation between Anjou and Touraine that stretches south from the town of the same name.

Fines Bulles—"fine bubbles"—is a Loire-trademarked name for the Chenin Blanc–dominant bubblies of the region, but you'll see other terms on labels as well. Those made according to the traditional Champenoise method are typically labeled Crémant de Loire or Méthode Traditionnelle. The steel-tank method that's used for Prosecco is also permitted; these wines are called Mousseux.

Frothy *méthode ancestrale* wines, too, are produced in the Loire. As in Bugey, this archaic style of sparkling wine tends to be low in atmospheric pressure—that is, the bubbles are less aggressive than they are in Champagne, Cava, or Prosecco—with low alcohol and noticeable sugar. Here are two personal favorites from Saumur that exemplify two styles: First, a polished *méthode traditionnelle*, then, a funky *méthode ancestrale*.

....

Bouvet "Excellence" Loire Brut Rosé ($$)

The Bouvet Ladubay house is owned by the Monmousseaus, known to many for terrifically affordable bubblies bottled under the family name. Loire tourists love dropping in at this impressive winery on the west edge of the town of Saumur: There's an art gallery in the former stables, and you can take a bicycle tour of the massive cellars. This Crémant is incredibly floral, with notes of red currant, candied orange peel, grapefruit pith, an ultra-frothy mousse, and a sensation of sweetness at the finish—Cabernet Franc like you've never tasted it before. And pretty "excellent" for $17 or so.

....

Melaric "Globules" Méthode Ancestrale
Loire Cabernet Franc Rosé ($$)

Winemakers Melanie and Aymeric Hillaire made a portmanteau of their names when they started up their artisanal label in 2006. Their winery is only a short drive from Bouvet Ladubay but the approach couldn't be more different. These vignerons practice biodynamic-ish agriculture, farm with the help of horses, and make this quirkily delicious bubbly observing natural techniques. It tastes like an earthy hard cider and is a forgiving match for a wide variety of foods.

François Chidaine
Touraine Rosé ($)

François Chidaine is widely admired for his Chenin Blancs from Montlouis and Vouvray. He farms his vineyards biodynamically, allows indigenous yeasts to guide fermentation, and softens his wines with lees aging. But whites aren't his only strength. He has a side venture in Murcia, southern Spain,[166] which vinifies a Monastrell-Tempranillo blend. And about 20 miles (32 km) southeast of Montlouis, where the vineyards follow the path of the Cher tributary, Chidaine grows Pinot Noir and Grolleau.[167] This raspberry-tinted pink is a blend of both. It has the supple texture of lees stirring, and flavors of pineapple, melon, and bitter herbs. A creeping finish ends with a final kick of energy. This wine's ideal match: Touraine's empanada-like *fouée*, a dough pocket stuffed with meat, mushrooms, beans, or cheese.

CHINON

Chinon is a subappellation of Touraine as well as the name of the town where Richard I "The Lionheart" ensconced himself in an impressive hilltop fortress. The appellation follows the path of the Vienne (a Loire tributary, as previously mentioned); and its sandy, gravelly soils and climate are ideal for the cultivation of Cabernet Franc. It makes a somewhat tart red wine with aromas of spring greens and river rocks that always makes me thirsty for grilled fiddleheads; it can bring herbaceousness and depth to many rosé blends. However, despite its green and gravelly notes, some sorcerers are able to coax something guileless and mellifluous out of Cab Franc in the form of a rosé.

Jean-Maurice Raffault
Chinon Rosé ($)

The Raffault family was growing grapes as far back as 1693, but Jean-Maurice Raffault really shook things up in the early 1970s by departing from old customs and taking radical (now more typical) steps, such as vinifying each vineyard parcel separately instead of throwing the whole lot into the fermenter together. His son Rodolphe Raffault, who has one of the best names I've ever heard, maintains his father's legacy,

---

[166] *Chidaine's wife, Manuéla, is from Spain. She's well known in wine circles for her riverfront bottle shop, "La Cave Insolite," in Montlouis-sur-Loire.*

[167] *Grolleau is a Loire red grape that is often diverted into rosé production due to its relatively high acidity and low alcohol.*

paying special attention to the roles of lees and oak in winemaking. His spontaneously fermented rosé is soft and juicy with sweet red-berry notes—just a touch of pepper hints that this is, in fact, Cab Franc.

SANCERRE

If you visit the hilltop town of Sancerre, be sure to climb the staircase of the fourteenth-century Tour de Fiefs for spectacular views of the valley. And don't miss tasting Crottin de Chavignol—the local goat cheese—which absolutely sings with the Sauvignon Blancs of Sancerre and neighboring Pouilly-Fumé.

Oenophiles say that the "flinty minerality" of the Sauv Blancs comes from the silex[168] and limestone soils. That flintiness shows

---

The Noble Jewel That Is Noble-Joué

Touraine Noble-Joué is the distinctive appellation for a distinctive style of pink. The grapes must be sourced from Touraine vineyards located between the Indre and Cher rivers in the area around Joué-lès-Tours, a suburb of the city of Tours. The wine is a blend of three "noble" grapes that also grow in Champagne: Pinot Noir, Pinot Meunier, and Pinot Gris. Because Pinot Gris is not technically a white grape, the three wines are shamelessly blended after fermentation.

Historians have found evidence of the Touraine Noble-Joué blend dating back to the ninth century, and fifteenth-century ruler Louis XI apparently slurped the stuff down when he was in residence at Château de Plessis-lès-Tours, in La Riche. There, the king also locked his prisoners into dreadful little iron cages before suspending them from the dungeon ceiling. Likewise, the wines can be forceful, yet airy.

Rousseau Frères Touraine Noble Joué Rosé   ($$)
This was a regular go-to summer wine for me before I ever knew the interesting story behind the Noble-Joué appellation. It has the white peach, pear, citrus, and ginger notes of a white and the sturdy body of a red—the oomph to please the rosé naysayers combined with aromatics reminiscent of a delicate Vouvray. It's like a pit bull wearing a flower garland. Which is a thing. Google it if you don't believe me.

up in Sancerre Pinot Noir and Pinot Gris as well. So keep plenty of that fresh chèvre on hand the next time you open a Sancerre rosé.

....

Matthias et Emile Roblin "Origine" Sancerre Rosé ($$–$$$)

The Roblin brothers are the fourth-generation winemakers at the humble Château de Maimbray, located in a village a few minutes northwest of Sancerre on a small Loire subtributary called La Belaine. Their rosé of Pinot Noir, made in a low-interventionist, traditional style, has an alluring floral perfume and a piquant finish. And although it's pink, it's certainly a sibling of white Sancerre, with its notes of sour lemon, brine, and terrific lingering acidity.

....

Domaine André Neveu "Le Grand Fricambault" Sancerre Rosé ($$–$$$)

A family estate in Chavignol makes this lean, frisky *saignée* rosé from Pinot Noir. Scented with the *fines herbes* you might find on a log of goat cheese, it's spicy on the palate, with a hoof-kick of acidity that will wake you up just in time for cocktail hour.

REUILLY

The small town of Reuilly, along with its neighbor, Quincy, is an island of viticulture east of Touraine and west of Sancerre. In addition to turning out Sauvignon Blanc and Pinot Noir, Reuilly has truly mastered the art of *vin gris* of Pinot Gris (called Pinot Beurot around these parts),[169] and plantings of the lavender-skinned grape have increased over the past few years. The Kimmeridgian soil of the eastern Loire[170] really comes into effect here—the very essence of yellow limestone, packed with tiny fossilized oyster shells, seems to seep into this briny, yellowy-pink wine.

....

Domaine de Reuilly Reuilly Pinot Gris ($$)

Nope, that's not a typo—the winery just has the same name as the wine appellation. And this is the second-best-selling rosé in importer Kermit Lynch's catalog, so it's twice as nice. Proprietor and

---

[168] *A flinty, sandy soil, containing a mix of clay, limestone, and silica.*

[169] *There are Reuilly rosés made from Pinot Gris and Pinot Noir, but the* vins gris *of only Pinot Gris are more interesting.*

[170] *This soil type is also influential in the wines of Chablis and Champagne.*

vigneron Denis Jamain farms his Pinot Gris organically (and practices biodynamics in his Sauvignon Blanc and Pinot Noir vineyards). He harvests oak from his own forest to make his barrels for the red; this minerally pink, like the rest of his wines, goes through spontaneous fermentation.

CÔTE ROANNAISE

Looking at a map, it is difficult to grasp that the Côte Roannaise is part of the Loire Valley. It's about two and a half times as far from Sancerre—which we typically consider to be the far east of the Loire—as it is from Lyon, the city that separates Burgundy from the Rhône. But the vineyards are on the southern section of the big river, so it's a "Loire" appellation.

This island around the town of Roanne is its own entity, focused on Gamay-based reds that can be quite Beaujolais-like, and selling most of its wine locally. A few producers have been branching off into Pétillant Naturel *(méthode ancestrale)* rosé lately, and I was delighted when I stumbled across this next wine, which is available in the United States. . . .

Domaine Sérol "Turbullent" Côte Roannaise Rosé   ($$$)

The grape here is a strain of Gamay unique to Côte Roannaise, called Gamay Saint Romain, that grows on southern-facing slopes. Again, we have an indigenous-yeast *méthode ancestrale* wine, low in alcohol. It's a luxuriant journey for the senses, with rose water, freesia, and lanolin on the nose, and rose-hip tea, tropical fruit, orange candy, and pear on the palate.

Burgundy

For oenophiles, Burgundy is the Côte de Beaune, the Côte de Nuits, Chablis, and all the acclaimed Villages and Grand Cru vineyards they contain. As for everything else to the south in the Saône-et-Loire *département*, well, that's Pinot Noir and Chardonnay, too, but it's just not the same. These aficionados might be surprised to learn that northern Burgundy is also home to some rowdy rosé-producing towns.

MARSANNAY

Located approximately 5 miles (8 km) south of the busy city of Dijon, the town of Marsannay-la-Côte doesn't have much in the way of scenic vistas or entrancing medieval architecture. But Marsannay is the only Burgundian appellation approved to label rosés under its own name; in fact, it was a pink-wine *Village* before it was ever acknowledged for its reds or whites.

Marsannay reds and whites have been accused of being rather flimsy, and the rosés, too, have been called something like the vinous equivalent of cheap perfume. However, the new guard of Marsannay is going gung-ho artisanal, making reds and pinks that could make a person delirious with the freshness of their black fruit and the ability to soak up oak-barrel spice as though it were expensive aftershave.

Domaine Sylvain Pataille "Fleur de Pinot" Marsannay Rosé ($$$$)

Bright young star Sylvain Pataille breaks from the bad old Marsannay habit of mechanized vinification-by-rote, lovingly farming his old-vine plots organically and vinifying with indigenous yeasts. His rosé is a total triumph: Spicy, smoky, and woody, it benefits from its lengthy hibernation (between eighteen and twenty-four months) in new and nearly new oak barrels. The fruit notes from the Pinot Noir, plus some Pinot Beurot (Pinot Gris, as we learned in Reuilly), are pure blackberry. This is a wine for the Burgundy collector eager to expand her horizons.

CÔTE SAINT-JACQUES

Just as the Côte Roannaise stretches the outline of the Loire

Valley, Burgundy jogs wayyy northwest to encompass Chablis, and even farther, Joigny, only about 93 miles (150 km) outside of Paris. While its hillside vineyards, overlooking the Yonne River, grow your typical Burgundian Pinot Noir and Chardonnay, the obscure Côte Saint-Jacques has a special thing going with Pinot Gris—aka Pinot Beurot. The chalky, slate-y soils here render a flavorful *oeil de perdrix*–colored *gris de gris* that looks like butter and leans toward notes of chamomile and spice.

Christophe LePage Côte Saint Jacques Bourgogne Pinot Gris ($$)

LePage's spontaneously fermented golden-pink Gris evokes the days before high-tech presses and crystal clarity in the glass. At the same time, it's Pinot Gris in 3-D. It's everything you'd expect from the white version—citrus, white pepper, some creaminess—with the added dimension of fruit tannins and an energy that pops. Give it a couple of years of cellar age.

Beaujolais

Stuck between two A-listers, Burgundy and Rhône, Beaujolais humbly makes its tutti-frutti nouveaus for the masses and its more feral, thorny, floral Villages- and Cru-level reds for those in the know. There's an opening here for rosé, and I hope more producers take it.

If farmed and vinified attentively, the resident Gamay grape divulges the floral, herbaceous, and red-berry notes that can be so provocative in a pink wine.

Jean-Paul Brun "FRV 100" Méthode Ancestrale ($$)

Pronounce this one's name as the French do and you get "eff-er-veh-sant," i.e., effervescent. Jean-Paul Brun represents the new face of Beaujolais, making artisanal, handcrafted wines without yeast additions. This deliciously low-alcohol treat has an initial nose of burnt cotton candy that turns to strawberries and cream. On the palate, there are raspberries, cherries, and a touch of sweetness.

Bordeaux

If you are going to drink a wine from Bordeaux, why not make it a powerful red, a waxy dry white, or a heartbreakingly delicious dessert wine? Why even bother with rosé?

None of the best Bordeaux Châteaux do, unlike the esteemed producers in Rioja and Tuscany, who see no shame in pink wine-making. So while there is a lot of pink Bordeaux produced, very little of it is any good. To wit: Bordeaux rosés command the lowest average price per bottle in Paris wine shops. If you must purchase a dry Bordeaux rosé that's not a *clairet* (see below), I suppose it's best to go for the one with the highest price. But I wouldn't know, because I've suffered through enough bad cheap pink Bordeaux to have sworn it off.

CLAIRET

The exception to the above is *clairet*. It has the same grape makeup as a "claret"—that's the British term for a Bordeaux red—and, like Spanish *clarete*, it's a rosé. All three words are derived from the Latin term for "clear." Today's *clairet* isn't very clear, though; it looks more like a light red. A cold maceration that can last up to a week brings out the flavor and deep beet color of the fruit, but not the tannins. The alcohol level tends to be quite reasonable—reminiscent of the red Bordeaux of, say, forty years ago.

....

Château Landereau Bordeaux Clairet ($$)

It's unusual for Malbec and Cabernet Franc to take up the bulk of a Bordeaux blend, but they account for 60 percent of this one, outnumbering the Cabernet Sauvignon and Merlot. But then, this isn't a red wine. It's the color of faded velvet and has notes of cassis, red cherry, and gravel. It's Bordeaux lite, and I think you'll like it.

PROFILE

AUSTRIAN ROSÉ

COLOR
peonies on Austrian
porcelain

AROMATICS
white stones, sour cherries,
nutmeg

PERSONALITY
cool, calm,
and collected

GOES WELL WITH
Helmut Lang,
Wiener Schnitzel

Riesling was once dismissed as a sugary, old-lady sort of drink. But now that Patti Smith qualifies as an old lady, Riesling is rock and roll. Today's wine-bar patrons aren't freaked out by a slight perception of sweetness. They declare with a wink that they're "high on acid." And they embrace the low-alcohol delicacy of Teutonic Riesling because it's the contrary of high-octane Cabernet Sauvignon. Which shines a bright spotlight on all the German-speaking viticultural regions.

Importers are shipping more German and Austrian wines our way these days, and those increasingly include reds and pinks. So it's time to turn up the Kraftwerk and party with our new best friends: Blaufränkisch, Zweigelt, Roter Elbling, Saint Laurent, Spätburgunder. Oh, and David Hasselhoff, of course.

For a while in the early aughts, Grüner Veltliner was the "it" grape variety. And Riesling has always been a big kahuna in Austria. But today, curious drinkers are looking past groo-vee to see what else Austria has to offer. Like Zweigelt, the red love child of Blaufränkisch[171] and Saint Laurent that's almost as captivating as an early-twentieth-century theatrical dance revue.[172] For those looking for a light Austrian wine, the rosés from these grapes represent something floral and fruity and new and different—a break from all that Grüner and Riesling.

Unfortunately for us, Austria's most interesting regional rosé specialties stay in state. For example: Schilcher, a wine made from the fragrant and historic Blauer Wildbacher grape variety, and a particular young pink out of Burgenland called Primus Pannonikus, which is what Transformers drink when they're done destroying things.

NIEDERÖSTERREICH

Austrian wine country hugs the nation's eastern border, basking in a warm climate (German wine country, on the other hand, chills out in the mountainous northwest). Niederösterreich, or "Lower Austria," is the northern chunk that borders the Czech Republic and Slovakia; the Danube River runs through it. The Groiss winery (below) is located in Niederösterreich's—and Austria's—largest quality subzone, called Weinviertel, or "wine quarter." While some Austrian rosés don't match Germany's for delicacy, this one does.

IJG Groiss Niederösterreich "Sommerwein" Rosé ($$)

One of my all-time fave rosés, scoring points for presentation as well as drinkability. The Audubon-esque botanical etchings on the label (see page 203) don't disappoint: Strawberries and white flowers are indeed present on the palate. There's also an intriguing sweet-and-sour tension atop a firm foundation of minerality. Winemaker Ingrid Groiss's estate is located in the hamlet of Fahndorf, in a zone of loess, gravel, and sand soils that winegrowers call "In der Schablau," or "In the Blue Saddle." Groiss is one of the young winemakers bringing back the old-school Austrian tradition of *gemischter satz*, or field-blend,[173] wine, but this triumph is all Blauburgunder, aka Pinot Noir.

Wachau

Wachau's big attraction is the Burgruine Dürnstein, a ruined castle where twelfth-century Richard I of England[174] (remember him from Chinon, page 195?) was held

---

[171]   *Known as Lemberger in Germany and Kékfrankos in Hungary.*

[172]   *I recommend drinking Zweigelt whilst watching the Ziegfeld Follies on YouTube.*

[173]   *The old tradition of co-planting a jumble of grape varieties together, harvesting them all at once, and vinifying this motley assortment.*

[174]   *In disguise and on the run, the "Lionheart" was shipwrecked in northern Italy, then captured by the Duke of Austria, who accused him of arranging a murder. These things happen when a person runs off on a Crusade.*

captive. These days, the region focuses its energies not on imprisoning world leaders but on worldly Grüner Veltliner and Riesling. These haughty whites are subject to a barrage of confusing Teutonic ripeness classifications,[175] which we thankfully needn't bother with. (Isn't rosé wonderful?)

Weingut Holzapfel Wachau "Pink" ($$)

The elegant baroque building that houses this winery, distillery, restaurant, and guest house is a notable work of architecture. It's also unabashedly pink. As for the wine, it's dry and crisp, but there's a sense of the baroque in its faint hints of candied cherry, dried orange peel, *agua fresca de Jamaica*, and Bosque pear.

Kremstal

Just up the Danube Cycle Path from Wachau, Kremstal is also part of the Wachau Valley, a collection of steep terraces and picturesque villages clustered along the banks of the Danube. Again, the focus is on Grüner Veltliner and Riesling. But where there is great white wine, the good lord sayeth, there will also be great pink.

Weingut Stift Goettweig Messwein Kremstal Rosé ($$)

Stift Goettweig is a palatial eleventh-century Benedictine abbey boasting hilltop views, a museum, a concert hall, and a restaurant that serves wild game from its expansive grounds. In partnership with Austrian vino impresario Fritz Miesbauer, the monks also grow grapes on the slopes of Mount Göttweiger. Their Messwein is an altar wine, made without additives and under the watchful eye of the bishop.[176] Pale gold in color, this rosé barely divulges its Pinot Noir identity. It's all heavenly fresh cream and citrus blossom.

BURGENLAND

Remember that glass-walled private clinic in the Alps where James Bond tracks down Dr. Madeleine Swann in *Spectre*? That's our idea of "Austria." But Burgenland—Austria's second-largest wine region—is more like . . . the Bahamas beach scene in *Casino Royale*. Located at the

---

[175] *Read more about these on page 207.*

[176] *Forget the notion that it should look like the blood of Christ, because in this corner of Austria, white Grüner Veltliner passes at Mass.*

western edge of Central Europe's Pannonian Plain, low-lying Burgenland glories in more than 2,000 hours of sunshine annually and the hottest temperatures in the nation.

....

Neusiedlersee

The hot spot for Burgenland bikini-wearers and bird-watchers is also ground zero for winegrowers: Neusiedlersee. The southeast end of Lake Neusiedl is a national park bordering Hungary, while the northern bank is a playground for people, whether sailing, swimming, or sunbathing. The region used to stake its reputation on sweet wines, but today, the new guard is focusing on deeply flavorful dry reds from Zweigelt and Blaufränkisch.

....

RoSée Connection "Jerry & Barry Für Fruchtige" Neusiedlersee Rosé ($)

When Markus Altenburger took over his family's winery, he switched the focus to high-end, single-vineyard, native-yeast Blaufränkisch and Chardonnay. Rosée Connection, one of his side projects, bills itself as "Austria's first rosé winery." It's not just the label that brings Ben & Jerry's ice cream to mind: The nose and

palate on this quirky Zweigelt-Blaufränkisch blend are nougat-y and off-dry. Serve it ice cold with piquant foods.

....

Biokult Österreich Rosé Secco ($$)

This juicy Pinot Noir rosé has a note of *mushkazone* (Hungarian spice cookie). And the "bio cult"[177] in question is a 5,000-acre (2,000-ha) certified-biodynamic farm in Pamhagen, a Neusiedlersee town that was torn apart by the Iron Curtain due to its location on the Hungarian border. Here, the Michlits family raises cattle and produces vinegar and beer; the vineyards climb the lower slopes of an extinct volcano. This is a side project of their Meinklang winery, known for its naturally fermented vegan wines. Although it isn't labeled "Sekt"—the standard term for Germanic sparkling wines—this is a bubbly, the cork held on with a *spago* (string) à la Prosecco.

---

[177] *I'm going with the assumption that "biokult" is a tongue-in-cheek name, and that the Michlits family members aren't all walking around like zombies in long flowing robes.*

PROFILE

GERMAN ROSÉ

COLOR
Claudia Schiffer's
flawless complexion

PERSONALITY
clean as a whistle,
confident despite obscurity

AROMATICS
spring flowers,
tree fruit, pine

GOES WELL WITH
Krautrock, sausages,
potato salad

I wish I could tell you all about the regional rosé specialties Schillerwein, Rotling, and Badisch Rotgold, but the Germans are very good at polishing their own gleaming trophy of an economy, so not much *rosewein* leaves Deutschland. Germany is the world's third-thirstiest consumer of pink, after France and the United States.

There's also the issue of messaging. Your typical top-shelf German Riesling label is littered with crazy-making insider terminology. Only groupies—like those *Avatar* geeks who go around speaking Na'vi to each other—are willing to take the time to work it out.

Unfortunately, the best German rosé follows the same rules. This style of wine, called "Weißherbst," is a direct-press pink made from one single grape variety. It's classified as a QbA or Prädikatswein—that is, of the highest quality. Good luck trying to sell a bottle of Winzergenossenschaft Königschaffhausen Steingrüble Spätburgunder Trockenbeerenauslese Weißherbst from the Rheinhessen to an English-speaking clientele.

Happily, a few producers make simple dry rosés for export and give them names like "Rosay." Because we Americans are simple people. And we like to drink, *ja*.

Note: Unlike the European nations we've visited previously,

Germany doesn't have large catchall wine regions that share borders with political states. So while both Mosel and Rheinhessen (up next) are located in the state of Rheinland-Pfalz (Rhineland-Palatinate), they are not subappellations.

MOSEL

After leaving the Vosges Mountains in France and passing through Luxembourg, the Moselle becomes the Mosel: A river valley whose 150 miles (240 km) of dizzying hairpin turns are lined by steep slopes and slippery with shards of slate. The stars here are the fairy-tale castles and the Riesling. But one can't survive on white wine and turrets alone. So stop off at the former wine-trade hub of Traben-Trarbach, where the colorful architecture is Art Nouveau. It's a good place to sip the nouveau wine of Germany, rosé.

....

Weingut Matthias Dostert "Rosay" German Rosé ($$)

Like that unlikely Olympic medalist in the feel-good sports movie, Roter Elbling is an obscure, unlikely grape that comes out of nowhere to kick major booty. Its skins are so pale that it can only make a *vin gris*, but oh, what a wine: drink-it-all-day low alcohol, lively spritz, gauzy softness. Plus all the pleasures of a delicious Kabinett or Spätlese Riesling: Apple-blossom perfume, a yuzu sour note juxtaposed against a tangerine sweetness and lime-stone minerality. Can you hear the inspirational music? These things always make me cry.

RHEINHESSEN

Germany's largest wine region follows the western bank of the Rhine River from Mainz to the evocatively named city of Worms. Its producers have been doubling down on quality in recent years, and Riesling vines now outnumber the often-insipid Müller Thurgau. The reds are an unusual lot, with names like Dornfelder and Blauer Portugieser. Saint Laurent, which we'll meet below, is an intensely fragrant Czech relative of Pinot Noir, like your cousin from out of state who wears too much cologne.

Architectural aside: *Trulli*, the little gnome huts[178] that dot the Puglian countryside (see page 142), make a guest appearance in Rheinhessen wine country. They popped up during the eighteenth century with the arrival of migrant quarry workers from Italy.

Wagner Stempel Rheinhessen Gutswein Rosé   ($–$$)

How often do you get to taste a blend of Saint Laurent, Frühburgunder,[179] Merlot, and Spätburgunder?[180] Wagner Stempel is a ninth-generation family *weingut* (winery), about an hour's drive from Frankfurt, specializing in indigenous-yeast, neutral-barrel-fermented Rieslings grown in certified-organic, porphyry-rich vineyards. The motley assortment of grapes takes this wine in different directions, from red berries to pears to lemon meringue, but altogether, it's a nice little package. P.S. A "Gutswein," by German labeling law, is just a good-quality, basic wine, culled from the winery's own vineyard holdings. Not some fancy-schmancy single-vineyard Riesling, but not rotgut, either.

---

[178]   Called weinberghäusch *(vineyard house) in German, or* wingertsheisjer *in the local dialect.*

[179]   *Also known as Pinot Noir Précoce, an early-ripening mutation of Pinot Noir.*

[180]   *Pinot Noir.*

PROFILE

UK ROSÉ

COLOR
coral cravat,
English roses

PERSONALITY
celebratory, effervescent,
suave

AROMATICS
tart raspberry,
wild strawberry

GOES WELL WITH
polo matches,
tea sandwiches

Who were the first Champagne makers? The Brits. Seventeenth-century English merchants imported sour northern French wines by the cask, adding sugar and bottling them on home turf. When the weather warmed in the springtime, the wines fermented a second time, resulting in delightful fizziness . . . and a rash of exploding bottles. British glassmakers designed stronger bottles, and Winston Churchill's favorite beverage was born.

Even today, the United Kingdom is still the top export market for Champagne. Also, Brits are the world's fourth-most-ravenous rosé consumers.[181] So there's a big market on that little island for pink fizz. Fortunately, Britain is a prime

place to make sparkling wine, since it just so happens to share two key characteristics with the most effervescent of French wine regions: chilly weather and chalky soil.

Like Champagne, England's southern coast is blustery and damp, and its Dover cliffs—only about 30 miles (50 km) from Calais—are famously chalk white. Nearly 70 percent of homegrown British wine is sparkling, and the majority of it comes from the southeastern counties of Kent and Sussex, where old country estates have been converted into Chardonnay, Pinot Noir, Pinot Meunier, and Pinot Blanc vineyards.

If there's a prevailing style here, it's minimalist—buttoned-up notes of crisp pear, starched

linen, and restraint—but in blind tastings, the best UK bubblies are indistinguishable from Champagne. Although not much makes it to American shores, give these delightfully frothy pinks a try the next time you visit London.

Gusbourne Traditional Method England Rosé ($$$$)

Gusbourne's original estate in rural Kent dates back to 1410 and is minutes from the High Weald natural area and the sea. An additional vineyard in West Sussex is inside the South Downs National Park. Dry and crisp, with pinprick bubbles and frisky energy, this wine has a honeyed tint, honeysuckle aroma, and honeycomb flavor, followed by mint on the finish.

Wiston Estate "South Downs" Brut Rosé ($$$$)

The 6,000-acre (2,400-ha) Wiston Estate in the chalky South Downs hills of West Sussex has been in the same family since 1743. Today, wine critics go gaga for the soft texture and red-berry allure of the genteel Wiston rosé. As is the case with so many Champagnes, this Pinot Noir–driven wine comes in both vintage and nonvintage forms—the richness of the vintage version, all from estate-grown fruit, makes it worth the few extra bucks.

---

[181] *Consumption data from the CIVP and the Comité Interprofessionnel du Vin de Champagne.*

PRETTY AND PINK

$$$$
Champagne
Savart

$$$$$
Champagne
Taittinger

$$$$$
Champagne
Henri Giraud

$$$
Jura
Tournelle

$$
Bugey
Renardat-Fache

$$–$$$
Loire
Roblin

$$
Niederösterreich
IJG Groiss

$$
Kremstal
Stift Goettweig

$$
Burgenland
Biokult

$$$$

Champagne

Camille Savès

$$$$

Champagne

Geoffroy

$$

Alsace

Dopff & Irion

$$

Loire

Domaine de Reuilly

$$$

Loire

Domaine Sérol

$$

Beaujolais

Jean-Paul Brun

$$

Germany

Matthias Dostert

$$$$

United Kingdom

Gusbourne

$$$$

United Kingdom

Wiston

New Rosés from the New World

In the Old World, tradition and bureaucracy rule the wine trade. In the New World, it's a free-for-all. Outside of the Eurozone, wine-growing regions aren't overburdened by regulations.[182] Vinetenders plant whichever grape varieties seem to suit the soil and climate, and winemakers are relatively unconstrained in the way they blend and vinify them. In rosé-making, this means that *saignée* is not frowned upon, and the blending of finished wines is not verboten.

Still, Europe is never far from a New World winemaker's mind. Most notably, the grapes of southern France have landed on every vinously inclined nation's shore. Rhône-style reds, and by extension rosés, are everywhere. And they can be quite nice.

Those looking for a detour can travel down the Natural Wine path to taste reverent reproductions of antiquated beverages. A rosé that tastes like it dates back to before the Age of Enlightenment can be wonderfully novel even while it's terribly outdated, like a bartender with muttonchops who's wearing a waistcoat. So contemporary! So old-fashioned!

But what can the New World offer that the Old isn't already doing? A haven for unusual grape varieties that never quite took flight back home. In South Africa, for instance, Pinotage has come into its own; and in Chile, Carménère has flourished as an expatriate.

If any single theme unifies the winegrowers of the New World, it's a fearless embrace of the unknown. It's a willingness to explore untrodden ground, plant something new, and vinify it differently. The rosés in this chapter won't present the polished finesse of Provence's most elite pink wines, but they'll keep adventurous drinkers engaged.

---

[182] *American winemakers will claim otherwise . . . unless they have tried to make wine in France.*

PROFILE

SOUTHERN HEMISPHERE ROSÉ

COLOR
clouds over a
Patagonian sunset

PERSONALITY
adventurous, inviting,
always in season

AROMATICS
tropical fruit, volcanic rock

GOES WELL WITH
shrimp on the barbie,
cueca music,
Trevor Noah on TV

Our ports receive regular shipments from the wine regions of Australia, New Zealand, Chile, Argentina, and South Africa. But not many of those wines are pink. Nearly 85 percent of the grapes grown in New Zealand are white, so there's that. And as of 2015, rosado wines accounted for only 2 percent of Argentina's overall production—those gauchos just love their high-octane reds.

But there's also the issue of the inversion of seasons. Most US rosé consumption happens between the months of May and September. So it didn't make much sense for producers in the antipodes to ship container loads of heavy glass bottles filled with rosé in October until now.

With the current demand for rosé lasting year-round, we should be seeing better and better imports from the southern half of our sphere in the coming years. Future books on rosé will, I hope, devote an entire chapter to each of the very disparate nations profiled here.

For now, let's rack up some frequent-flyer miles and go on a whirlwind tour of three continents—Australia, South America, and Africa—to get to know some rosés that might be worth traveling across half the globe to taste.

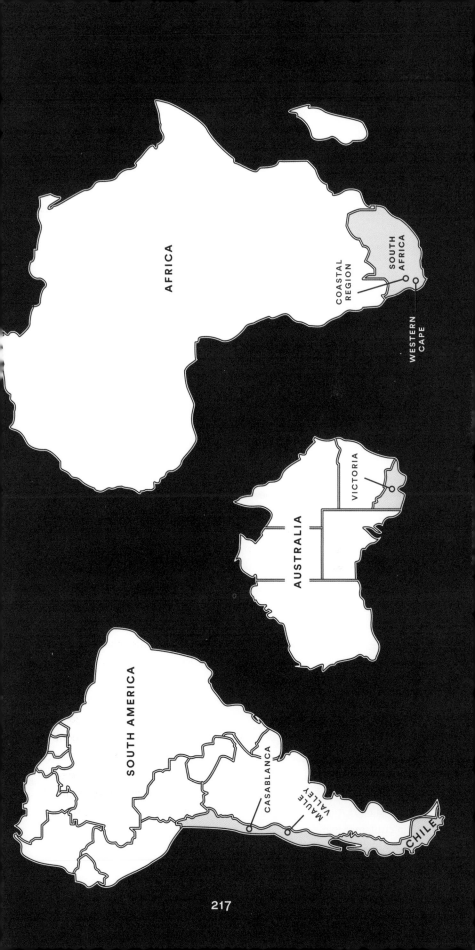

AFRICA

COASTAL
REGION

SOUTH
AFRICA

WESTERN
CAPE

AUSTRALIA

VICTORIA

SOUTH AMERICA

CASABLANCA

MAULE
VALLEY

CHILE

Australia

Rosé may account for less than 2 percent of total Australian wine exports annually, but this nation is poised for a rosé revolution. The three big grape varieties from southern French rosé—Syrah (called Shiraz here), Grenache, and Mourvèdre—thrive in the vineyards of Australia.

The land of Oz is ahead of the curve in terms of contemporary winemaking techniques and technical know-how, so oenologists don't struggle to produce stable, clean, crisp pink wines. At the same time, there's a movement in Australia to explore previously uncharted territory. Obscure Italian grapes, indigenous yeasts, biodynamic agriculture, and other offbeat approaches are increasingly showing up in the Aussie wine media. So the possibilities for the future are vast. For now, let's meet one wine that's a straight shooter, and another that's exploring an alternative path.

VICTORIA

Southeastern Australia is a winemaking powerhouse defined by the Australian Alps, the Eastern Highlands, the Murray River, and the Bass Strait. While dry inland zones such as Rutherglen support more robust varieties like Shiraz and Cabernet Sauvignon, the temperate areas near the coast's seaside clifftops are lush and green. Here, subappellations such as Yarra Valley and Mornington Peninsula grow cool-climate grapes such as Chardonnay and Pinot Noir, and produce vibrant, edgy rosés.

scare off the impatient with its initially off-putting odor. Just relax and give it a minute in the glass or, alternately, allow it to age for a year before opening it. Then you'll get an elemental smokiness, almonds, muskmelon, and vanilla. This is the wine to drink with damper, the old Aussie settlers' soda bread, which was traditionally baked on the coals of a campfire.

Tournon "Mathilda" Victoria Rosé ($)

Michel Chapoutier is either the most brilliant vigneron in France's Rhône Valley or the enfant terrible of the southern French wine-making community. Whatever you believe, you can't deny that his ideas have made an impact. Maison Chapoutier is a many-tendriled vine, with biodynamic and organic winemaking ventures throughout the South of France, Alsace, Portugal, the United States, and Domaine Tournon[183] in Australia. Here, his vineyards are in the rangy foothills of the Victoria Pyrenees, approximately 70 miles (110 km) north of Melbourne in the state of New South Wales. This wine, named after Chapoutier's daughter Mathilde,[184] is all whole-cluster-pressed, spontaneously fermented Grenache. It's a very pale onion-skin color and might

Taltarni "Taché" Méthode Traditionnelle South Eastern Australia Chardonnay-Pinot Noir-Pinot Meunier ($$)

Victoria-based Taltarni is a sister winery to Clos du Val in California's Napa Valley as well as two other operations, in Australia and Languedoc. This classic Champenoise-style blend of grapes sourced from Victoria— as well as neighboring South Australia and the wild, wind-chilled island of Tasmania—is a pale cantaloupe color. With its notes of citrus, crème brûlée, caramel, and kiwi, it's quite popular among Sydney's chic set. Taché is French for "stained."

---

[183] *The word "Domaine" does not appear on the label but does appear in descriptions.*

[184] *Spelling the name with an A is a reference to the Australian folk song "Waltzing Matilda."*

Chile

Chile is a major wine producer but, unlike Australia, a minor wine consumer. All that juice has got to go somewhere. Approximately 70 percent of the grapes grown in Chile are red, providing plenty of raw materials for rosé. And the United States is Chile's top export market. Ipso facto, as Chilean vintners experiment with rosado, their wines are sent our way. The following examples range from clean and crisp to arcane and experimental.

Two imposing natural barriers make Chile tall and slim: the South Pacific Ocean on the west and the Andes Mountains to the east. This skinny nation is striated into a stack of valleys that are also DOs.[185]

CASABLANCA

If you don't live under a rock, you've seen the film *Casablanca* and you're aware of Chile's best-known wine region, near the cities of Santiago and Valparaíso. The Casablanca Valley is known for its serviceable Sauvignon Blancs and its sinewy reds made from Carménère, Chile's flagship red grape. But the Casablanca Valley has so much more to offer: namely, an array of fragrant whites and bracing Pinot Noirs.

Bodegas RE
Casablanca Pinotel   ($$)

Bodegas RE breaks from the rather corporate Casablanca mold. It's chockablock with terra-cotta amphorae, clay-coated vats, and big oak casks. "Pinotel" is the winery's term for a blend of Pinot Noir and aromatic old-vine Pink Muscat. Both are fermented and aged in large neutral oak casks to achieve an oxidative effect of allspice and gasoline that will either attract or repel you, depending on your level of tolerance for natural wines. This salty, spicy, sultry, spritzy, elemental wine, with its slap-in-the-face acidity, pushes the boundaries of rosado. Serve with cilantro-flecked green pebre sauce on grilled bread.

MAULE VALLEY

The valley carved out by the Río Maule is the nation's oldest winegrowing zone, having been initially planted by settlers way back in the sixteenth century. (That would be the era when the Spanish arrived and unkindly mauled the Incas.) Today, Maule still has plenty of old vines. Being closer to the South Pole, Maule has a cooler climate than Casablanca, and accordingly its fine wines are a bit friskier. But this region's oeno industry was built on bulk sales,[186] and the idea of farming and vinifying for quality rather than quantity is relatively new. An interesting intersection between the old way of viticulture and the new is the return to the rustic country grape, aptly named País.[187]

Miguel Torres "Santa Digna Estelado" Secano Interior Uva País Brut Rosé ($$)

Spain's preeminent viticultural family produces a wide range of Spanish wines and runs a sister estate in California in addition to Miguel Torres Chile, which has been in operation since 1979. País is the ubiquitous workman grape of the Chilean countryside, first planted by the Spanish centuries ago, that has never earned much notice until now. Its thin skins, light flavor, and lack of pigment make it ideal for sparkling rosé production, so Torres Chile has developed relationships with subsistence farmers to purchase their organically dry-farmed País grapes. This wine is Fair Trade–certified and has created economic opportunities for rural Chilean farmers thanks to its role as a test subject. The remarkable quality of this efferves-

cent wine proves that some simple attention to viticulture can improve the quality of País dramatically, bringing out its floral aromas and clean palate. "Secano Interior" is a special appellation for wines made from País and Cinsault grapes in southern Chile.

Apaltagua Maule Valley Reserva Carménère Rosé ($)

Phylloxera, that nasty root louse that seems to come up in every wine discussion, practically obliterated the blue-skinned Carménère grape from France.[188] The variety is enjoying a second act as the star of Chilean winemaking. This fresh, yellow pale rosado is nimble, with notes of passionfruit, pomelo, and some Chilean cilantro. The Apaltagua winery is located in the Apalta subzone of the Colchagua Valley, but owns six large vineyards in five distinct DOs. The Huaquén vineyard, overlooking the Mataquito River in the Coastal Range foothills of Maule, is the source of this Carménère.

---

[185] *Denominación de Origen, just like in Spain.*

[186] *Maule harbors the most vineyard acres of any Chilean region.*

[187] *Country.*

[188] *So far, phylloxera hasn't made it to Chile due to its remote location.*

South Africa

Sun-soaked South African wine country is just ridiculously beautiful. Every vineyard seems to be on or near a sparkling body of water, and backed by a dramatic rocky mountain that juts straight up out of the valley floor like some surreal diorama. Between the bright sun and the driving winds, this is a country that's cashing in on alternative energy.

That same winning combination of sun and wind elicits ripe flavor from grapes while warding off mold, toughening tannins, sharpening acidity, and creating wines with a hold-on-for-dear-life vitality.

WESTERN CAPE

Until the very few fine wines from the Northern Cape become available in the US, Western Cape, for all intents and purposes, means "South Africa," because this over-

arching appellation encompasses all the major wine-growing regions in the nation.

....

Graham Beck "Méthode Cap Classique" Western Cape Chardonnay-Pinot Noir Brut Rosé ($$)

The grapes in this cuvée were sourced from two different places. It's difficult to fathom how Chardonnay for such an elegant wine could be grown in the desert-like Robertson region, but ice-cold nights there lock in acidity. The Pinot Noir, for its part, hails from the breezy Stellenbosch appellation on False Bay, where it's protected from the driving winds off the South Atlantic. This yeasty, aggressively bubbly rosé has notes of mango and the South Africa aromatic shrubland—like *garrigue* —called *fynbos*. *Méthode cap classique* is the South African term for Champagne-style, or *méthode traditionnelle*, sparkling winemaking.

....

Coastal Region

The Coastal Region, covering South Africa's southwestern

shores, is the nexus of the nation's finest winegrowing subzones. Standout producers here are rewriting the playbook[189] by growing grapes from Bordeaux and southern France and blending complex dry red wines. Although it used to be scorned, the secret sauce in many of these mixes is Pinotage. This rather off-the-wall red grape—a savory cross between Pinot Noir and Cinsault—has become synonymous with South Africa.

Pinotage can be rather tannic and unappetizing if not farmed and vinified carefully. But it has the potential to turn out wonderfully complex purply black wines with notes of soy sauce and balsamic vinegar. In rosé form, the tannins are dialed back and that sweet-and-salty character shines through, standing out on its own or bringing an element of the unexpected to pink blends. Try it with South Africa's signature curried meat custard dish, bobotie.

Boschendal Coastal Region "The Rose Garden" ($$)

South Africa's second-oldest wine estate is a stunning example of the unique, lacy-edged Cape Dutch architectural style. Today, the property includes a large farm, an on-site artisanal butcher, three restaurants, a spa, horse and carriage rides, hiking trails, and, the eponymous rose garden, plus former slave quarters and a role in South Africa's awful history of inequality. But hey—we Americans have our own ghastly legacy to be embarrassed about, so let's just drink some nice rosé. This, one of three Boschendal pink wines, is a lightly spicy blend of Merlot, Pinotage, Shiraz, and Cinsault, with notes of baked pineapple, tart summer berries, dry twigs, and scallions.

---

[189]   *In the past, South Africa's sole entrant on the international fine-wine stage was a sweet dessert wine called Vin de Constance.*

The Cape Doctor Is In

South Africa's cool southern coast is an exciting region for wine production and holds great promise for rosé. Winds blasting north from Antarctica, along with the famous "Cape Doctor"—a driving gale from the southeast—discourage rot and make for frisky flavor and bright acidity in grapes. At their best, South African rosés taste a bit like spray from a windblown ocean.

PROFILE

USA ROSÉ

COLOR
red, with white
and blue tones

AROMATICS
blackberries, raspberries,
gun smoke

PERSONALITY
brash, exploratory,
irreverent

GOES WELL WITH
burgers, country music,
corn on the cob

Our young wine industry may not be able to solve our messy nation's most pressing social problems, but it's trying hard to keep up with our sudden, fervent need for rosé. We're now the second-most-ravenous consumer of pink wine after France, and our vintners are facing the challenge head-on.

Many American winemakers don't own estate vineyards, instead sourcing fruit from far and wide. (Where it's a noteworthy event when a Soave producer tries his hand at Cerasuolo, no one bats an eyelash when an Oregon winemaker vinifies Washington grapes.)

Unfettered by the restraints of land ownership, they're fearless in their willingness to try nontraditional grapes and techniques. Sometimes the results are rapturous. Other times, not so much. Still, the climate of curiosity that pervades our domestic winegrowing ethos makes every American rosé encounter exciting.

But out of so many tasty American rosés, which deserve our close attention? Those that make a statement about the genre by aiming to establish a benchmark for regional style. Those that reflect the climate and soils of the winegrowing region. And those that inspire wonder in oenophiles.

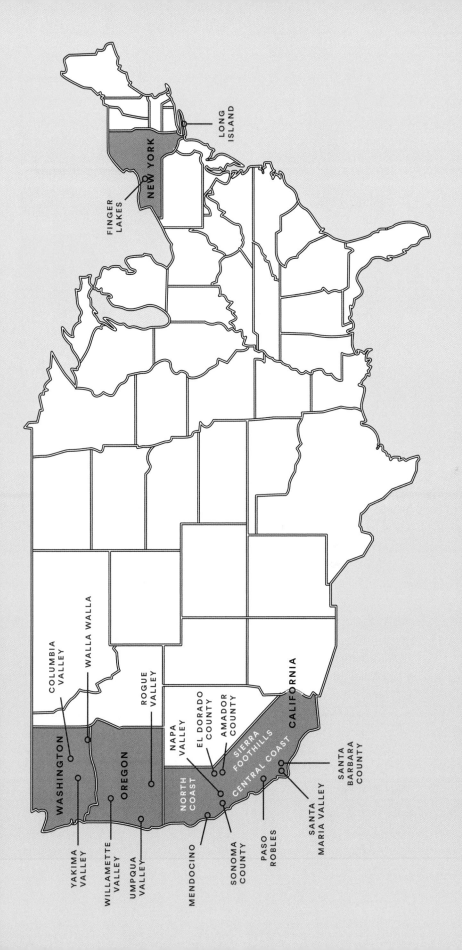

FINGER
LAKES

NEW YORK

LONG
ISLAND

COLUMBIA
VALLEY

WALLA WALLA

ROGUE
VALLEY

CALIFORNIA

NAPA
VALLEY

EL DORADO
COUNTY

AMADOR
COUNTY

SIERRA
FOOTHILLS

CENTRAL COAST

SANTA
BARBARA
COUNTY

WASHINGTON

OREGON

NORTH COAST

YAKIMA
VALLEY

WILLAMETTE
VALLEY

UMPQUA
VALLEY

MENDOCINO

SONOMA
COUNTY

PASO
ROBLES

SANTA
MARIA VALLEY

New York

New York is the nation's third most oeno-productive state, but much of its wine doesn't make it into books like this one because it's made from folksy native and hybrid grapes.

While there are some promising fine wines coming from other appellations such as the Niagara Escarpment, pink lovers should focus their attention on the Finger Lakes and Long Island. The top winemakers in these two regions are toning down flabby fruit and emphasizing acidity to make rosés of distinction.

FINGER LAKES

This heart-shaped region spans, roughly, west to east from Rochester to Syracuse and south toward Corning. And it surrounds a group of—yes, you guessed it—finger-shaped, glacial-carved lakes, along with many scenic waterfalls. The moderating effect of all that water, not to mention nearby Lake Ontario, spares the vineyards from the extreme heat and cold that the northeastern United States is known for.

The Finger Lakes hangs its hat on aromatic, acid-driven white Riesling, whether vinified dry or as a dessert wine. The Germanic influence continues with the cool-climate red grapes Pinot Noir (or Spätburgunder, if you like), and Lemberger. The most successful rosés, however, are the syntheses of Germanic-style high-acid, low-tannin winemaking with

Cabernet Franc, the red grape of the Loire and Bordeaux. These examples of clearly defined fresh-fruit flavor and minerality have become so iconic that the wine-makers of the Finger Lakes hold an annual event called "Discover Dry Rosé."

Atwater Finger Lakes Cabernet Franc Dry Rosé ($)

This pleasant, onion-skin-pale sipper isn't trying to be anything other than enjoyable, with a soft texture and notes of citrus and stone fruit from the addition of some Pinot Noir. From a long-established winery on Seneca Lake, this exemplifies the unfussy ethos of the Finger Lakes winemaking scene.

Kelby James Russell "Nutt Road Vineyard" Finger Lakes Cabernet Franc Dry Rosé ($$)

At the opposite end of the spectrum, this raspberry-colored wine comes from the new guard—Russell is the young winemaker for Red Newt Cellars and débuted his own label with this dry, restrained rosé. It betrays its Cab Franc-ness with uncontrived notes of green pepper, pencil shavings, and river stones, but then finishes with

upbeat fruitiness. Bonus points to the winemaker for including the bone-dry residual sugar level as well as a suggested music pairing on his highly informative back label.

LONG ISLAND

The Hamptons is a fantastic place to sell rosé. It's not, frankly, a fantastic place to make rosé, because autumn nighttime temperatures don't typically dip low enough to seal in terrific acidity at harvest time. Thus, there's a tendency here to make oaky, condensed red wines. But the vignerons of Long Island will not be dissuaded from giving the pretty, pleasure-seeking populace what they want.

And, to be fair, where some vintages may lack that thrill of soul-piercing acidity, the same could be said of many southern French and Italian pink wines.

Also, Long Island has the Atlantic Ocean, which brings briny, foamy notes to rosés, rendering them irresistible in situations such as clambakes and lobster boils.

By easing up on the throttle—as they must do, since rosé winemaking is, by definition, minimalist—producers allow the surf-sand-and-seashell terroir to show through.

Wölffer Estate "Summer in a Bottle" Long Island Rosé Table Wine ($$)

The bottle is worthy of a "Best Dressed" list, and the wine slips on easily. Mostly Merlot, it's got Cabernet Franc, Chardonnay, and Gewürztraminer, which adds a touch of SweeTarts. The combination ticks all the boxes: texture (soft), fruitiness (citrus, pineapple), and verve (there's spritz to make up for any lacking acidity). In its ongoing effort to meet the needs of the region's deprived populace, the winery also produces a basic rosé ($$) that suggests the salty surf off Hampton Beach, and a more sumptuous "Grandioso" ($$$) that's as creamy and cozy as an alpaca throw. I must admit: The "Summer in a Bottle" is anthemic and as such, gets top billing in this paragraph, but I'd personally rather settle down with the Grandioso and a good film. Plus, Wölffer makes a sparkling rosé ($$$), and another rosé grown and vinified way down in Mendoza, Argentina, ensuring a year-round supply.

Channing Daughters Home Farm Vineyard Long Island Rosato di Refosco ($$)

Like Wölffer Estate, Channing Daughters brings forth a great deal of pink wine. But the approach is dissimilar. Winemaker James Christopher Tracy presents a lineup of six different whole-cluster-pressed pink wines—five single varietals and one blend, all $$—as well as a series of limited-release ramato-style bottlings ($$$). These spicy "orange" wines are delicious party tricks, but I'm more intrigued by his guileless study of his seaside landscape, viewed through the lens of five different grapes vinified à la rosé. We'll revisit the northeastern Italian Refosco grape in the next chapter (pages 265–272), as we explore Slovenia and Greece; Long Island may well be another good landing spot for this slightly bitter, blue-skinned variety. Gently pressed and vinified by Tracy, it's a ramble through rustic Friuli by way of the Hamptons, testing the limits of the surroundings and the possibilities of the grape.

Washington

The United States' second-most-productive wine industry, after California's, can be as businesslike as a Microsoft executive, as stolid as a sailor on the Alaskan fishing fleet, and as alluring as an apple orchard in full bloom. Its bolder side turns out substantial reds of the Bordeaux and Rhône persuasion. Its more thoughtful side produces far more Riesling than any other US state. Its rosés fall somewhere in between: aromatic yet powerful.

While Seattle sucks up all the commerce, tech, and trade, Washington's winegrowing action is concentrated on the east side of the state, in wheat-farming and cattle-ranching country.[190] The hot, dry summers here make for ripe Bordeaux- and Rhône-style grapes, and call for frequent infusions of ice-cold rosé.

COLUMBIA VALLEY

The big daddy of Washington wine regions covers just about everything east of the Cascade Mountains. The range acts as one helluva rain shadow, leaving Seattle, the coast, and the islands in a near-constant state of dreary drizzle until, oh, August.

[190] *While the vast majority of Washington's vineyard land is east of the Cascade Mountains, a good number of wineries are located in and around the city of Seattle.*

Meanwhile, much of the Columbia Valley gets cold, snowy winters and scorching-hot summers. I'm not sure if anyone, other than the wine grapes, comes out a winner.

This is an elemental landscape, scoured bare by Ice Age floods. Its defining feature is the mighty Columbia River, which runs south from Canada before turning west and tracing the Oregon border. This massive aqueous force has carved out cliff walls, powered cities with its dams, propelled countless windsurfers and kiteboarders, and cooled off an awful lot of vineyards. So what of the wines?

Hmm, well, the Columbia Valley wine region is larger than the entire nation of Denmark. So the wine is . . . whatever you want it to be. Robust red varieties tend to grow at the more desert-like east end, while more delicate grapes can be found to the west, toward the Pacific Ocean. From Rhône to Bordeaux to Loire, every sort of French wine grape is grown, not to mention a number of Italian varieties, as well.

A region of this size attracts equally large business ventures, so if anything, the wineries of the Columbia Valley tend to be corporate rather than boutique. But with that scale comes an assurance that the wines will be technically flawless.

Seven Hills Columbia Valley Dry Rosé ($$)

As is typical for Washington, Seven Hills has a Walla Walla winery but sources its fruit from four different vineyards throughout the Columbia Valley. This pink is a blend of the minor Bordeaux grapes Cabernet Franc, Petit Verdot, and Malbec, intentionally farmed for rosé and picked a few weeks before the red wine harvest. Overall, the style is restrained, contained, spritzy and light, with green-pepper and herbaceous notes counterbalanced by tropical fruit.

Canoe Ridge Vineyard "The Expedition" Columbia Valley Rosé ($–$$)

Canoe Ridge's flagship vineyard is in the Horse Heaven Hills, atop a butte that explorers Lewis and Clark described as resembling an overturned canoe. This rosé is a blend of mostly Rhônish varieties—strawberry-scented Grenache, hearty white Roussanne, and some peppery Counoise—with a dose of Lemberger, aka Blaufränkisch, because sometimes you've just gotta bring a German to a French party. There's nothing about the body or aromatics of this rosé that screams "Rhône varieties," but it ticks all the boxes, delivering tangerine juiciness and fresh acidity.

....

Division Villages "L'Avoiron" Columbia Valley
Rosé of Gamay Noir   ($$)

Those same climate conditions that make Washington a great Riesling-growing region also elicit fragrance and charm from grapes like Gewürztraminer, Chenin Blanc, and Gamay Noir. This fresh, floral, delightful wine is evidence of the porosity of the Washington-Oregon border: The grapes are from Washington, but the vinification happened in a Portland urban winery space that is shared by eleven small producers. It's an understated declaration of independence from the Columbia Valley establishment.

....

Yakima Valley

The oldest and best-known of the Columbia Valley's subappellations, the Yakima Valley surrounds three smaller winegrowing subzones[191] and encompasses more than a third of the state's grapevines. As with the Columbia Valley, that's more than can be adequately summed up in a sentence; depending on their location, these vineyards can grow frisky Riesling or full-bodied Merlot.

The Yakima River and the town of Yakima take their name from the people of the Yakama Nation, who fished, hunted, and foraged here, and are the only ones who can spell the word "Yakama" properly. For European settlers, this golden, grassy land became cattle-ranching and orchard country. Today, Latin-American farm laborers and their families make up nearly half the population. Cinco de Mayo is more popular than the rodeo these days, and that's just fine for rosé fans, since a steaming-hot tamale, straight from the corn husk or banana leaf, is a wonderfully fortuitous match for an ice-cold glass of cherry-scented Washington rosé.

....

Tranche "Pink Pape" Blackrock Vineyard
Yakima Valley Rosé   ($$)

Tranche's Blackrock Estate Vineyard is on the eastern edge of the Yakima Valley AVA. Never mind that no rosé is produced in Châteauneuf-du-Pape. (It's next door to Tavel, after all.) This faux-"Pape" pink is Cinsault, Counoise, and Grenache, gently pressed and

---

[191] *Red Mountain, Rattlesnake Hills, and Snipes Mountain.*

softened up by three months of lees contact. It's a grassy, herbal wine, punctuated by black pepper notes from the Counoise; serve it with garlicky foods. Tranche[192] is a sister brand of Corliss, a producer of power reds.

WALLA WALLA

The Walla Walla Valley provides two types of vineyard terrain: breezy, sunny ridges and slopes, or Rhône-like rocky riverbeds. More than 40 percent of its vineyards

---

Charles Times Two Equals $$$$

Take two marketing geniuses with terrific palates, add an unquenchable demand for rosé, and you've got a bulk-wine business success story. Charles & Charles is a collaboration between two prominent wine impresarios with the same first name. Charles Smith is a wild-haired former rock-band manager who landed in Walla Walla and founded a multi-label juggernaut responsible for wines ranging from the $12 "Kung Fu Girl" Riesling to the burly $50-and-up reds of the K Vintners label.

Floppy-haired French-born Charles Bieler, whose family previously owned the rosé powerhouse Château Routas in Provence, runs his own wine empire from New York City. His projects include the popular Bandit boxed wines; The Show reds from California and Argentina; Gotham Project wines on tap in the New York City area; and Bieler Père et Fils, a rosé from Coteaux d'Aix-en-Provence. Together, the two savvy Charleses source Columbia Valley grapes to make America's top-selling rosé in its price range (which would be all of $10 to $12).

....

Charles & Charles Columbia Valley Washington State Rosé ($)

This Syrah-Mourvèdre-Grenache-Cabernet Sauvignon-Cinsault-Counoise *négociant* blend is refreshing, although some of its melony notes teeter on the edge of overripe. Insider gossip: Trinchero Family Estates, of Sutter Home fame (see pages 34, 239) manages sales, marketing, and distribution for the brand.

fall on the Oregon side of the state line, but the town and most of the wineries fall on the northern side. Which is a plus, because "Walla Walla Washington" trips off the tongue so much more fluidly than "Walla Walla Oregon."

The semi-arid Channeled Scablands of Eastern Washington are bone-dry Wile E. Coyote country. But the name Walla Walla, translated from the indigenous Sahaptin dialect, means "many waters." Streams tumbling down from the Blue Mountains create an oasis where delicious sweet onions and some of the most exciting wines in the west both grow.

For rosé lovers, the grape varieties to watch are those found in the Rhône, most notably Syrah and Grenache. These grapes roar when vinified as red wines here, and can barely contain their raw energy as rosés.

Waters "Patina Vineyard" Walla Walla Valley Rosé ($$)

Like a grizzly bear stuffed into a tutu, this whole-cluster-pressed Syrah from a tiny riverbed vineyard nearly bursts the seams of its bottle. Behind a perfectly rosé-appropriate lemonade flavor, the Syrah growls out notes of black pepper, mint, roasted game, and gravel. For those seeking something with more tulle and fewer claws, this Syrah-focused winery also releases a more rounded, fragrant Washington State rosé ($$) that's co-fermented Syrah and Viognier.

---

[192]   *The name is an inside joke for wine geeks. In Bordeaux, futures go on the market in stages, or "tranches," before any consumers have even tasted the wine. Tranche sells its wines on release and does not take itself so seriously.*

Oregon

Washington's Puget Sound is a welcome mat for damp, cold weather, and the Cascade Mountains act like a giant overstuffed sofa, forcing the drizzle to sit down and stick around the Seattle area. In Oregon, however, a unique topology makes west-side cool-climate viticulture a better bet. First, the Coast Range filters nasty weather coming in off the Pacific. Second, the Ice Age floods that roared west from Montana and carved out the Columbia Gorge turned south when they hit the Coast Range, dropping rich soil deposits and forming the fertile Willamette Valley. Between the abundance of fresh produce grown here and the salmon, tuna, crabs, and clams from the coast, it's rosé night every night in Oregon, no matter the season.

Oregon's winemaking industry is dominated by this garden of Eden, to the point where outsiders think that Pinot Noir and Pinot Gris, the signature grapes of the Willamette Valley, are the only wines coming out of the state. Not so. In both Oregon and Washington, the Columbia Gorge is a dynamic growing region, and as we've just learned, Walla Walla is partly in Oregon. In addition, three major valleys continue to sketch the line of the winegrowing zone farther south, all the way to the California border.

WILLAMETTE VALLEY

Despite the protection of the Coast Range and the onslaught of global warming, the Willamette Valley still suffers through its share of stormy springs, gray summer days, and cold autumn downpours. So the Pinot Noir doesn't always get quite as ripe as winemakers would choose. *Saignée* to the rescue.

Thus, until recently, rosé was mostly viewed as a side course in the Willamette Valley. But as demand has skyrocketed of late, winegrowers have begun to see the value in rosé for its own sake. In addition, rafts of investors from California, France, and elsewhere have arrived over the past decade, transforming what was once a cluster of small family-run wineries into a sleeker, more sophisticated collection of grand estates. There has been a significant jump in the number of vines planted, and Pinot Noir is no longer the scarce commodity it once was. The result: More wineries are branching out, allotting one portion of their Pinot Noir toward bubbly production, and another toward serious dry rosé.

The rosé renaissance that's happening right now ranges from "white" Pinot Noir, like flat Champagne, to funky skin-fermented Pinot Gris, maybe even vinified in a house-made terra-cotta amphora (see page 26). It represents an exciting opportunity, because while American vintners aren't treading over any new ground with their many iterations of southern French–style pink wines, there's no existing precedent for high-end, flat Pinot Noir rosé in Burgundy, outside of one or two vignerons in Marsannay. As an Oregonian myself, I'm eagerly awaiting the next chapter in this still-developing story.

....

Soter "Mineral Springs" Yamhill-Carlton Brut Rosé ($$$$)

Tony Soter was a Napa Valley superstar winemaker before opening his namesake place in Oregon. His Mineral Springs Ranch is an idyllic hilltop farm raising sheep and heirloom vegetables in Yamhill-Carlton, a subzone of the Willamette Valley that tends to bring out black-cherry-cola-like flavors in Pinot Noir. This *méthode traditionnelle* bubbly serves up plenty of red fruit flavor, counterbalanced by a bit of hazelnut-crème luxury.

JK Carriere "Glass" Willamette Valley White Pinot Noir ($$)

Winemaker Jim Prosser was an early adopter of the idea that Willamette Valley rosé could be more than a byproduct of red-wine production. Although it's flat, "Glass" is inspired by methods used in Champagne to make white sparkling wine from midnight-blue Pinot Noir grapes. Prosser's whole-cluster-pressed, spontaneously fermented Pinot rests for four months in neutral oak barrels on Chardonnay lees, a process that leeches color and broadens the midpalate of the wine. The winery also produces an onion-skin-colored sparkling *blanc de noir* ($$$$).

Ponzi Vineyards Willamette Valley Pinot Noir Rosé ($$)

One of the first families to plant Pinot Noir in the Willamette Valley, the Ponzis consistently turn out polished, elegant wines like this perfumed and succulent rosé, with its strawberry notes and laser-beam acidity. Winemaker Luisa Ponzi has a deft touch with whites and, by extension, rosé; she also produces small quantities of sparkling rosé.

Antica Terra "Angelicall" Willamette Valley Rosé Wine ($$$$$)

This would be a red Pinot Noir if the juice had not been separated from the skins, mid-ferment, and transferred to barrels after a week of maceration. The wine then ages on the lees for a year. Open the bottle in the morning and let it breathe all day before digging in. Then recork it and continue to taste it every day over the next week . . . it gets more nuanced and interesting the more oxygen it drinks in. The color is faded red roses, and the aroma and flavor are reminiscent of a fine old Bordeaux or Burgundy: dried rose petals, leather, cloves, and allspice. Winemaker Maggie Harrison learned her trade at Sine Qua Non (see page 250), and her label has become its own cult phenomenon, with a price tag to match.

UMPQUA VALLEY

The three most prominent appellations of the state's southern half are all valleys: the Umpqua, the Rogue, and the Applegate. The northernmost follows the Umpqua River and its tributaries through a landscape of low mountains and wilderness, shade and plain, offering the opportunity to grow everything from Tempranillo to Riesling.

....

Abacela Umpqua Valley Grenache Rosé ($$)

Earl Jones, aided by his world-renowned viticultural climatologist son, Greg, searched all over the nation for a place to make wines like those of Spain's Ribiera del Duero before settling in the Umpqua Valley with his wife, Hilda. Abacela has gone on to garner critical acclaim for its Tempranillos and Albariños. It's odd that this rosé—er, rosado—doesn't go by the name "Garnacha," as the style is more Spanish than French: unabashedly bold in color, with exuberant ripe strawberry and cherry notes, accented by salty olives. A slurper.

ROGUE VALLEY

Further south, the Applegate River defines the Applegate Valley appellation. And surrounding it is southern Oregon's best-known winegrowing zone, the Rogue Valley. Cradled between the Cascade and Siskiyou Mountains, this California borderland enjoys a warm, dry climate that favors southern French grape varieties.

Dark, brooding reds—the usual suspects from the Rhône and Bordeaux, as well as Zinfandel—are particularly successful here. And where there are reds, there can be pinks. And thank goodness for them, because what else could a person drink with fresh, pungent Rogue Valley asparagus each spring?

....

Quady North Rogue Valley Southern Oregon Rosé ($)

Herb Quady, former assistant winemaker at Bonny Doon (see page 247) approaches Syrah, Cabernet Franc, and Viognier in the way that his northern neighbors approach Pinot Noir, releasing multiple single-vineyard bottlings and geeking out over site-specific clones. He vinifies single-variety rosés that are only available in local markets; but this slightly viscous blend of cool-climate Syrah, Grenache, and Mourvèdre is more widely available. It's mostly whole-cluster-pressed and is perfumed with stone fruit and white flowers, finishing with orange peel. He calls his label "Quady North," because his parents run Quady winery in Madera, California, where vermouth, dessert wines, and fortified wines are the house specialties.

California

Back in the late eighteenth century, Franciscan brothers planted California's first wine grapes.[193] The variety, called "Mission" or "Viña Madre," is not in wide use anymore. But some subsequent plantings, most notably Zinfandel beginning in the 1820s, have thrived in California for well more than a century. Known as Primitivo in southern Italy, this grape can make syrupy, high-alcohol fruit bombs when vinified as a red wine in California. It's also, of course, the source of the infamous semi-sweet White Zinfandel.

At the same time, California's current crop of inquisitive growers and vintners are planting obscure grape varieties with the intention of making rosé. And a new generation of winemakers is preaching the gospel of low alcohol, minimum intervention, neutral oak, and spontaneous fermentation.

NORTH COAST

When North Coast winemakers like Robert Sinskey (page 243) began

[193] According to legend, they scattered mustard seed at the same time. So in sunny California, you'll often see sunny yellow mustard blossoms blooming between vine rows.

vinifying fine dry rosé in the 1990s, the wine world took note. Because in the American oenophilic cosmos, California's North Coast is the center of the universe. The wine country north of the city of San Francisco cradles the crème de la crème of American viticulture. Misted and cooled by the Pacific Ocean, basking in the glow of the California sun, this is the seat of some of the nation's finest restaurants and most fabulous fortunes. (Plus groovy, agrarian Mendocino.)

Not Subtle, but Sutter Home

In 1971, Bob Trinchero decided to make the most of a cold vintage. He bled some juice out of a tank of macerating Zinfandel to make a more concentrated red.

His friend Darrell Corti—a globe-trotting food importer and retailer—tasted the remaining pinkish-white *saignée* and suggested that Trinchero bottle it and name it after Switzerland's ultra-pale *oeil de perdrix* Pinot Noir rosé. But US labeling regulations demanded an English description of California's first commercial rosé of Zinfandel: It was dubbed "Oeil de Perdrix—A White Zinfandel Wine."

By 1987, Sutter Home White Zinfandel was sweet, and classified as a Type 2 Narcotic. Just kidding. Actually, it was the bestselling wine in the United States, and "white zin" had become a household name. By the early 1990s, Sutter Home was the second-largest family-owned winery in the United States.

Today, the Trinchero Family Estates portfolio includes forty-five different wineries, five liquor brands, and one cider house. There are many Trinchero Family rosé iterations, but more than two million cases of Sutter Home White Zinfandel continue to sell annually, proving that for many drinkers, this American institution never went out of style.

....

Sutter Home "The Original" California White Zinfandel   ($)
Another Trinchero Family Estates rosé, the Ménage à Trois "Folie à Deux" California Rosé ($), is America's top-selling rosé in its price range of $9 to $12 and reeks of mushy, overripe strawberry and raspberry jam. The Sutter Home white zin, by comparison, isn't half bad. A medium-sweet wine at 8.5 percent alcohol, it smells and tastes like vinified raisins and could be a decent match for spicy foods. Give it a try for old times' sake.

Arnot-Roberts North Coast Rosé of Touriga Nacional ($$$)

Just off the main drag in the charming Sonoma town of Healdsburg, Arnot-Roberts is a workmanlike winery run by childhood friends Duncan Meyers and Nathan Roberts, who crafts the cellar's oak barrels himself. The two source the very Portuguese grapes Bastardo (aka Trousseau) and Touriga Nacional from a vineyard in the Clear Lake appellation, just north of Sonoma County. In the 11 percent alcohol zone, this wine is, at first glance, nothing like the powerful and spicy reds of the Douro. But it does have a certain slate-y, leathery, iron-like toughness that belies its pale onion-skin color.

Mendocino

Shaded by tall redwoods, sparsely populated Mendocino County is a free-spirited place where organic farming and marijuana farming (sometimes in tandem) are two of the most popular occupations. The winemaking style reflects the population: gentle and mellow. Most wineries fill the hilly area between the towns of Redwood Valley, Yorkville, and Navarro; the western tong of that wishbone is the Anderson Valley subzone, noted for its bright Pinot Noirs and delicate sparkling wines.

LIOCO "Indica" Mendocino County Rosé ($$)

Carignan, well known in the Languedoc and Spain, found traction in California in the mid-twentieth century. LIOCO winery is located in Santa Rosa, but as is so often the case with West Coast wineries, its proprietors and winemaker have an ability to sniff out prime vineyards—in this case, growing dry-farmed, head-trained[194] old Carignan—in neighboring regions. Ripe apricot, lime zest, and citrus blossom make this a lovely summer rosé; bonus points for completed malolactic fermentation, which counterbalances the gristle of those old vines.

County Line Anderson Valley Rosé ($$)

Eric Sussman, proprietor of the cult fave Rhône-leaning winery Radio-Coteau in Sebastopol, débuted his Pinot Noir–oriented County Line label with this dry rosé in 2003. It's a whole-cluster-pressed Champagne clone of Pinot from Elke Home Ranch near Boonville. The wine is earthy and brambly, with a wild-berry note.

Sonoma County

From the architecturally significant beach houses of Sea Ranch down to stunning Point Reyes, Sonoma County is an Instagrammable tourist magnet that also turns out a ton of good wine. The region encompasses, at last count, seventeen subappellations, representing a dizzying array of soil types, terrain, and microclimates.

When I started researching this section, I figured I would end up writing about the distinguished Pinot Noir rosés from the foggy, chilly Sonoma Coast and the neighboring Russian River Valley— Flowers, Cep (Peay Vineyards), Red Car, and Gary Farrell spring to mind. That didn't happen because I kept coming back to outlier—or outlaw?—wines from warmer parts of the county. These rosés defy categorization, and I love them for that.

The vibe is lower-key in Sonoma than it is in the Napa Valley, just across the Mayacamas Mountains. Alaska-based Russian explorers established a coastal colony here in the early 1800s and planted vines; today, that history and sense of adventure are reflected in the name of the wine region's major defining feature, the Russian River. *Vaše zdorovie!*

Bedrock Wine Co. "Ode to Lulu" California Old Vine Rosé ($$)

Joel Peterson, founder of Sonoma's Ravenswood winery, is known as the "Godfather of Zin." His son Morgan Twain-Peterson is now a winemaker in his own right and was en route to earning his Master of Wine—one of the world's most difficult distinctions to earn—as I wrote this. From his winery in the town of Sonoma, Peterson sources Mourvèdre, Grenache, and Carignan from multiple old-vine vineyards to make this pink. And when I say old, I mean these vineyards were planted between 1888 and 1922. Low alcohol, whole-cluster-pressed, and native-yeast fermented, this lovely rosé is a study in silky restraint, with minerality, citrus, and strawberry blossoms. A pleasant surprise from the son of the man whose marketing motto is "No Wimpy Wines."

Broc Cellars Sonoma County White Zinfandel ($$)

From his urban winery in Berkeley, winemaker Chris Brockway

---

[194] *Head-trained or bush-trained vines are a common sight in the Old World, but they can be a delightful surprise in the New World.*

sources organically and biodynamically farmed fruit from all over the state, focusing on northern regions like Sonoma and Mendocino. The Zinfandel for this wine came from Arrowhead Vineyard in the breezy Sonoma Valley and Buck Hill Vineyard in foggy Russian River—both are chilly Sonoma County subzones. And Brockway harvested his fruit early, to capture freshness rather than jamminess. There's no law stating that Zinfandel rosé must be sweet, so Brockway's wine is dry, with a curious crabapple aroma and flavor. Broc Cellars makes two other rosés, most notably the earthy "Love" cuvée ($$) showcasing the unusual Napa Gamay, a red grape that's known as Valdiguié in Languedoc.

Napa Valley

Ah, the la-la land of baronial estates, baroque wines, limousines, and four-star restaurants.

In reality, the Napa Valley is a multiform place, home to a diverse population. Viticulturally speaking, it's a collection of unique subappellations channeled between the Vaca and Mayacamas Mountains, from northern Calistoga to American Canyon.

Yes, it's overrun with tourists. But it's also—even after all these years of blockbuster winemaking—

a place of viticultural promise. A few experimental producers here are rethinking what Napa Valley wine should look and taste like. For them, crisp and quirky rosé, rather than inky, concentrated red, is a central part of the vision. And that vision doesn't fit with our stereotype.

Domaine Carneros "Cuvée de la Pompadour" Carneros Méthode Champenoise Brut Rosé ($$$)

The Carneros subappellation straddles the southern ends of both Napa Valley and Sonoma County and is regularly blanketed in a cold fog coming off San Pablo Bay. This downright dreary climate is ideal for sparkling-wine production, which is why the Taittinger Champagne house invested in the region. The magnificent Domaine Carneros palace's brick detailing is inspired by Taittinger's HQ, the Château de la Marquetterie in Champagne. Madame de Pompadour is an appropriate mascot for this decadent blend of organic Pinot Noir and Chardonnay, with its notes of caramel, crème brûlée, baked apples, and white pepper. The winemaking is a hybrid of the two rosé Champagne methods: Some of the Pinot Noir for the base wine macerates with the skins, and the color is pumped up post-fermentation by the addition of a bit more still Pinot.

....

Robert Sinskey Vineyards Los Carneros Vin Gris of Pinot Noir ($$$)

When you're at a sporting event and a teenage girl walks to the center of the field and opens her mouth to sing with cameras focusing on her face, there's a moment of tension. Then, when you ascertain that she has total command of the material, you experience the most glorious release. "This girl is going to hit that high note," you think, "and I'm going to weep a little." Robert Sinskey's *vin gris* gives the wary palate that release. You might have seen the words "Pinot Noir" and assumed that the rosé came to be as a *saignée*,

---

Turley Turns, Turns, Turns the Tide

Turley Wine Cellars is a California icon, with a Napa Valley winery and tasting rooms in Paso Robles and Amador County. Since its founding in 1993, the house's focus has been on limited lots of single-vineyard Zinfandel—the really good stuff.

Christina Turley, born in 1984, is too young to have the negative associations with Zinfandel that babies of the sixties and seventies wrestle with. So, in 2010, when she came back home to work for her family winery after an illustrious early career as a New York sommelier, she convinced the rest of the Turleys to put their qualms aside and vinify a White Zinfandel. A really good one.

....

Turley Napa Valley Zinfandel ($$)

This wine isn't labeled "white" and it isn't a regular thing—the 2015 vintage, for example, didn't happen. But it has made the concept of a dry, low-alcohol, serious, native-yeast fermented, neutral-oak-aged Zinfandel rosé cool again. The certified-organic, head-trained, dry-farmed[195] estate Zin grapes were picked specifically for rosé and pressed after a short maceration.

---

[195] *Not irrigated. An increasingly important goal for any vinetender, in light of California's water crisis, dry farming is also considered a mark of quality, on the theory that the roots of dry-farmed vines reach deep below the soil's surface. Dry farming is de rigueur in many parts of the Old World.*

to darken and enrich a red Pinot Noir bottling. But you would have been wrong. Night harvested, whole-cluster-pressed organic fruit makes a wine of exceptional refinement, like a soprano knocking an aria out of the park.

Matthiasson California Rosé Wine ($$)

Irreverent Steve Matthiasson grows varieties such as Refosco, Ribolla Gialla, Tocai Friulano, and Schioppettino at his home vineyard on the northern outskirts of the town of Napa. But put the thought of Italian grapes aside for a moment, as this rosé is a full-on Rhônish blend of Syrah, Grenache, Mourvèdre, and Counoise. While the Syrah comes from the Napa Valley, the remainder of the grapes are sourced from the inland Dunnigan Hills—hence

the "California" appellation. Subtle, smooth, and understated, this minerally wine is pale rose-gold in color with nuanced notes of sandalwood on the nose and palate.

Ehlers Estate "Sylviane" St. Helena Napa Valley Rosé ($$)

Moving northwest, farther into the valley, we find a wine that's more stereotypically "Napa" without losing that rosé freshness. The stone barn and vineyard at Ehlers Estate date back to the late nineteenth century. (The organically farmed vines are younger, due to a post-phylloxera replanting.) This watermelon-stained wine is all Cabernet Franc and has a heady nose of flowers and fruit. The palate on a recent warm-vintage bottling was dried blueberries and dry earth, making this the sort of rosé that could please a Dry Creek Zinfandel devotée. Never mind the price (it's approximately $28): This wine must, at all costs, be paired with a burger, right off the grill.

SIERRA FOOTHILLS

On the east side of the state, gold-panning ghosts roam the spare foothills of the Sierra Nevada. Many small subzones fall inside this lonely stretch of historic Highway 49, from the Tahoe National Forest to Yosemite National Park, but only a couple harbor noteworthy vinous treasures. Rhône varieties dominate the rosés here currently, but with the Central Coast (see page 246) vinifying those grapes so expertly, the smart vinetenders and winemakers are still looking around for the right fit. At high elevations, cool-climate grapes might be the answer, and as we'll see, Portuguese reds hold promise for the lower, hotter spots.

El Dorado County

The dry and high El Dorado subappellation is a grouping of mountainside vineyards growing a broad assortment of grapes. The California Gold Rush began here, and early miners planted vines as far back as the mid-nineteenth century. Their grape of choice, Zinfandel, lives on in leathery, brambly reds. Something tells me that the "49-ers" weren't making delicate rosés. But if the following wine is an aberration, it's as American as a pioneer striking out for the unexplored.

Edmunds St. John "Bone-Jolly" El Dorado County Witters Vineyard Gamay Noir Rosé ($$)

Beaujolais doesn't immediately spring to mind when one is driving toward South Lake Tahoe, but at 3,400 feet (1,035 m) of elevation, not far from the snow line, Gamay grows just fine. Except in the years when it freezes, and Steve Edmunds loses part or all of his vintage. But that is a risk Edmunds is willing to take. The Berkeley-based vintner scours the far corners of California for unusual grape varieties growing in unexpected places—or, as he did in this case, he convinces vineyard owners to take a leap of faith and plant something unexpected. "Bone-Jolly" is a play on "Beaujolais," and sure enough, this rosé has the cleansing acidity, tart raspberry, cool stones, and thyme notes of a nice glass of Beaujolais Villages.

Amador County

Just south of El Dorado, the vineyard elevations are slightly lower and the temperatures are slightly balmier. Also, there is a large concentration of old vines—again, some date as far back as the nineteenth century. That all adds up to wines of depth and concentration. The frontier spirit lives on in the wide variety of grapes planted, and the willingness to try something anomalous.

Forlorn Hope "Kumo To Ame" Dewitt Vineyard Amador County Rosé   ($$)

Matthew Rorick is another California iconoclast who seeks out overlooked varieties. The grapes in this "clouds and rain" (from the Japanese)[196] rosé are a Douroesque field blend of Touriga Nacional with Tinta Roriz, Tinto Cão, and Trincadeira; but the effect is more López de Heredia than anything Portuguese I can think of. The wine making regime is whole-cluster-pressing; native-yeast fermentation; and no fining or filtering, which is highly unusual for a rosé. A recent vintage, tasted at the age of three, had the petrol note of an aged Riesling, but hadn't lost its youthful spritz, minerality, mango, lilac, seafoam, salt, or spice. And did I mention the pleasantly low alcohol, at around 11 percent? Rorick also makes an intriguing orange wine, the Sierra Foothills "Dragone" Ramato of Pinot Gris ($$$).

CENTRAL COAST

It takes four to five hours—on a good day—to drive from San Jose to Santa Barbara. That entire north-south stretch falls under the heading of "Central Coast." Such a huge region is widely variable, but tends toward endless sunshine, a long growing season, and windblown hillsides close to the Pacific Ocean.

If any part of California is emerging as a rosé powerhouse, it's the Central Coast. A strong allegiance to Rhône grape varieties and a spirit of adventure here have raised rosé to a level that can't be matched by any other region in the United States. While Pinot Noir is also strong, grapes like Grenache and Mourvèdre are moving the needle, making purple and pink wines fragrant with the wild fennel, milkweed, and sagebrush that dot the high grasslands.

---

[196] *According to Rorick: "The name was drawn from James Clavell's novel* Shōgun, *where it is used by geishas to refer to the moment of ecstasy."*

Bonny Doon Done Rosé

Since 1984, Randall Grahm has been making his Rhône-style, Mourvèdre-based "Vin Gris de Cigare," which draws its name from a law in Châteauneuf-du-Pape prohibiting "flying cigars" (UFOs) from flying overhead. But only with the American dry rosé awakening has the wine become a big seller. As of the 2015 vintage, Grahm's Bonny Doon winery had bumped production of Vin Gris de Cigare up to 14,000 cases to meet demand and rolled out four additional experimental pink wines. Here are three of them:

Bonny Doon Vineyard "Vin Gris Tuilé[197]: Brick Pink Wine of the Sun & Earth" Central Coast Pink Wine ($$$)

This glass carboy-aged *vin gris* basked in direct sunlight for nine months and wasn't released until the age of three. Its color is cloudy gold and its aroma is Sherry, chamomile, snickerdoodle dough, turmeric, and curry.

A Proper Pink Tannat-Cabernet Franc California Pink Wine ($$)

Grahm's "A Proper Claret" line is devoted to Bordeaux-ish wines that don't fit his Rhône Ranger reputation. This ruddy blend of Tannat and Cabernet Franc claims to have been made in the style of an old-fashioned *clairet*. Its spritz and lively strawberry and raspberry notes are counterbalanced by ponderous graphite and cola.

Bonny Doon Vineyard "Il Ciliegiolo" Tracy Hills Rosato ($$)

This quickly pressed, early bottled Ciliegiolo (yep, the same Ligurian-Tuscan grape we met on page 133 grows in California!) occupies the no-man's-land between rosato and red, with an uplifting quality that could win over the most staunch white-wine drinker. On the palate are notes of blueberries, plums, black olives, black cherries, and black pepper.

---

[197] *The term translates as "brick wine." Grahm has made something like the rosé from Domaine Les Hautes Collines de la Côtes d'Azur à Saint Jeannet, a very traditional cellar near Nice where wines are set out in glass* bonbonnes *to absorb sunlight. The* vins doux naturels *of the Languedoc-Roussillon also utilize the glass-under-the-sun technique. These dessert wines are also referred to as* tuilé.

Tablas Creek on the Table

In 1989, the Perrin family—famous in this book for its partnership in Miraval (see pages 80–83), and everywhere else for its Château de Beaucastel in Châteauneuf-du-Pape—purchased a ranch in the Las Tablas district of Paso Robles in partnership with American importer Robert Haas. The Perrins were convinced that the dry, sunny climate and the chalky limestone soils were similar enough to the conditions at home that they could make great Rhône-style wines here.

Dissatisfied with the grapevines available in the United States, the family decided to import cuttings from their own château vineyard. Over time, they established a nursery and sold vines and rootstock to other vineyards in the area. These Beaucastel offspring were dubbed the "Tablas Clones."

Today, Tablas Creek organically and biodynamically farms Mourvèdre, Grenache Noir, Syrah, Counoise, Roussanne, Viognier, Marsanne, and Grenache Blanc. A menagerie of animals—including sheep, chickens, and donkeys—patrols the property to weed, fertilize, and scare off pests. The winemaking style is subtle and decidedly French: Fermentations are natural and large neutral-oak barrels are favored. Tablas Creek has inspired numerous other wineries to make Rhône-style wines in Paso Robles—next-door neighbor Halter Ranch, for example.

Tablas Creek Vineyard "Patelin de Tablas"
Paso Robles Rosé ($$)

This ultra-pale blend of mostly Grenache (with Mourvèdre, Counoise, and Syrah) is sourced from seven Paso Robles subzones. The Grenache and Syrah are direct-pressed, while the Mourvèdre and Counoise additions are from *saignée*. The tasting experience is more about creamy texture—thanks to extended lees contact—and spice than fruit. Tablas Creek also makes the limited-edition "Dianthus" Rosé ($$$), a blend of original estate-grown Mourvèdre, Grenache, and Counoise that comes on stronger, with notes of blackberries, plums, raisins, rhubarb, and spice.

Paso Robles

In Hearst Castle country, the landscape looks Provençal, with rows of lavender lining driveways and boutique olive farms selling zesty extra-virgin oils. This is Paso, aka the "Rhône Zone," a large area surrounding the eponymous town. Like the castle, the wines are brash all-American reinterpretations of something the southern French do very well: Think fiercely peppery reds, and rosés with herbaceous power. These wines rock with locally grown and brined olives, or a seafood salad studded with San Luis Obispo County avocados.

Halter Ranch Paso Robles Rosé ($$)

Visitors to this nineteenth-century livestock ranch and racing-horse farm can tour all 281 gorgeous acres (113 ha) in a Land Rover Defender 110. Don't you love California? As for the rosé: This pale beauty is mostly Grenache, with a bit of Mourvèdre and Syrah, but most interestingly, it's more than 20 percent Piquepoul Blanc, causing one to reminisce about the Languedoc. Tart green tannins and restrained starfruit notes are counterbalanced by a punch of acidity, making this full-bodied wine immensely refreshing.

Santa Maria Valley

Contrary to what you might expect, temperatures dip the farther south you travel down the California coast. (Case in point: That time you brought your swimsuit to San Diego and never used it.) Icy water from the Pacific deep washes up on this stretch of coast, chilling maritime breezes and sending fog into the hills above the town of Santa Maria. So the grapes here tend toward Burgundian varieties, but everything from Aligoté to Tocai Friulano grows here. You might even come across an oddity from Savoie. Regardless of the grape, bracing acidity is this California region's secret weapon, making a mean match for equally unexpected foods, like the locals' favorite fruits, cherimoya and sapote.

Clendenen Family Vineyards "Bien Nacido Estate Plantings" Santa Maria Valley Mondeuse Rosé ($–$$)

Jim Clendenen is a legendary figure among California's Burgundy-minded for his longtime commitment to balanced, finessed Chardonnay and Pinot Noir, most famously under the Au Bon Climat label. This understated rosé may not rock your world, but let's just back up and repeat the fact that it's Mondeuse.[198] From California.

....

Santa Barbara County

The Santa Maria Valley (above) actually falls within Santa Barbara County, but it deserved its own category. Now let's examine two additional Santa Barbara County wines from lesser-known areas to the east. The first is from the Cuyama Valley, an outlier on the far side of Los Padres National Forest in the Sierra Madre Mountains. The second is in Happy Canyon of Santa Barbara, an official subzone, which defines the eastern edge of the Los Olivos and Santa Ynez Valley subappellations. Its location in the foothills of the San Rafael Mountains attracts warm, dry weather; during Prohibition, locals would "take a trip up Happy Canyon" to buy moonshine off the farmers here, and the name stuck.

As with Paso Robles, the predominant influence here,

Sine Qua Non, Without Which Nothing

How does a winery become a cult phenomenon? Ask Manfred and Elaine Krankl, proprietors of Sine Qua Non, a winery based in Oakview, south of Santa Barbara in Ventura County. Their first four and a half barrels, bottled under the name "Black & Blue" in 1992, were a runaway hit, and the Krankls have never looked back.

Today, there's a mile-long wait list for the honor of purchasing bottles directly from the winery, and retailers and auction houses offer the wines at prices that range from the hundreds to the thousands. As we learned in Chapter 1 (see page 14), a single bottle of 1995 Sine Qua Non "Queen of Hearts" California rosé sold at auction for a record-breaking $42,000.

I can't write up one of Sine Qua Non's rosés for you. Not just because they're so expensive, but because the wines are constantly subject to change. Manfred Krankl, an Austrian by birth, creates different unorthodox label designs annually, never using the same name or making the same wine twice. Rhône varieties from the Central Coast are Sine Qua Non's specialty, and a rosé is always in the lineup. If it's priced in the thousands, it's not exactly "essential"—as "sine qua non" translates—but it's certainly a curiosity.

especially for rosé production, is southern France. The grapes are of the Rhônish G-S-M group and the wines—whether red or rosé—speak of the intense sunshine and sea breezes of this gorgeous place, which coaxes unabashed, all-American fruit from the crumbly soil.

....

A Tribute to Grace "Santa Barbara Highlands Vineyard" Santa Barbara County Rosé of Grenache ($$)

New Zealand native Angela Osborne vinifies Grenache and nothing else. At 3,200 feet (975 m) of elevation in the Cuyama Valley, Santa Barbara Highlands Vineyard experiences wide diurnal shifts, ensuring full ripeness without mushy oversweetness. There's a

supple roundness to this peachy wine, and the alcohol is noticeable but balanced by acidity.

....

Liquid Farm "Vogelzang Vineyard" Happy Canyon of Santa Barbara Mourvèdre Rosé ($$–$$$)

Fresh, low-alcohol, and earthy, softened by neutral barrel fermentation and aging, this elegant rosé has a light herbaceous quality and restrained Asian pear fruit. Liquid Farm is a fairly new label whose winemaker trained at Dragonette Cellars, another producer of delicious Happy Canyon rosé.

---

[198] *Mondeuse is the high-acid red grape of France's out-of-the-way Savoie region.*

PRETTY AND PINK

$$
Australia
Taltarni

$
Chile
Apaltagua

$$
South Africa
Boschendal

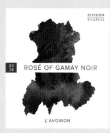

$$
Washington
Division Villages

$
Washington
Charles & Charles

$$
Washington
Waters

$$$$$
Oregon
Antica Terra

$$
California
County Line

$$
California
Matthiasson

THE NEW WORLD

$$

New York

Kelby James Russell

$$

New York

Wölffer Estate

$$

Washington

Seven Hills

$$$$

Oregon

Soter

$$

Oregon

Abacela

$

Oregon

Quady North

$$

California

Edmunds St. John

$$$

California

Bonny Doon

$$

California

Tablas Creek

Exotic Rosé Regions, from Corsica to Africa

Winemaking has been happening for decades, centuries, and even millennia, in places that might surprise you. Rosés are vinified in Morocco and India. Rosés are made in the state of Georgia and the Republic of Georgia. Rosé is part of the winemaking culture in the Greek province of Macedonia and the nation of Macedonia.

In fact, more than a century ago, a certain Monsieur Dugast found the rosés of Algeria to be refreshing and delicious, declaring, "Les vins rosés n'ont pas le defauts de vins rouges et des vins blancs; ils en ont en quelque sorté—chose rare—seulement les qualités. Ils ont une couleur rose vif claire et sont légèrement toniques tout en se laissant boire sans fatigue."[199]

And as I was finishing this chapter, I happened to be in Mexico's Yucatán Peninsula, and wouldn't you know it . . . I found Mexican rosés on wine lists there. Even the Indonesian island of Bali produces rosé—the wine is "salty," I'm told.

The wines of western Europe and the New World are duly imported to our shores and distributed to our retail stores and restaurants. But as globalism expands, so does our understanding of the breadth and depth of the vinous planet. This chapter will take us to some of the most unimaginable places to grow grapes, let alone make pink wine, and will uncover some of my favorite rosé regions on the planet. (Between the Canary Islands and Corsica, I'm done for.)

If there's any characteristic that unites these far-flung winegrowing regions, it's the courageousness of their vinetenders. Whether facing monsoons or sandstorms, mortar shells or Soviet strongmen, these viticulturists have believed in the value of their grapes, to bring people together in the name of peaceful pleasure.

---

[199] *"The rosé wines do not have the defects of red wine and white wine; they have somehow—something rare—only the qualities. They have a clear bright pink color and are somewhat like tonic, allowing drinking without fatigue."* — Dugast, Les Vins d'Algérie, 92–93.

CANARY ISLANDS

MOROCCO

SARDINIA

CORSICA

SLOVENIA

MEDITERRANEAN SEA

HUNGARY

GREECE

BULGARIA

ISRAEL

LEBANON

ARABIAN SEA

INDIA

CORSICAN-SARDINIAN ROSÉ

COLOR
the *spiaggia rosa*—pink
sand beach—of Budelli, in
the Maddalenas

PERSONALITY
proud and independent,
musical

AROMATICS
sage, juniper, olive, starfruit,
strawberry

GOES WELL WITH
brandade, garlicky white
beans, grilled artichokes

One is French, the other is Italian, but Corsica and Sardinia are closest, geographically, to each other. During the last ice age, these two Tyrrhenian Sea islands were conjoined and close enough to present-day Italy that Paleolithic hominids settled on them. They are rugged and mountainous, with cliffs dropping to sparkling azure water and the same fragrant *maquis* that so marks the rosés of Provence and the Languedoc. The steep inclines and combination of igneous and sedimentary soil types create the ideal conditions for vinetending. So while tourists frolic on the pristine beaches, they sip wines made from grapes grown in the inland wilds.

Due to their strategic locations, both islands bounced between occupying empires over the centuries. Today, their native populations are fiercely independent, with their own unique languages, music, cuisine, customs, and subversive state flags that feature the profiles of revolutionaries. Today, however, there's a revolution happening in quality winemaking. *Vive la rosé!*

Corsica

For some seven centuries, Corsica was ruled by the Genoese. Then, after a too-brief period of independence, France took control in 1768. So road signs on the island are in French, Italian, and Corsican, and the wines, too, have a transnational flair to them: They combine the rustic, savory charm of the Italian with the tannins and polish of the French.

More than half the wines vinified on this island are pink. As rosés, the red indigenous grapes Sciacarello and Nielluccio, and pink-skinned Barbarossa, express themselves with acidity and strength, herbaceousness, and brine. Their major downfall is price. The good stuff is rare, and the import channels aren't fully established yet. So buy this wine because it's interesting and an adventure. And if it was good enough for Napoléon, it's good enough for you.

Clos Alivu
Patrimonio Rosé   ($$)

Patrimonio is an AOP on Corsica's north shore that specializes in Nielluccio, a red grape that may or may not be related to Sangiovese. In any event, it's short on pigment,

which makes it an ideal candidate for rosé. Winemaker Eric Poli's old-vine plot renders a flavorful quaff, redolent of wild berries, rose water, and olive brine.

Yves Leccia "Y Leccia
Domaine d'E Croce"
Patrimonio Rosé   ($$$)

This rich, coral-colored pleasure is earthy and fruity—a red wine hiding in the body of a pink. It's about four-fifths Nielluccio, completed by Grenache. Its sibling, the Yves Leccia "YL" Ile de Beauté Rose ($$) is lighter and spicier, with notes of citrus and minerality. M. Leccia and his wife, Sandrine, farm their slate-soiled Domaine d'E Croce estate, located at the base of Cap Corse, organically.

Domaine de Marquiliani
Vin de Corse
Rosé de Sciaccarellu   ($$$)

In the 1950s, the Amalric family took possession of an estate that had burned to the ground on the eastern Costa Serena and replanted it with the indigenous Sciaccarellu grape, a red that manages to maintain high acidity levels and fresh red-berry flavors in the Corsican heat. The current proprietor, Anne Amalric, made a name for herself as one of Corsica's finest olive oil producers before focusing on winemaking. With its hint of effervescence, and notes of wet stones and pink grapefruit, this seashell-pink delight is delicious minimalism. "Vin de Corse" is an AOP designation that encompasses the entire island.

The Advent of Abbatucci

French Revolutionary hero General Jean-Charles Abbatucci was a comrade-in-arms of Napoléon Bonaparte. His descendants have been active in a different movement—that to save the endangered indigenous grape varieties of the island.

At the family estate in the Ajaccio AOP, on the southwestern side of the island, Count Jean-Charles Abbatucci practices biodynamic agriculture and plants new vines using the *sélection massale* method—cultivating cuttings from the strongest, most flavorful plants to establish new vines. He works his soil with plow-pulling horses and sends a herd of sheep down the vine rows to dine on weeds. He even occasionally plays traditional Corsican music—soothingly woven polyphonic voices—in his cellar, to inspire the wines.

Domaine Comte Abbatucci "Faustine"
Vin de France Rosé   ($$$)

Sciacarello's juicy sweet-and-sour notes of red berries and bright acidity are tempered by the soothing effect of six months of aging on the lees. Herbaceous notes of Corsican *maquis* complete this classic rosé. Abbatucci does not use the Ajaccio appellation in protest of the French AOP rules regarding the use of endemic Corsican varieties.

Sardinia

The Mediterranean's second-largest island is rich in turquoise swimming spots, underwater caves, and sleek mega-yachts harbored along the Costa Smeralda. Inland, where Sardinian is spoken, stone structures from the island's unique Bronze Age Nuragic civilization still stand—archaeologists believe, by the way, that the Nuragici made wine way back when. Despite the Mediterranean heat in the hills, a strong wind, the sirocco, keeps vineyards well ventilated and cool at night.

I must take a moment to mention the culinary influences of Moorish pirates, three centuries of rule by the Spanish, and the natural resources of the island. Seasonings include locally foraged myrtle, wild fennel, and saffron. Mullet eggs, dried and then shaved like Parmesan cheese, make an odorous condiment called bottarga. Spit-roasted lamb and wild boar are local specialties, as are pungent cheeses. Accordingly, the wines, including the rosati, are rich, tending toward a sunburned color and alcohol levels on the higher end of the spectrum, the better to stand up to the robust cuisine.

Argiolas "Serra Lori" Isola dei Nuraghi Rosé ($)

Antonio Argiolas established Sardinia's first quality-oriented winery, in the village of Serdiana, in 1938 and has long been a champion of the native grape varieties that were domesticated from the wild by early islanders so long ago. This brick-tinted rosato is a blend of Cannonau—actually the same thing as Grenache or Garnacha—with Monica, Carignano, and Bovale Sardo[200] grown in the Trexenta hills. Its heady richness reflects the heat waves that can hit the island during the summer and early autumn. There's an aroma of red roses, and the palate is soft and cinnamon-accented, with a fruity component. There are some twenty DOP zones on the island; Isola dei Nuraghi is an IGP encompassing all of Sardinia.

---

[200] *Monica was a popular R&B recording artist in the 1990s. She is also a Sardinian red grape with Spanish origins. Bovale Sardo is the same thing as the Spanish red grape Graciano, and Carignano is the same thing as Carignan.*

SAHARAN COASTAL ROSÉ

COLOR
the shimmering scales
of the Alfonsino fish

AROMATICS
ash, tropical flowers, Canary
Islands–grown aloe vera

PERSONALITY
hardy, adventurous,
an outlier

GOES WELL WITH
timple guitar music,
papas arrugadas,
Palmero cigars

I really wish this section could start with the Balearic Islands, just west of Sardinia. You've surely heard of Ibiza, the celebrity magnet that vies with Rio de Janeiro for the title "party capital of the world." (If you go there, don't take a pill of dubious origins, OK?) Ibiza's responsible big brother, Mallorca, is home to a thrilling winemaking scene fueled by exotic indigenous grapes with names like Callet, Escursac, Fogoneu, Manto Negro, and Prensal.

Sadly, few importers ship Mallorca's red and white wines to North American shores. Plus, beach-going visitors to the island greedily guzzle down all the rosados before they ever leave the island. So, sorry, folks: No Mallorca for us today. Instead, let's travel 1,600 miles (2,575 km), off the coast of Africa. Here, about 90 miles (145 km) east of the Morocco–Western Sahara border, are the Canary Islands—one of the world's most improbable winegrowing regions.

The only things keeping temperatures in check here are altitude—the foothills of snow-topped mountains like Teide[201] are relatively cool—and a godforsaken, unrelenting gale. Which can be a huge nuisance. A few times a year, a windblown sandstorm called the *calima* rages in from the Sahara Desert, filling the air with a thick fog of dangerous dust particles.

Rain? It's overrated. Tractors? Who needs them when you've got

---

[201] *The highest peak in Spain at 12,000 feet (3,650 m).*

camels? The soil is porous sand, so the islands have never known phylloxera and the vines are self-rooted. Year-round temperatures are so balmy that grapevines don't go dormant over the winter. Plants need their sleep in order to regenerate, so vineyard owners must prune drastically to kick-start the spring renewal process. Vinetenders in Morocco battle similarly trying conditions, if not quite so extreme.

Canary Islands

Don't try to understand winegrowing on the Canaries because your brain might melt down. On the island of Tenerife, *viticultores* stoop or kneel to work their wind-dodging grapevines, which crawl along the ground in "braided cords" (*cordónes trenzados*). On Lanzarote, vines grow from ebony-black volcanic ash in large pits called *hoyos*. These act as reservoirs for precious morning dew, bringing the roots closer to the more nourishing soil that lies beneath the ash. Aided by low rock walls, the hoyos also protect the leaves, flowers, and fruit from being yanked off by maritime gusts.

Yet despite the strong sea gales, the black ash, and the camels, or, maybe because of them, Canary Island rosados are thrilling, delicious treasures, delicately floral and fragrant with tropical fruit notes. Perhaps this is a consequence of the islands' remote location. To go to the trouble of importing one of these wines, you've got to be pretty excited about it.

The grape to know here is Listán Negro. Nearly identical to the Mission grape planted by the Spaniards in the early days of California winegrowing, it's juicy, somewhat peppery, and low in tannins, redolent of ripe black cherries. For me, this grape makes a heartbreakingly beautiful rosado—and not just because I know how arduously the vines and the vine-tenders struggle to make it.

Bermejo Lanzarote Listán Rosado ($$)

The Lanzarote DOP covers the island of the same name, the east-ernmost of the Canaries. It gets the worst of the Saharan winds and has a desert climate, but its wines can be surprisingly nuanced. This rosado is direct-pressed Listán Negro. It's a rare, cantaloupe-colored treat with aromas of delicate white flowers and jasmine. The palate is soft and juicy and the long finish comes in waves of acidity and salinity.

El Grifo Lanzarote Rosado ($)

In operation since 1775, El Grifo is one of Spain's oldest wineries;

its Wine Museum is a popular stop for tourists and some of its vines planted in the nineteenth century are still going strong. This vivacious Listán Negro rosé is the color of cactus fruit. Food-friendly and festive, it's savory and spicy, with notes of wild sage, roasted red pepper, and tomato, accompanied by a just-took-a-shower, scrubbed-clean mouthfeel.

Frontón de Oro Gran Canaria Rosado ($$)

From the DOP that covers the island of the same name, this wine is Listán Negro grown at head-spinning elevations of around 3,200 feet (1,000 m) in the zone of San Mateo. Thirty hours of macer-ation make for a watermelon color and aroma. The palate is honeydew seasoned with cayenne pepper and Moroccan spices.

Viñátigo Ycoden Daute Isora Tenerife Listán Negro Rosado ($$)

Viñátigo proprietor and professor Juan Jesús Méndez and his oenologist wife, Elena Batista, work with the Rodríguez Virgili University in Tarragona to study, preserve, and vinify imperiled indigenous grape varieties. Méndez has collaborated on additional viticulture and winemaking projects in other parts of the Canaries and even in Uruguay, a nation with strong ties to the islands. The couple's rosado of Listán Negro is voluptuous and sexy, with notes of red cherries, Campari, and the spiced honeyed rum that the Canary Islands are known for.

Morocco

Now let's check out the scene on the mainland. As you may recall, our friend Monsieur Dugast was charmed by the rosés of Algeria back in 1900. This was during a period of French military control of northern Africa that lasted more than a hundred and thirty years. In Morocco, the French expat population sniffed out particularly prime vineyard land and set up wineries. The market—and production—crashed post-Moroccan independence, but it's bouncing back now.

The current king and his father both studied in France and have encouraged foreign investment to revitalize the commercial wine industry. Despite the fact that Islam is the state religion, the better restaurants offer wine lists, and it's not uncommon to see winemaking in rural villages.

Rosé is a specialty of the nation, and the Castel Group produces a ubiquitous Moroccan *vin gris* called Boulaouane that's just as iconic as its Languedoc brand, Listel. Domaine des Ouled Thaleb (below), on the Ben Slimane plateau, dates back to 1923. Overall, a good Moroccan rosé is delicate and fragrant, with notes of ripe melon. Pair it with a harissa-spiced vegetable couscous or kebabs with mint-yogurt sauce.

Ouled Thaleb Zenata Moroccan Rosé ($)

Zenata, just northeast of Casablanca, is noted for its Médoc-like shale and gravel soils. This northern coastal location gets cool Atlantic breezes and vies with the mountainous Meknès region for the title of best winegrowing zone in the nation. This blend of Syrah, Grenache, and Cinsault is a simple but expertly made quaffer with notes of oranges and lime pith. Drink it ice-cold on a scalding-hot day.

PROFILE

GREEK ROSÉ

COLOR
Santorini sunset

PERSONALITY
idiosyncratic:
a young-at-heart old soul
in a fisherman's cap

AROMATICS
capers, Greek oregano,
figs, Ambrosia melon

GOES WELL WITH
Greek salad, fried
eggplant, flowing linens

While they were ahead of the rest back in the amphora days, Greek winemakers fell behind between the fifteenth and twentieth centuries. First, the Ottomans effectively shut down overseas wine trade. Then, when phylloxera hit mainland Europe, a newly independent Greece put all its energy into growing Corinthian currants, which, once dried, wouldn't rot en route to France, where they could be turned into—dreadful—wine. Then the French figured out how to outsmart the root lice, the market for currants tanked, and Greece got phylloxera. So, yeah.

Things have turned around since 1981, when Greece joined the EU. Spend some time there today and you'll feel like a lotus eater: The wine is so good when you're sitting at a seaside bar noshing on mezethes that you'll never want to leave. But the economy is depressed, and the written language continues to tangle up overseas trade. Although export bottles are printed with Anglicized labels, no one can agree how to spell the names of Greek grapes in the Latin alphabet, and Greek winery websites are labyrinths of poorly translated confusion.

It would be as foolish to make a sweeping statement about Greek rosé as, say, to try to sum up *The Iliad* or *The Odyssey* in a single sentence or free-form riff.[202] Scores of native varieties grow in a

---

[202] *"Trojan War, Agamemnon, plague, fighting, Hector, Ajax, fighting, fighting, chariot race somewhere in there, fighting…"*

plethora of winegrowing regions, and on top of that, techniques and grapes have been imported from western Europe, making for a mishmash of styles. That said, to make a gross generalization, the bottles that have come across my desk have tended to be light-bodied yet deeply colored, with a tomato-paste tint and a hibiscus-tea flavor.

At any rate, the next time you come across a bottle of Greek rosé in the US, throw out some feta and olives and give it a try. We owe a place with 4,000 years of winemaking history that much.

....

Skouras "Zoe" Peloponnese Rosé ($)

George Skouras studied oenology in Dijon, France. In 1988, he released the groundbreaking Megas Oenos. The Greek equivalent of the Italian Super Tuscan, it is a blend of Aghiorghitiko[203] and Cabernet Sauvignon, aged in new French *barriques*.

Skouras didn't read the Provençal playbook, however, when he developed his rosé. It could pass as a pale red wine with its deep color and concentrated notes of raspberry, blackberry, spice, bougainvillea, sand, smoked Marasca cherries, wild rosemary, unripe blueberries, and sticky

tannins. The winery is located in Argos in the northeastern Peloponnese.

....

Nico Lazaridi Drama Rosé ($)

Does a name determine one's fate? One sip of this wine evokes images of the cast of *Mamma Mia!* singing ABBA on a Greek island for reasons that were never entirely clear. "Drama," it turns out, is the name of a viticultural subzone of the Macedonia appellation, but I prefer to think of Meryl Streep's free-flowing tresses when I drink this wine. Don't be put off by the label description stating that it is "medium sweet," because its notes of *hortas* (wild greens) counterbalance any tragicomic strawberry sweetness. Acidity and expressive tannins tie everything together in a surprisingly poised denouement. The Nico Lazaridi brand is popular in Greece, particularly for its Bordeaux-style "Magic Mountain" red.

---

[203] *Also spelled Agiorgitiko, this fruity, midnight-skinned grape is the most widely planted variety in Greece.*

What to Drink When Mercury Is in Retrograde

On the west coast of the Peloponnese, Greece's second-longest continuously operating winery occupies the pristine Ichthis peninsula. Less than 20 miles (30 km) from the archaeological site of Olympia, Mercouri Estate is the place that time forgot: peacocks and horses strut the grounds, and the estate house is overgrown with vegetation. There's a small chapel, and a crumbling old stable is filled with implements and artifacts dating back to the estate's 1864 beginnings.

Winery founder Theodoros Mercouri planted Refosco grapes here in the late nineteenth century, spawning a still-extant local clone called "Mercouri." With phylloxera ravaging the vineyards of western Europe, Mercouri shipped his wines to Trieste for distribution. The winery still exports a full 40 percent of production.

Today, fourth-generation brothers Vassilis and Christos Kanellakopoulos make the dessert wine "Chortais," vinified from raisined Mávrodaphne[204] and Korinthiaki, or Corinthian currant, in an irreverent nod to the estate's history as a currant farm. Their rosé exemplifies this family's cross-cultural approach to winemaking, as it's a mix of Greek, Italian, and French grapes.

....

Mercouri Estate "Lampadias" Ilia Rosé   ($$)

Syrah, Negroamaro, and Aghiorghitiko release ambrosial orange-blossom and lemon-chiffon aromas followed by a soothing botanical sensation that's like having your tongue massaged with lotion. Ilia is a PGI (Protected Geographical Indication)—the same thing as the French/Italian/Spanish IGP.

---

[204] *It's similar to the Greek Port-like dessert wine Mavrodaphne of Patras. Apparently the cheaper versions are made from raisined currants and sun-dried Mavrodaphne grapes, as per the Chortais. Dried grapes are frequently used in dessert-style winemaking. Dried currants, not so much.*

PROFILE
CENTRAL EASTERN EUROPEAN ROSÉ

COLOR
Serbian gold

PERSONALITY
cautiously optimistic,
industrious

AROMATICS
paprika, roses,
Hungarian chamomile

GOES WELL WITH
goulash, kalocsai motifs

The rich winemaking traditions of eastern central Europe were hobbled by a half century behind the Iron Curtain. Forced to manufacture wine for quantity rather than quality, the nations of the Eastern Bloc largely lost their viti-vinicultural identities. Then, after the dissolution of the Soviet Union, there came financial distress and the Yugoslav wars.

Today, nations like Slovenia, Croatia, Hungary, Romania, Macedonia, and Bulgaria are recognized among oenophiles as diamonds in the rough. We know that they have long winemaking traditions and that they harbor terroir that could be great. For now, the few rosés we get from these nations represent the first tentative steps in a long journey of recovery.

Hungary and Bulgaria

Stephen, the first king of Hungary, ordered monks to plant vineyards around monasteries; thanks to his foresight, the nation is known internationally for two unique wines. The first is sweet, precious Tokaji Aszú. The second is Egri Bikavér, or "Bull's Blood," a savory dry red blend based on the peppery-flavored blue-skinned grape

Kékfrankos, which is the same thing as the Austrian Blaufränkisch and German Lemberger. Today, Hungary is diversifying into other wine styles, including rosé.

As with Hungary, Bulgaria's viticulture is influenced by the Danube River. Winemaking has been happening here since the Stone Age, although a half-millennium of Turkish occupation slowed things down a bit. More recently, under Communist rule, Bulgaria's wine factories churned out enough swill—particularly from the Cabernet Sauvignon grape—to earn the title of the world's second-biggest wine exporter. Those days are over, and Bulgaria is upping its game. The rosés echo the reds in their dry brothiness—these aren't wines for sipping on the porch in the heat of summer, but for slurping down alongside meat-packed börek pastries.

....

Sauska Villányi Rosé ($$)

Hungary's Sauska owns vineyards in both Tokaj, where the famous Tokaji Aszú dessert wine is made, and Villányi, where red-grape vines grow on warm southern-facing slopes near the Croatian border. This hearty blend of Kékfrankos, Cabernet Franc, Cabernet Sauvignon, Merlot,

Pinot Noir, and Syrah is, in essence, a pink "Bull's Blood." Minimalist winemaking and natural yeast fermentation make for a savory rosé with ripe orange slices on the nose and a salty, satisfying palate.

....

Veni Vidi Vici "Vini" Thracian Valley Rosé ($)

Bulgaria's Thracian Valley is defined by the Balkan Mountains, Turkey, and the Black Sea. Roses[205] have always grown in the wild in its northern "Valley of Roses" and today are farmed for the perfume trade. And as aficionados know, where you can grow rose bushes, you can grow wine grapes. This blend of Pinot Noir and Syrah is an odd aromatic combination of fresh-cut chives (lots) and rose water (a bit). The price can't be beat—I found it recently for just $8—but why Syrah and Pinot Noir? It makes a person wonder what a rosé made from Bulgaria's indigenous grape varieties might taste like, if grown with careful contemporary viticultural techniques.

---

[205] *As in the flowers, not the wine.*

Republic of Slovenia

Northeastern Italian Friuli and western Slovenia's Primórska share a Mediterranean climate and crumbly marine-sedimentary soil. Vineyards cross the national border, especially in the viticultural hotspot of the Gorizia Hills, aka Collio Goriziano,[206] or Goriška Brda. Both Slovenian and Friulian are spoken by the locals. Between the cherry and olive groves are terraced rows of endemic grape varieties like Ribolla Gialla, aka Rebula; and Refosco, aka Refošk.

On both sides of the border, super-old-school winemaking techniques have enthralled the wine-erati in recent years. You might recall reading about an "auburn wine," or, as the Italians call it, ramato, from Radikon in Chapter 1 (page 26). Now let's meet one of these iced-tea-like, archaically styled wines from the Slovenian side, made from the Sivi—Pinot Gris/Grigio—grape.

....

Klinec Medana Brda "Gardelin—Villa de Mandan" Pinot Sivi ($$$)

In the mid-to-late eighteenth century, Empress Maria Theresa and her son, Joseph II, overhauled the wine industry of the Hapsburg empire. Villages were ranked in much the same way that Bordeaux would be classified under Napoléon III. Medana—also known today as "Villa de Mandan" due to its Greco-Roman origins—came out as top-tier. Klinec is an organic (and essentially biodynamic) family farm, inn, and rustic eatery. In addition, it's a natural winery that dates back to 1918. This lusty *gris de gris* is a nectarine-gold color thanks to five days on the skins and maturation on the lees in acacia barrels for two years prior to bottling. The overall effect is orange brick dust, rose hip tea, and rhubarb bitters—which together make a terrific match for Slovenian prosciutto.

---

[206] *Often referred to simply as "Collio."*

ROSÉS OF
THE MID TO FAR EAST

COLOR
terra-cotta and rose water

PERSONALITY
brave, historically
significant, sumac-scented

AROMATICS
frankincense, myrrh,
pomegranate

GOES WELL WITH
bangles, gladiator
sandals, harem pants

In Chapter 1, we learned about the "amber" or "fire opal"–colored wines made in the Republic of Georgia according to methods devised thousands of years ago (see page 25). Georgia's neighbors in the cradle of civilization zone likely made similar beverages back in the early BCs.

So it seems ludicrous that we haven't all been drinking Lebanese and Israeli wines—not to mention rosés—all this time. After all, the Roman Empire's international wine trade never really went away. But the Levant has struggled with political unrest, war, warming global temperatures, and, last but definitely not least, the Islamic prohibition of alcohol consumption.

There are, however, some promising wines coming out of the region. There are a few delightful rosés available from Turkey, although tracking down a bottle of the current vintage can be a challenge.[207] Farther east, 14 percent of India's population may be Muslim, but a fast-growing, increasingly urbanized economy is spurring a new interest in wine. So let's go globe-trotting, shall we?

---

[207] *As I wrote this chapter, I was awaiting a ghost shipment of wines from Turkey that never arrived. C'est la vie.*

Lebanon

First there were the Canaanites. Then the Phoenicians, the Assyrians, the Persians, and Alexander the Great and the Macedonians. Somewhere in there, during the pre-Byzantine period, Jesus showed up and turned water into wine.

Yep, the Lebanese have been making wine for a loooong time. But more recently, the 1970s brought civil war and Syrian occupation, and the eighties were marked by the Israeli invasion. Since then, rival factions have provoked periodic squabbles, and just next door, Syria has descended into its own miserable civil conflict. Longtime Lebanese winegrowers casually mention tanks rumbling through vineyards; shells dropping around wineries; roadblocks; and even entire vintages lost to war.

Most of the vineyards are located in the verdant, high-elevation Bekaa (also spelled Beqaa) Valley, about a half-hour east of Beirut on the Syrian border. One snowcapped mountain range protects this lush ecosystem from the Syrian desert; another blocks incoming storms from the Mediterranean. The valley gets both winter freezes and scalding summers, and as climate fluctuations become more pronounced, new vine plantings are creeping higher and higher into the mountains.

Where does rosé fit into this sacred landscape? I'll tell you where: in the chicest clubs in Beirut and Tel Aviv, where the music is thumping, the people are dancing, and the need for a fine local dry rosé might provoke a political incident if it's not addressed immediately.

....

Château Ksara Bekaa Valley "Sunset" Rosé ($)

In 1857, Jesuit monks planted grapevines in Lebanon. They converted ancient Roman tunnels under their monastery into a wine cellar and founded what is today the nation's largest and oldest continuously operating winery. Château Ksara produces a wide range of wines as well as Arak, an aniseed brandy aged in clay jars that's the Lebanese national drink. The portfolio includes three rosé wines, including a *gris de gris* of Carignan and Grenache Gris. But the spicy Cabernet Franc and Syrah

---

Musing on Musar

How many of us know what our ancestors were up to seven centuries ago? The Hochar family traces its roots back to knights who traveled to Lebanon from Picardy, France, during the Crusades.

They maintained strong links to France, especially Bordeaux, and founded their winery in 1930 on a hillside overlooking Jounieh Bay, 15 miles (24 km) north of Beirut. During the Lebanese Civil War, the château's cellars served as a bomb shelter for the residents of the town of Ghazir.

Château Musar follows a totally natural regimen: no additives, no sulfur, no filtration. Some wags claim that the wines are flawed, while others find them beguiling—similar to the Bordeaux of the 1960s, or perhaps, even, the wines the Crusaders drank in the days of the early Christian Roman empire.

....

Château Musar "Musar Jeune" Bekaa Valley Cinsault Rosé ($$)

While Musar uses indigenous grapes for its white wines, this rosé is a *saignée* of Cinsault. It's a pale cherry color, fading around the edges, almost like a very light red. Notes of pomegranate and caramelized orange peel are accompanied by spice, leather, and—yes—mothballs. Just when you think there might be something terribly wrong with it, you come back to the glass and are blown over by its beauty. This is the magic of Musar.

"Sunset" is the winery's best-known pink, and it's the one you'll find flowing freely in the rooftop bars of the party capital of the Middle East, Beirut. I have seen it priced at $7 a bottle, so you really have no excuse not to try it. Woot, woot— cue the latest Malikah album!

Israel

Winemaking should be a slam-dunk for Israel. It's in the Bible, right? But the Holy Land teeters on the too-hot zone for viticulture. Plus, kosher wines were notoriously bad in past decades due to pasteurization. But as winemaking techniques have improved, so has quality.

The best Israeli viticultural area—apart from the geopolitically risky Golan Heights—is Galilee, at the far north of the nation on the Lebanon border. High-elevation sites here are relatively cool and get some halfway decent—miraculous, maybe—rainfall.

I have had gawd-awful rosés from Israel. But my mind and heart are open. The grapes are French these days,[208] and the wine is coming along. There's no direction to go with the reds in this climate other than big and bold, but the following rosé is nicely balanced.

Galil Mountain Upper Galilee Rosé ($)

Galil Mountain is a project of Israel's prominent Golan Heights Winery group, which includes the well-known Yarden brand. The winery is located on a collective farm, Kibbutz Yiron, and manages six vineyards in the Upper Galilee mountains. This rosé is a blend of mostly direct-press Sangiovese, topped off with *saignées* of Pinot Noir and a teensy bit of Grenache. It's a satisfying wine, part umami, part pomegranate juice, that should pair well with roasted meat. It is not *mevushal*, meaning it hasn't been flash-pasteurized at a high temperature.

---

[208]   *Readers may be surprised to learn that the famous kosher wine Manischewitz is an American brand, made with native American grapes in New York state.*

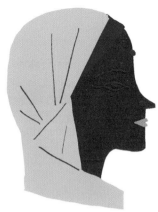

India

Get ready for the wines of the Near and Far East. In China, where big reds rule, rosé isn't particularly popular yet, but some wineries are betting big on it. Like Moët Hennessey, which has installed an outpost of its Chandon sparkling-wine brand in the Ningxia region and is pushing pink bubbles.

In India, the tips of iconic lotus blossom petals are a color of national pride. "Rani pink," or "the queen's pink," is frequently seen on painted walls and fabrics. So there are no hangups about drinking pink wine.

It's too early to wax philosophic about the rosé style of any particular Indian wine region, other than to simply note that the enthusiasm level is high. However, the climate is ideal for pink wine quaffing, and the food-pairing possibilities are to die for. Spices like cayenne and turmeric match beautifully with rosés with slightly higher alcohol and residual sugar levels. And the following wine could pass for a pink from the Rhône or Provence. *Globalisme est arrivé.*

Grover "Art Collection" Nandi Hills Rosé ($)

An entrepreneur whose work took him to France planted Grover Zampa's first vineyards in 1992, retained superstar oenologist Michel Rolland as a consulting winemaker, and eventually merged with another winery to form a conglomerate producing nine different lines. The company owns two vineyard and winery sites: one in the Nashik region in northern India, and the other in the Nandi Hills in the south near Bangalore. Here, at an elevation of 3,000 feet (920 m), Rhône grapes do particularly well in the red loamy and gravelly soil of the Grover vineyard. The "Art Collection" wines feature the work of prominent Indian artists on their labels. Heat and humidity are constant concerns,[209] but this Shiraz rosé is well made, reminiscent of a Rhône with its ripe melon fragrance and flavor. The alcohol is noticeable but brings a welcome glycerine texture to the wine.

---

[209] *According to associate winemaker Karishma Grover, pruning and harvest are timed to finish prior to monsoon season. The vines are trained to grow tall, to minimize reflected heat. And in the hottest months, irrigation cools them down.*

PRETTY AND PINK

$$	$$$	$$$
Corsica	*Corsica*	*Corsica*
Clos Alivu	**Yves Leccia**	**Domaine de Marquiliani**

$	$$	$$
Canary Islands	*Canary Islands*	*Canary Islands*
El Grifo	**Frontón de Oro**	**Viñátigo**

$$	$$$	$
Hungary	*Slovenia*	*Lebanon*
Sauska	**Klinec**	**Château Ksara**

EXOTIC ROSÉ REGIONS

$$$

Corsica

Domaine Comte Abbatucci

$

Sardinia

Argiolas

$$

Canary Islands

Bermejo

$

Greece

Skouras

$

Greece

Nico Lazaridi

$$

Greece

Mercouri Estate

$$

Lebanon

Château Musar

$

Israel

Galil Mountain

$

India

Grover

Online Rosé Retailers

BROOKLYN WINE EXCHANGE
brooklynwineexchange.com
138 Court St., Brooklyn, NY
(718) 855-9463
This charming shop between Brooklyn Heights and Cobble Hill has a solid website, offering a survey of classics, nerdy stuff, and rosés you didn't know existed but now maybe cannot live without.

CHAMBERS STREET WINES
chambersstwines.com
148 Chambers St., New York, NY
(212) 227-1434
The online shop for this TriBeCa institution is confusing to navigate, but the enthusiasm for rosé is infectious. While searching by color isn't an easy option, because that would make too much sense, one can sort wines by their organic, biodynamic, or low-sulfur status.

CRUSH WINE & SPIRITS
crushwineco.com
153 E 57th St., New York, NY
(212) 980-9463
A selection of interesting rosés anchored by a thick catalog of vintage rosé Champagnes.

DOMAINE L.A.
domainela.com
6801 Melrose Ave., Los Angeles, CA
(323) 932-0280
Chic, cutting-edge assortment of semi-obscure, highly coveted pink wines to go with your outfit from Tenoversix. Because why would you want to shop anywhere other than Melrose Avenue when in L.A.?

K&L WINE MERCHANTS
klwines.com
3005 El Camino Real, Redwood City, CA
(650) 364-8544
and two more locations
With retail stores in Redwood City, San Francisco, and Hollywood, K&L offers a quality selection of California rosés as well as solid values and geeky finds from all over the wine world.

KERMIT LYNCH WINE MERCHANT
kermitlynch.com
1605 San Pablo Ave., Berkeley, CA
(510) 524-1524
The importer who brought us Domaine Tempier, Corsican rosés, and other delights also runs a retail website and shop.

LUSH WINE AND SPIRITS
lushwineandspirits.com
2232 West Roscoe St., Chicago, IL
and two more locations
This Chicagoland chain offers a year-round rosé club for diehard pinkos who need a regular fix, and bottles a California Mourvèdre Rosé under its own private label, Nomad.

WINE.COM
wine.com
Online only
As reliable as a utility, wine.com is easily underestimated. Sure, it's stocked with a long list of big names and bargains, but it also surprises with its pink offerings from places like Greece and New Zealand.

Five Top Fives

FIVE BANG-FOR-YOUR-BUCK ROSÉS

Anne Pichon "Gris Montagne" Ventoux Rosé	$	*France*
Apaltagua Maule Valley Reserva Carménère Rosé	$	*Chile*
Nortico Vinho Minho Dry Rosé	$	*Portugal*
Sinfo Cigales Rosado	$	*Spain*
Weingut Matthias Dostert "Rosay" German Rosé	$	*Germany*

FIVE WINE-GEEKY ROSÉS

Forlorn Hope "Kumo To Ame" Amador County Rosé	$$	*United States*
Frank Cornelissen "Susucaru" Terre Siciliane Rosato	$$$	*Italy*
Klinec Medana-Brda "Gardelin—Villa de Mandan" Pinot Sivi	$$$	*Slovenia*
Valentini Cerasuolo d'Abruzzo	$$$$$	*Italy*
Viñátigo Ycoden Daute Isora Tenerife Listán Negro Rosado	$$	*Spain*

FIVE AGEWORTHY ROSÉS FOR THE LONG HAUL

Antica Terra "Angelicall" Willamette Valley Rosé Wine	$$$$$	*United States*
Château Musar "Musar Jeune" Bekaa Valley Cinsault Rosé	$$	*Lebanon*
Château Simone Palette Rosé	$$$$	*France*
Clos Cibonne "Cuvée Tradition" Côtes de Provence	$$$	*France*
R. López de Heredia "Viña Tondonia" Rioja Gran Reserva Rosado	$$$	*Spain*

FIVE ROSÉS TO IMPRESS

Château d'Esclans "Garrus" Côtes de Provence Rosé	$$$$$	*France*
Domaines Ott* Château Romassan Bandol	$$$$	*France*
Taittinger "Comtes de Champagne" Rosé Champagne	$$$$$	*France*
Ferghettina Franciacorta Rosé	$$$$	*Italy*
Soter "Mineral Springs" Yamhill-Carlton Brut Rosé	$$$$	*United States*

FIVE ROSÉS FOR PEOPLE WHO DON'T LIKE ROSÉ

Librandi Calabria Ciró	$	*Italy*
Cepa 21 "Hito" Ribera del Duero Tempranillo	$$	*Spain*
Defesa Alentejano Aragonez Syrah Rosé	$	*Portugal*
Domaine Ilarria Irouléguy Rosé	$$	*France*
Jean-Jacques Lamoureux Rosé des Riceys	$$$	*France*

The ABCs of
Wine Classification

A decade ago, European Union economists sat down and tried to solve a pressing problem: A recent proliferation of bargain-priced table wines from the New World had left Europe with more low-quality wine than it could sell. The EU has since diminished this glut—referred to, figuratively, as the "wine lake"—by subsidizing the conversion of surplus juice into cheap brandy, sugar syrup, and even ethanol (to make biofuel). And it has paid vignerons to pull out their vines and find other jobs.

In addition, the EU standard-ized quality classifications in 2009 in an effort to make the existing industry more competi-tive. That said, as I was pounding away at my keyboard to compose this tedious paragraph in 2016, wineries and regions throughout Europe were still dragging their feet about implementing the new taxonomy in their labeling, so the old designations were continuing to be used widely. Since I don't have a crystal ball at my desk, I'll adhere to the new terminology in this book, except in the case of a quote or for historical context.

You might want to guzzle rosé and hum the tune of the Jackson 5's "ABC" as you suffer through the following lexicography. I have tried to make the process less painful by limiting myself to Europe's three largest wine-producing nations, since these terms were most likely to pop up throughout this book.

APPELLATION D'ORIGINE PROTÉGÉE (AOP): Formerly Appellation d'Origine Contrôlée (AOC), this is the standard French designation for a fine regional wine. Libertarians will shudder to learn that in order to use the title of a European AOP—such as "Côte de Provence"—on their labels, wineries must follow a pro-scribed set of strict requirements carved into stone by each regional wine authority. This includes a list of allowable grape varieties and what percentage of each variety is permitted in red, white, or rosé blends.

CRU: The French term for a single vineyard that was declared to be great by a bureaucrat at some point in time, allowing its owners to charge exorbitant prices for its wines.

INDICATION GÉO-GRAPHIQUE PROTÉGÉE (IGP):

A larger, less-prestigious geographical area than an AOP, an IGP generally has looser rules regarding which grape varieties can be used. These wines tend to offer terrific bang for the buck. Today's IGP designation encompasses the old "Vin de Pays" (simple country wines) as well.

DENOMINAZIONE DI ORIGINE PROTETTA (DOP):

The Italian equivalent to the French AOP, the DOP was formerly known as Denominazione di Origine Controllata (DOC).

DENOMINAZIONE DI ORIGINE CONTROLLATA E GARANTITA (DOCG):

An even-tonier-than-DOC designation that now falls under the general DOP umbrella, to the chagrin of everyone who sells DOCGs at higher prices than DOCs. Unsurprisingly, I am still seeing "DOCG" on the neckbands of wine bottles as I type this in 2016.

INDICAZIONE GEOGRA-FICA PROTETTA (IGP):

Formerly known as Indicazione Geografica Tipica (IGT), this is Italy's version of the French IGP.

DENOMINACIÓN DE ORIGEN PROTEGIDA (DOP):

Equivalent to the Italian DOP or French AOP, this is supposed to be the replacement for Spain's old Denominación de Origen (DO) designation, but funny thing . . . I really haven't seen it on any Spanish regional wine labels yet.

DENOMINACIÓN DE ORIGEN CALIFICADA (DOCA):

A higher rung than DO. Again, this is purportedly being phased out in the way DOCG is, but according to a spokesperson from the Wines from Spain trade organization, "there has been a lot of red tape and backlash."

INDICACIÓN GEOGRÁFICA PROTEGIDA (IGP):

Like France's IGP and Italy's IGP. The Spanish still stubbornly use the old term, Vino de la Tierra (VT).

Bibliography

Anson, Jane. "Business as usual at Pitt and Jolie's Château Miraval, says winemaker," Decanter. September 28, 2016; http://www.decanter.com/wine-news/business-usual-pitt-provence-wine-miraval-332308/.

Brager, Danny. U.S. Wine Trends: Battle for the Next Pour. Yountville, CA: Wine Market Council and Nielsen, 2016.

Clarke, Oz. The History of Wine in 100 Bottles: From Bacchus to Bordeaux and Beyond. New York: Sterling Epicure, 2015; 113.

De Lorenzis, Gabriella, Ramaz Chipash-vili, Osvaldo Failla, and David Maghradze. "Study of Genetic Variability in Vitis vinifera L. Germplasm by High-throughput Vitis18kSNP Array: The Case of Georgian Genetic Resources," BMC Plant Biology. 15 (2015): 154; accessed June 14, 2016, doi: 10.1186/s12870-015-0510-9.

Dugast, J. Les Vins d'Algérie. Giralt: Paris, 1900; 92–93.

Fisher, M. F. K. Musings on Wine and Other Libations, ed. Anne Zimmerman. New York: Sterling Epicure, 2012; 105.

Johnson, Hugh. The Story of Wine. London: Mitchell Beazley, 2004; 79.

Liebling, A. J. Just Enough Liebling: Classic Work by the Legendary New Yorker Writer. New York: Farrar, Straus and Giroux, 2004; 46–48.

Liebling, A. J. "Memoirs of a Feeder in France: Just Enough Money," New Yorker, April 18, 1959; 49.

Lukacs, Paul. Inventing Wine: A New History of One of the World's Most Ancient Pleasures. New York: Norton, 2012; 61–62.

Martin, Neal. Robert Parker's Wine Advocate 202 (August, 2012).

McGovern, Patrick E. Ancient Wine: The Search for the Origins of Viniculture. Princeton: Princeton University Press, 2003; 8.

Paoletti, Jo B. Pink and Blue: Telling the Boys from the Girls in America. Bloomington: Indiana University Press, 2012; 98.

Parker Jr., Robert M. Parker's Wine Buyer's Guide No. 7. New York: Simon & Schuster, 2008; 1266.

Phillips, Rod. French Wine: A History. Berkeley: University of California Press, 2017; 42–32, 96.

Phillips, Rod. A Short History of Wine. New York: Ecco, 2000; 75.

Pliny (the Elder), The Natural History of Pliny, Vol. 3, trans. John Bostock and H. T. Riley. London: H. G. Bohn, 1855; 250.

Prial, Frank J. "Updating a Heritage," The New York Times, October 13, 1991.

Prial, Frank J. "Zinfandel: Beloved No Longer," The New York Times, February 24, 1985.

Redding, Cyrus. A History and Description of Modern Wines. London: Henry G. Bohn, 1851; 80, 141, 190–91.

Ribaut, Jean-Claude. "Les conditions d'un bon rosé," M: Le Magazine du Monde, August 8, 2007. Accessed June 18, 2016; http://www.lemonde.fr/vous/article/2007/08/08/les-conditions-d-un-bon-rose_942885_3238.html.

Robinson, Doris J. "Sparkling Rosé Wine Punch: Musician Phil Moore Serves California Rosé Wine Punch to Spark Conversation among Guests," Ebony, September 1, 1963; 188–190.

"Rosé's Rise is Unstoppable," Market Watch, April 22, 2016. Accessed June 18, 2016; http://marketwatchmag.com/wine-files-rose-april-2016/.

"Sacha Lichine Aiming to Make Provence the 'Champagne' of Rosé," Shanken News Daily, June 28, 2013; http://www.shankennewsdaily.com/.

St. Aubyn, Edward. The Patrick Melrose Novels. New York: Picador, 2012; 58.

Thach, Liz. "Time for wine? Identifying differences in wine-drinking occasions for male and female wine consumers," Journal of Wine Research 23, no. 2. (2012): 134–154.

"Wine Buying with the Mystery Removed," LIFE, April 12, 1954; 112–121.

Index

ACKNOWLEDGMENTS
The author thanks Peter, Cece, and Bitsy Cole for their
toleration and adoration. She also thanks Teague Wiebe
and Evelynn Moz for their determination, Peter Miller for
the introduction, Michael Jacobs for the conceptualization,
Doug and Kathie Raff for the foundation, Laura Dozier
for the direction, Sebit Min for the creation, Mercedes
Leon for the illustration, and her friends for their general
lack of moderation.

Editor: Laura Dozier
Designer: Sebit Min
Production Manager: Denise LaCongo

Library of Congress Control Number: 2016945920

ISBN: 978-1-4197-2410-7

Abrams Image books are available at special discounts when
purchased in quantity for premiums and promotions as well
as fundraising or educational use. Special editions can also
be created to specification. For details, contact special-
sales@abramsbooks.com or the address below.

ABRAMS The Art of Books
195 Broadway, New York, NY 10007
abramsbooks.com

SOUTH AFRICA
Western Cape

CHILE
Casablanca

AUSTRALIA
Victoria

NORTHERN FRANCE
Riceys

AUSTRIA
Kremstal

NEW YORK
Finger Lakes

WASHINGTON
Walla Walla

CALIFORNIA
Sierra Foothills

OREGON
Willamette Valley

SOUTHERN FRANCE
Provence

SOUTHERN ITALY
Calabria

WASHINGTON
Columbia Valley

SPAIN
Cigales

**REPUBLIC OF
GEORGIA**

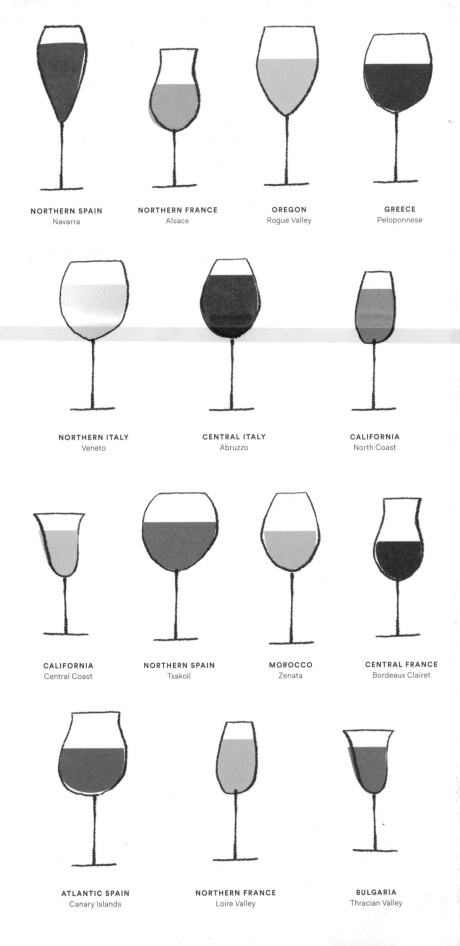

NORTHERN SPAIN
Navarra

NORTHERN FRANCE
Alsace

OREGON
Rogue Valley

GREECE
Peloponnese

NORTHERN ITALY
Veneto

CENTRAL ITALY
Abruzzo

CALIFORNIA
North Coast

CALIFORNIA
Central Coast

NORTHERN SPAIN
Txakolí

MOROCCO
Zenata

CENTRAL FRANCE
Bordeaux Clairet

ATLANTIC SPAIN
Canary Islands

NORTHERN FRANCE
Loire Valley

BULGARIA
Thracian Valley